DAILY LIFE OF

PIRATES

Recent Titles in
The Greenwood Press Daily Life Through History Series

DAILY LIFE OF

PIRATES

DAVID F. MARLEY

The Greenwood Press Daily Life Through History Series

 GREENWOOD

AN IMPRINT OF ABC-CLIO, LLC
Santa Barbara, California • Denver, Colorado • Oxford, England

Library of Congress Cataloging-in-Publication Data

Marley, David, 1950–
    Daily life of pirates / David F. Marley.
        p. cm. — (Greenwood press daily life through history series)
    Includes bibliographical references and index.
    ISBN 978-0-313-39563-5 (hardcopy : alk. paper) —
ISBN 978-0-313-39564-2 (ebook)
    1. Pirates—Juvenile literature.   I. Title.
    G535.M326   2012
    910.4'5—dc23   2011035019

ISBN: 978-0-313-39563-5
EISBN: 978-0-313-39564-2

16   15   14   13   12   1   2   3   4   5

This book is also available on the World Wide Web as an eBook.
Visit www.abc-clio.com for details.

Greenwood
An Imprint of ABC-CLIO, LLC

ABC-CLIO, LLC
130 Cremona Drive, P.O. Box 1911
Santa Barbara, California 93116-1911

CONTENTS

ACKNOWLEDGMENTS

They are very bad subjects, who believe they have not been put in the world except to practice brigandage and piracy. Enemies of subordination and authority, their example ruins the colonies, all the young people having no other wish than to embrace this profession for its libertinage, and ability to gain booty.

— Governor Jean-Baptiste Ducasse's
opinion of Saint-Domingue's
flibustiers, summer 1692

The author would like to acknowledge the generous assistance provided by Dr. Basil Kingstone and Graham Staffen of the University of Windsor, Ontario, Canada; M. Raynald Laprise of Quebec City, Canada; M. Roberto Barazzutti of Paris; Dr. William Autry; Lic. Leonor Ortiz Monasterio, directrix of the Archivo General de la Nación, Mexico; Dr. Pedro González García, director of the Archivo General de Indias, Seville; Professor Joel H. Baer of Macalester College, Saint Paul, Minnesota; Miguel Laburu Mateo of the Sociedad de Oceanografia de Guipúzcoa of San Sebastián, Spain; Walter Nebiker of the State of Rhode Island and Providence Plantations Historical Preservation Commission of Providence, Rhode Island; Dr. Ronald B. Prud'homme van Reine of the Nederlands Scheepvaartmuseum, Amsterdam; Capitán de Fragata Jorge Ortiz Sotelo of the Instituto de Estudios Histórico-Marítimos of Lima, Peru; Ms. Hendrika Ruger and Ms. Joan Magee of Windsor, Ontario; Dr. Jean Starr of Edinburgh; M. Christian Pfister of Dunkerque, France; Dr. Charles T. Gehring of the New Netherland Project of Albany, New York; and many other countless friends and colleagues who have helped with this project.

NOTE ON DATES: OLD-STYLE JULIAN VERSUS NEW-STYLE GREGORIAN CALENDAR DATES

Throughout this book, all dates are given in the modern Gregorian style, unless specifically marked as O.S. to designate the old-style English dates that were still in use in Britain and its overseas colonies during the great age of piracy, from 1650 to 1720. This older version of dating was also known as the Julian calendar, in honor of its ancient Roman reviser, Julius Caesar, and lagged 10 days behind those of other European nations.

This divergence had emerged from the political antagonisms and prejudices prevailing at the time of this changeover, during the late 16th century. Because the Julian calendar had become so outdated as to no longer coincide with the seasons or new moons, the Catholic Church spearheaded a drive to revise and universally apply a corrected alternative. After lengthy studies by the Neapolitan astronomer Aloysius Lilius and debates among many other leading scholars, Pope Gregory XIII issued a bull in March 1582 that declared that a new calendar was to be introduced: in practical terms, the day following the feast of Saint Francis in church rituals—which fell on October 4, 1582. But rather than being reckoned as October 5, the feast day was instead designated as October 15 to restore all subsequent equinoxes to their proper cycle.

This shift was accepted and implemented in most of Italy, Spain, Portugal, and their overseas empires. France adopted it two months afterward, and the French dates passed from December 9 to 20, 1582.

Most of the provinces of The Netherlands and Germany introduced this new Gregorian calendar as of 1583, and in fact it remains the version that we still recognize and use throughout the modern world today.

Protestant England, however—being at that time deeply opposed to any hint of Catholic suzerainty—refused to comply, so that, as of 1582, its old-style Julian calendar would continue to lag behind and remain out of sync with the new-style Gregorian calendars coming into common usage among the Spanish, French, Dutch, and Portuguese. And as a further complication, English calendars would moreover retain their ancient observance—especially in legal or financial documentation—of the new year as falling on March 24–25, necessitating a double indication in ordinary correspondence for any date that happened to fall between January 1 and March 24.

For example, in a dispatch sent by King Charles II in August 1669 to Sir Thomas Temple, his governor for Nova Scotia, it was mentioned that "His Majesty did by his letters of 8th March 1668/9 signify his final pleasure"—alluding to a previous communiqué dated only a few months previously in that very same year, on March 8, 1669 (O.S.). Such discrepancies became even more convoluted whenever corresponding from abroad, as when the English ambassador William Lockhart wrote a report from the French court to Secretary of State John Thurloe in London, dated "Paris, January 27/17, 1656/57"—having to combine the correct new-style date of January 27, 1657, used in France, with the old-style date of January 17, 1656, still recognized in England.

Foreign treaties or arrangements involving English interests would routinely feature double dates as well. For instance, the Dutch government at The Hague, in the immediate aftermath of the Third Anglo-Dutch War, issued a passport dated January 8/18, 1675 "for the *Hunter* man-of-war, Captain Richard Dickenson, which His Majesty of Great Britain is sending to convoy the ships *America* and *Hercules* to Surinam in pursuance of the 5th Article of the Treaty of 9/19 February 1674," to withdraw its English occupying forces.

CHRONOLOGY OF MAJOR WARS AND PIRACY (1650–1720)

Late July 1650	Four Cuban warships disgorge 450 militiamen on Roatán, failing to catch any of its English settlers.
August 1650	A Puerto Rican expedition overwhelms the tiny English colony on Saint Croix but is dispossessed a few weeks later by 160 French fighters from Saint Kitts.
May 26, 1651	Two dozen Franco-Dutch raiders sack the Mexican coastal town of Alvarado.
July 1651	Five French privateer vessels make a surprise assault on the Venezuelan port of La Guaira.
October 25, 1651	A commonwealth squadron arrives off Barbados, imposing the new republican rule of Sir Oliver Cromwell after a two-month blockade.
January 1652	French buccaneers from Tortuga Island (Haiti), occupy the Cuban town of Baracoa.
May 28, 1652	French and English raiders pillage the Mexican Gulf coast town of Minzapa.
Summer 1652	Two French vessels are sent under Timoléon Hotman, Chevalier de Fontenay, to reassert company rule over the Huguenot settlers on Tortuga

	Island. He grants privateering licenses against the Spaniards.
Late August 1652	French buccaneers ravage the Cuban town of San Juan de los Remedios.
February 9, 1654	Four Dominican ships bearing 200 soldiers and 500 volunteers dislodge the French colony on Tortuga Island.

CONQUEST OF JAMAICA AND UNBRIDLED BUCCANEER OFFENSIVES (1655–1663)

Noteworthy commanders: George Brimacain, William Goodson, Richard Guy, William James, Sir Christopher Myngs, Lewis Scott, Robert Searle, Kempo Sibata, Adriaen van Diemen Swart, Sir Thomas Whetstone, and Maurice Williams

April 23, 1655	Some 2,500 English troops under General Robert Venables, plus another 5,000 Antillean recruits, surprise the peacetime Spanish garrison at Santo Domingo, only to be sapped by diseases and sail off in defeat by May 12.
May 20, 1655	The English expedition penetrates the main anchorage on Jamaica, and its Spanish residents capitulate next day.
July 5, 1655	Admiral William Penn departs Jamaica for England with his battle fleet, leaving Vice Admiral William Goodson as naval commander, with a dozen lesser warships.
August 8, 1655	The small Spanish garrison is withdrawn from Tortuga, so that this island is reoccupied next year by English and French buccaneers under Elias Watts.
August 10, 1655	Goodson sorties with most of his Jamaican squadron, surprising Santa Marta on October 3, whose residents do not return for seven years.
October 15, 1655 (O.S.)	Cromwell's Puritan government declares war against Spain.
April 25, 1656	Goodson sallies from Jamaica with 10 warships, surprising Ríohacha in early May.
July 21, 1656	Goodson weighs to await the Mexican treasure fleet off western Cuba, detaching five warships for England a month later.

January 6, 1658	De Fontenay makes an unsuccessful attack on Buenos Aires, with five minor vessels.
February 20, 1658 (O.S.)	Christopher Myngs returns to Jamaica as its new naval commander.
April 1658	De Fontenay blockades Buenos Aires again, before being killed in a battle against three Dutch vessels.
May 20, 1658	Four Mexican transports deposit 550 sickly soldiers in north-central Jamaica, who are beaten when Governor Edward d'Oyley appears on June 25 with 700 soldiers aboard 10 ships under Myngs.
September 3, 1658 (O.S.)	Cromwell dies unexpectedly in England.
October 1658	Myngs burns Tolú and returns to Jamaica with three Spanish prizes, sold to men who will all prove formidable rovers: Robert Searle, Dutch-born Laurens Prins, and John Morris.
April 2, 1659	Myngs's four state frigates and a dozen freebooter vessels land 600 to 700 raiders, who devastate Cumaná. Myngs then hurries west to fall on Puerto Cabello and races to make a third rich haul at Coro. Regaining Jamaica, he is suspended from command and ordered home to stand trial because of stolen booty.
November 7, 1659	France and Spain end two dozen years of warfare with the Treaty of the Pyrenees, ignored by West Indian *boucaniers*.
March 27, 1660	The Dominican border town of Santiago de los Caballeros is sacked by 400 French buccaneers, under a letter of reprisal issued by Tortuga's governor Watts. Shortly thereafter, he sails for New England, making way for a French governor.
May 1660	Charles II is restored to the English throne, amid popular rejoicing.
Early 1662	A 30-man Jamaican expedition under Colonel James Arundell lands on Tortuga, failing to displace its French governor Frédéric Deschamps de La Place.

August 11, 1662 (O.S.)   Lord Windsor reaches Jamaica as its first royal governor, announcing a vigorous new privateering offensive. Myngs clears Port Royal six weeks later with 1,300 volunteers aboard a dozen vessels, storming Santiago de Cuba by October 19, leveling it and returning with six prizes.

Late October   Windsor resigns as Jamaican governor.
1662 (O.S.)

December 12,   Jamaica's deputy governor, Sir Charles Lyttleton,
1662 (O.S.)   allows Myngs to recall privateers for another expedition against the Spaniards.

Early January 1663   The Jamaican privateer Robert Blunden and retired naval captain Abraham Langford depart Port Royal to try to wean the *boucaniers* of Tortuga over to English rule.

February 10, 1663   Myngs assaults Campeche with almost 1,000 men. Wounded, he is succeeded by Edward Mansfield, leader of the privateers. The raiders depart two weeks later with fourteen prizes and considerable booty.

SECOND ANGLO-DUTCH WAR AND BUCCANEER SELF-INTEREST (1664–1667)

Noteworthy commanders: Michel d'Artigue, Abraham Crijnssen or "Captain Crimson," Edward Mansfield, David Martien, Colonel Edward Morgan, John Morris, Jean-David Nau (alias l'Olonnais or Capitaine François, the "French Captain"), Laurens Prins, Robert Searle, and Maurice Williams

June 14, 1664   Sir Thomas Modyford arrives as Jamaica's new governor, proclaiming "that for the future all acts of hostility against the Spaniards should cease."

September 1664   The privateer Robert Searle brings two Spanish prizes into Port Royal, which are restored to Santiago de Cuba, and his ship is impounded.

February 2, 1665 (O.S.)   Charles II authorizes English officials to begin granting privateering licenses against the Dutch.

February 11, 1665   The Dutch-born Jamaican subject Laurens Prins sacks the Dutch island of Bonaire, with 61 freebooters aboard Searle's frigate *Cagway*.

Mid-February 1665	A rogue expedition of 200 Jamaicans under John Morris and Dutch-born David Martien sack Villahermosa de Tabasco.
March 14, 1665	England declares war against The Netherlands.
April 28, 1665	Jamaica's governor Modyford dispatches Colonel Edward Morgan with 650 buccaneers in a preemptive strike against the Dutch in the Lesser Antilles.
April 30, 1665	The Dutch admiral Michiel de Ruyter attacks Barbados, bombarding its defenses and destroying an English convoy.
June 29, 1665	After stealthily ascending Nicaragua's San Juan River, Morris and Martien sack the inland capital of Granada.
July 17, 1665	Colonel Morgan dies from a heart attack upon disembarking on Dutch Sint Eustatius, but his men overwhelm all resistance. Early next year, his subordinate captains Searle and Steadman will raid the Dutch settlements on Tobago.
November 1665	Because of continual victimization of neutral Spanish Americans by English privateers, Jamaica's governor Modyford recalls 600 rovers into Bluefields Bay to remind them of their duty against the Dutch.
January 26, 1666	Louis XIV declares war against England.
Early March 1666	Modyford bows to popular demand and authorizes "letters of marque against the Spaniard," despite London's peaceful relations with Madrid.
March 19, 1666	News of the outbreak of Franco-English hostilities reaches Martinique.
April 8, 1666	Mansfield leads several hundred buccaneers in an unsuccessful invasion of Costa Rica.
April 22, 1666	A battle is fought between Saint Kitts's English and French residents at Pointe de Sable; the 350 French defenders—outnumbered four-to-one—decimate the vanguard of 260 Jamaican buccaneers under Lieutenant-Colonel Thomas Morgan, leading to a collapse of all English resistance.

May 25, 1666   Mansfield appears off Spanish-held Providencia Island with five vessels, disembarking 100 English and 80 French buccaneers to reconquer it the next day.

June 1666   Jean-David Nau and Michel d'Artigue raid Venezuela's Laguna de Maracaibo with 400 French buccaneers, emerging two months later with great booty.

August 4, 1666   An expedition under Governor-General Lord Willoughby of the English Windward Islands is destroyed by a hurricane off Guadeloupe; almost all of its 20 ships and more than 1,000 men are lost.

Late August 1666   A force of 500 Spaniards out of Portobelo recuperates Providencia Island.

Early September 1666 A single French bark out of Grenada tricks the English garrison on Tobago into surrendering.

Late October 1666   The Dutch privateer Gerart Bogaert recruits 100 refugees from French-held Saint Kitts, plus 50 French soldiers, to besiege the remnants of Thomas Morgan's Jamaican occupiers on Sint Eustatius.

November 4, 1666   A French fleet materializes off Antigua flying false English colors, capturing the island a couple of days later, then taking Sint Eustatius and Montserrat by February 1667.

February 26, 1667   Zeeland's Commodore Abraham Crijnssen, known as "Captain Crimson," reclaims Surinam from its English occupiers.

May 24, 1667   Louis XIV declares war against Spain to uphold his wife Maria Teresa's claim to Brabant and other parts of the Spanish Netherlands.

June 11, 1667   Crijnssen appears off Chesapeake Bay, devastating the tobacco convoy assembling up the James River.

July 31, 1667   The Treaty of Breda reestablishes peace between England, France, and Holland but does not mark an end to Franco-Spanish hostilities. Spain ignores any foreign claims in the Antilles, so that friction will persist.

HENRY MORGAN'S HEYDAY (1667–1671)

Noteworthy commanders: Joseph Bradley, Edward Collier, Gerrit Gerritszoon or "Rok Brasiliano," Jelles de Lecat (known on Jamaica as "Captain Yellowes"), John Morris, Jean-David Nau (alias l'Olonnais or Capitaine François, the "French Captain"), Laurens Prins, Manuel Rivero Pardal, and Robert Searle

August 1667	After pillaging San Juan de los Remedios, Nau l'Olonnais slaughters 90 crewmen of a 10-gun Spanish galliot sent from Havana, sparing a black slave to carry news of this massacre.
February 1668	Buccaneers again raze the hapless Cuban town of San Juan de los Remedios, whose citizens petition Madrid to relocate.
March 1, 1668	Morgan blockades Santiago de Cuba's entrance with a dozen ships and 700 men, his subordinates including many *flibustiers.*
March 27, 1668	Morgan lands to raid the inland Cuban town of Puerto Príncipe (modern Camagüey).
May 2, 1668	The Treaty of Aachen or Aix-la-Chapelle ends hostilities between Spain and France.
May 29, 1668	The Jamaican privateer Robert Searle assaults Saint Augustine, Florida.
July 10, 1668	Morgan's boats arrive near Portobelo, Panama, capturing it next daybreak.
January 2, 1669 (O.S.)	Preparing off Ile-à-Vache to lead 900 to 1,000 freebooters against Cartagena, Morgan's flagship *Oxford* explodes and sinks with almost all hands.
March 9, 1669	Morgan penetrates the Laguna of Maracaibo, sweeping its interior. Barred from exiting on April 25 by the Armada de Barlovento, he outwits it and sails away.
Spring 1669	The Jamaican privateer Joseph Bradley raids into the Gulf of Mexico along with Dutch-born Rok Brasiliano and Jelles de Lecat.
June 24, 1669	Jamaica's governor Modyford proclaims the English Crown's latest prohibition against anti-Spanish hostilities.
January 3, 1670	Governor Pedro de Ulloa of Cartagena issues a privateering license to Manuel Rivero Pardal to attack English interests throughout the West Indies.

Early May 1670   The lawless *boucaniers* of Tortuga Island riot against monopolistic restrictions imposed by France's West India Company.

Late Spring 1670   Prins, Harris, and Ludbury push up Colombia's Magdalena River to sack Santa Cruz de Mompós, only to be checked.

July 9, 1670   Incensed by Rivero's corsair raids, Modyford and the Jamaican Council commission Morgan as admiral and commander-in-chief of all privateers, with orders to retaliate against Spanish interests.

August 17, 1670   Prins, Harris, and Ludbury seize the new Fort San Carlos de Austria on the San Juan River, then steal across Nicaragua's lake to surprise Granada.

August 1670   Three Spanish ships and 14 piraguas from Saint Augustine threaten the new English settlement of Charleston, South Carolina.

October 24, 1670   Collier's half dozen English privateer vessels capture Ríohacha, along with the anchored Spanish corsair vessel *Gallardina*.

October 1670   Off southeastern Cuba, Morris's 10-gun privateer *Dolphin* captures Rivero's 14-gun *Fama*.

October 29, 1670   Prins, Harris, and Ludbury return to Jamaica from their Central American rampage, being mildly reproved by Governor Modyford for attacking Spanish America without permission, and then are sent to join Morgan.

December 18, 1670   Morgan's 38 vessels with more than 2,000 English, French, and Dutch freebooters, quit Ile-à-Vache to attack Panama.

January 6, 1671   Morgan's vanguard—three ships bearing 400 freebooters under Bradley—wrest Fort San Lorenzo at Chagres from its 360 defenders.

January 12, 1671   Morgan's fleet enters Chagres, despite his flagship *Satisfaction* and another four vessels sinking after striking a reef.

January 28, 1671   After trudging across the isthmus, Morgan's buccaneers capture Panama City.

March 16, 1671	With scant booty, Morgan hastily departs Chagres, regaining Jamaica to find English policy reversed, attacks against Spanish America now being out of favor, so that he and Modyford will be arrested three months later to face trial in London.
July 1671	Commodore René de Gousabats, Sieur de Villepars, arrives off Saint-Domingue with a French squadron to restore government rule.

THIRD ANGLO-DUTCH WAR AND FRANCO-SPANISH HOSTILITIES (1672–1678)

Noteworthy commanders: Jurriaen Aernouts, William Barnes, John Coxon, Cornelis Evertsen de Jongste ("Kees the Devil"), Pierre de Frasquenay, Sieur de Grammont, Diego Grillo, Pierre La Garde, Charles François d'Angennes, Marquis de Maintenon, Edward Neville, and George Spurre

March 31, 1672	Marauders burn the San Román shipyard beside Campeche.
Late June 1672	Various small islands in the Dutch Antilles are captured by English and French forces.
December 18, 1672	The English seize Dutch Tobago.
February 1673	San Juan de los Remedios, Cuba, is raided by buccaneers.
February 25, 1673	Governor d'Ogeron's 50-gun *Ecueil* runs aground near Arecibo, Puerto Rico, and more than 500 survivors are imprisoned by the Spaniards.
March 13, 1673	The French governor-general de Baas unsuccessfully assaults Dutch Curaçao.
March 1673	Zeeland's commodore Cornelis Evertsen de Jongste arrives off Surinam to raid in the New World.
June 1673	The Cuban-born mulatto buccaneer Diego Grillo intercepts a merchant frigate outward bound from Havana, then defeats a ship and two frigates sent in his pursuit, executing all 20 peninsular-born Spaniards aboard.
August 7, 1673	Evertsen reoccupies New York City.
Mid-October 1673	Governor d'Ogeron, having escaped from Puerto Rico, leads 500 *flibustiers* from Tortuga Island to Aguada in hopes of rescuing his captive men.

October 15, 1673	France declares war against Spain.
March 6, 1674	The second Treaty of Westminster reestablishes peace between Britain and The Netherlands.
Early July 1674	The Dutch corsair Jurriaen Aernouts arrives at New York.
July 20, 1674	The Dutch admiral de Ruyter is defeated before the French stronghold of Fort Royale, Martinique.
December 15, 1675 (O.S.)	Jamaica's governor Lord Vaughan, proclaims that English privateers must refrain from serving under foreign flags, because England is at peace—but many ignore this injunction.
June 30, 1676	Some 800 buccaneers attempt to penetrate Costa Rica's Matina Valley, only to be defeated at Moin Beach by 500 Spanish militiamen and 200 native archers.
January 23, 1677	Eleven privateer vessels under Charles François d'Angennes, Marquis de Maintenon, raid the Venezuelan island of Margarita.
March 7, 1677	An Anglo-French buccaneering force out of the Laguna de Términos, sacks the Mexican town of Jalpa.
Late June 1677	The French privateer Pierre La Garde, backed by the English mercenaries John Coxon and William Barnes, sack Santa Marta in Colombia.
November 9, 1677	Pierre de Frasquenay leads 400 *flibustiers* in a night march to surprise Santiago de Cuba, guided by a Spanish simpleton named Juan Perdomo—who meanders so much that one column mistakenly fires upon another in the gloom, ending their attempt.
May 11, 1678	The victorious French admiral Comte d'Estrées, sailing from Saint Kitts to attack Curaçao with 18 royal warships and dozen *flibustier* craft, runs aground on the Aves Island group and loses a third of his strength.
June 10, 1678	Rather than retreat with d'Estrées following his mass shipwreck, 2,000 *flibustiers* venture into the Laguna de Maracaibo to attack the neutral Spaniards under their veteran chieftain Grammont.

July 9, 1678	The English buccaneers George Spurre and Edward Neville, armed with French commissions, attack Campeche with 160 freebooters.
August 10, 1678	Louis XIV makes peace with The Netherlands, then signs a separate treaty with Spain in September—yet, since the latter does not extend to the Americas, *flibustiers* will continue campaigning.

BUCCANEER GLORY AND PACIFIC EXPANSION (1679–1688)

Noteworthy commanders: Gaspar de Acosta, Juan de Alarcón, Michiel Andrieszoon, Joseph Bannister, Felipe de la Barreda, Jean Bernanos, Pierre Bot, Pierre Bréha, Edmund Cooke, John Cooke, John Coxon, Edward Davis, Cornelius Essex, Laurens de Graaf, Sieur de Grammont, François Grogniet (alias "Chasse-marée"), Peter Harris, Pierre Le Picard, Thomas Paine, Jean Rose, François Le Sage, Richard Sawkins, Bartholomew Sharpe, and Jan Willems

February 11, 1679	Santiago de Cuba's defenses are damaged by an earthquake, tempting the French corsair Pierre Bot into an unsuccessful assault.
February 21, 1679	Grammont lands 600 *flibustiers* on Cuba's north coast, ransacking empty Puerto Príncipe (modern Camagüey), then fighting 600 Cuban militiamen and suffering 70 killed, before being rescued by Dutch-born Laurens de Graaf.
Late April 1679	Grammont departs Petit-Goâve with 200 *flibustiers* to prowl outside Havana.
June 1679	Bot and Pierre Bréha split off from Grammont's formation to attack Spanish salvors off eastern Florida, compelling their native divers to continue working and coming away with 200,000 pieces of eight.
August 26, 1679	Santa Marta, Colombia, is sacked in a surprise attack by buccaneers.
September 26, 1679	Coxon, Bartholomew Sharpe, and Cornelius Essex capture a Spanish merchantman in the Bay of Honduras, smuggling its cargo into Jamaica for sale.
Late December 1679	Coxon, Essex, Sharpe, Robert Allison, and Thomas Magott meet at Port Morant, Jamaica, agreeing to assault Portobelo.

February 6, 1680	Piraguas, out of Campeche under Felipe de la Barreda, surprises logwood cutters in the Laguna de Términos. A second expedition several weeks later will net a 24-gun English merchantman.
February 17, 1680	Coxon leads 330 Anglo-French raiders in a sneak attack against Portobelo, ransacking its dwellings and warehouses.
April 17, 1680	A third Spanish expedition out of Campeche bursts into the Laguna de Términos, seizing almost 40 foreign craft and 163 Baymen.
April 15, 1680	After hiding their ships on Golden Island, Coxon leads 332 buccaneers across the Isthmus of Panama, massacring the Spanish mining camp of Santa María el Real before seizing coastal craft in the Pacific and blockading Panama City.
	Coxon is voted out as admiral on May 5, retracing his route and leaving Richard Sawkins as leader of the pirates. The latter is killed at Remedios, so that Sharpe assumes command over the 186 freebooters remaining in the Pacific.
June 26, 1680	Grammont slips ashore with 47 raiders at La Guaira, Venezuela, surprising its 150-man garrison and hastily sacking before escaping back to his boats.
November 6, 1680	Sharpe lands 48 buccaneers to resupply at Ilo, Peru, brushing aside its 60 defenders and burning a small sugar mill inland.
December 13, 1680	Sharpe lands at Coquimbo, pushing inland to pillage La Serena, whose residents offer 95,000 pesos to be spared.
December 30, 1680	Four Dutch frigates and a fire ship arrive at Port Royal with three prizes, having been commissioned by the elector of Brandenburg to conduct anti-Spanish reprisals in the West Indies.
Early January 1681	Sharpe's buccaneers, unwilling to quit the Pacific yet, vote him out in favor of John Watling, who leads 90 men ashore at Arica on February 9. This Chilean town proves too big, with 600 to 700 militiamen pressing the raiders back after four hours of heavy fighting, during which Watling is killed and his head paraded through the streets

on a pole. The wounded buccaneers, who are left behind in a ransacked church, are also slaughtered, except for their two surgeons.

Only 47 buccaneers stagger back aboard ship, and Sharpe is restored to command, after which 50 freebooters soon separate to recross the Isthmus of Panama under John Cooke. Sharpe's 70 loyal hands finally capture two rich prizes in July and August 1681.

June 28, 1681	West Indian rovers penetrate Costa Rica's Matina Valley, sacking numerous plantations until expelled by a Spanish militia force out of Cartago.
November 1681	Sharpe rounds Cape Horn, reaching Barbados by February 7, 1682, and proceeds to Saint Thomas in the Danish Virgin Islands to dispose of his Spanish prize and slip back into civilian life.
	Disembarking as a passenger at Plymouth, England, by March 25, 1682 (O.S.), Sharpe is arrested two months later on suspicion of piracy, charges that later will be dismissed for lack of witnesses.
February 10, 1682	Five French corsair vessels under Grammont and de Graaf burn the Saint Augustine ship *Candelaria* aground in the Florida Keys.
July 1682	The Spanish frigate *Princesa* is captured off Puerto Rico by de Graaf, 50 of its 250 crewmen being killed or wounded. De Graaf's 140 *flibustiers* release their prisoners from Samaná Bay, retaining *Princesa* as his new flagship.
August 1682	The French buccaneer Captain Jean Foccard raids Tampico, seizing 30 captives and slaughtering cattle before departing.
March 1683	Bréha, John Markham, Dutch-born Jan Corneliszoon of New York, Thomas Paine of Rhode Island, and Conway Wooley raid Saint Augustine under French colors, looting the countryside.
April 7, 1683	Grammont and de Graaf hold a huge pirate gathering on Roatán Island, agreeing to a joint assault against Veracruz.
May 1683	The Cuban corsair Captains Gaspar de Acosta and Tomás Uraburru attack Charles Town (modern Nassau).

May 17, 1683   De Graaf and Grammont slip into the sleeping city of Veracruz with 800 buccaneers, subduing all resistance next dawn. Buildings are ransacked over the next four days before the pirates transfer thousands of prisoners offshore to Sacrificios Island, awaiting ransoms before finally weighing.

August 4, 1683   The four warships of Spain's Armada de Barlovento intercept a pair of French privateer vessels at Little Cayman, freeing a Spanish prize from Veracruz.

August 8, 1683   HMS *Francis* sights Jean Hamlin's 32-gun pirate frigate *Trompeuse* at anchor off Saint Thomas (modern Charlotte Amalie in the Danish Virgin Islands), torching it after nightfall.

Late November 1683 De Graaf and several consorts appear off Cartagena, so that three Spanish ships are manned with 800 men; they sortie under naval Captain Andrés de Pez by December 23. The seven smaller pirate craft swarm and capture them, with de Graaf claiming the largest as his new flagship before releasing his prisoners on December 25—with a message thanking the Spanish governor for the Christmas gifts.

January 19, 1684 (O.S.) The Cuban corsair Juan de Alarcón surprises Nassau with two *barcos luengo,* inflicting many casualties. After doing the same to Eleuthera, he returns and burns down Nassau's remnants on November 15, 1684 (O.S.).

Early February 1684 The English renegade John Cooke rounds Cape Horn with his 36-gun *Bachelor's Delight,* soon sighting *Nicholas* of London under John Eaton, while the 16-gun *Cygnet* of Charles Swan has also gained the Pacific to trade illegally.

Spring 1684   Spain declares war against France but is so enfeebled that Madrid cannot launch any significant offensives.

May 30, 1684   Bearing a commission from the French governor of Saint Croix, Jean Bernanos leads five vessels and some Carib allies in capturing a new Venezuelan fort on the Orinoco River.

June 12, 1684	Cooke dies near the Gulf of Nicoya, being succeeded by his mate Edward Davis, who reverses course.
July 5, 1684	A small band of Jamaican freebooters under Peter Harris "the Younger," sacks the Spanish outpost at Santa María el Real, then reaches the Pacific and defeats a Spanish flotilla off Panama's Pearl Islands.
August 3, 1684	Harris meets Swan in the Gulf of Nicoya. Swan's crew—tired of trying to trade with South America—presses to join the buccaneers. Swan insists that *Cygnet*'s owners receive a share in any prize money before both contingents steer south.
August 15, 1684	European frictions are suspended by a 20-year truce signed at Ratisbonne or Regensburg, calling for peace "within Europe and without, both on this side of and beyond the Line."
November 3, 1684	Swan, Harris, Davis, and Eaton's 200 men overrun Paita, for scant booty. Their attempt to surprise Guayaquil in early December 1684 is foiled when their Indian guide escapes, and, deeming their strength insufficient for any greater enterprise, they veer north to Panama to summon more pirates from across the isthmus.
June 3, 1685	Their numbers augmented to almost 1,000 men, a dozen pirate captains hope to intercept the Peruvian treasure fleet, but it slips past them into Panama City, then emerges from a shower four days later to engage the blockaders off Pacheca Island. The five Peruvian ships and two auxiliaries, manned by more than 1,400 soldiers and sailors, scatter the buccaneers westward next morning; the French and English blame each other for this defeat.
Early July 1685	Davis, Swan, and Grogniet briefly reunite to attack the Panamanian town of Remedios, then proceed northwest as separate groups.
July 6, 1685	De Graaf and Grammont land hundreds of pirates from more than 30 vessels, capturing and holding Campeche for almost two months before torching its buildings and departing.

September 13, 1685   The Armada de Barlovento flagship and vice flag spot de Graaf's *Neptune* east of Alacrán Reef, only to have him outmaneuver and escape them next day.

November 1, 1685   Grogniet and his Pacific *boucaniers* enter Realejo, Nicaragua, finding it already devastated by an English assault.

January 9, 1686   Grogniet briefly occupies Chiriquita, Panama.

March 5, 1686   Grogniet approaches Remedios at night to forage for food, only to be ambushed by three small Spanish vessels, suffering more than 30 casualties.

March 1686   De Graaf leads seven freebooter ships into Ascensión (modern Emiliano Zapata) Bay, Yucatán, marching 500 buccaneers to within half a dozen miles of Valladolid before inexplicably giving the order to retreat.

April 7, 1686   Despite some residual ill will, Townley and Grogniet—having reunited two weeks previously—land 345 men at Escalante, who fight their way into Nicaragua's capital of Granada three days later, for little plunder. The pirates endure numerous ambushes before fighting through Masaya on April 16 and regaining their ships.

April 30, 1686   Grammont intends to surprise Saint Augustine, but is swept past three days later, going on to South Carolina and eventually being lost with all hands off the Azores.

June 9, 1686   Half of Grogniet's men vote to join Townley, leaving 148 *flibustiers* to accompany him westward into the Gulf of Fonseca. Another 85 then continue northwest to waylay the Manila galleon off Baja California, while Grogniet returns to Central America with only 60 followers aboard three piraguas.

July 4, 1686   Two Royal Navy frigates catch the English renegade Joseph Bannister careening his 30-gun *Golden Fleece* in Samaná Bay, beating it to pieces from the shallows; but upon regaining Jamaica, the captains are reproved for not destroying Bannister's prize as well, and he has fled by the time they return.

July 22, 1686   Townley bags 300 Spanish captives near Panama
                                     City, two of their heads being sent to the Audien-
                                     cia President to compel him to supply the pirates
                                     while negotiating for release of five freebooter
                                     prisoners. This truce is broken when three ships
                                     manned by 240 Panamanians slip out of Perico
                                     Island to surprise Townley's resting flotilla on
                                     August 22, 1686; they are viciously defeated.
                                     Wounded, Townley sends 20 more heads ashore,
                                     eliciting conciliatory gestures from the Spaniards
                                     before he dies and is succeeded by George Dew.

August 1686   A galley and two piraguas bearing 100 Spaniards
                                     from Saint Augustine destroy the new Scottish
                                     colony at Port Royal, South Carolina, then ram-
                                     page north until a hurricane compels them to
                                     retire. The settlers wish to retaliate by commission-
                                     ing two French privateers for a counterattack but
                                     are forbidden by their newly arrived governor.

November 16, 1686   James II of England and Louis XIV of France
                                     agree to restrict the activities of their buccaneers
                                     in the New World.

Late November 1686   Five Biscayan privateer vessels arrive in the West
                                     Indies, hired by Madrid to supplement the inef-
                                     fectual antipiracy patrols of the Armada de Bar-
                                     lovento.

January 23, 1687   Grogniet encounters Dew in the Gulf of Nicoya,
                                     and, after ravaging that area together for a month,
                                     they weigh to surprise Guayaquil.

February 7, 1687   Captain Thomas Spragge reenters Port Royal
                                     from the Mosquito Coast, with the English ren-
                                     egade Bannister and his accomplices dangling
                                     from HMS *Drake*'s yardarms.

March 9, 1687   Governor de Cussy of Saint-Domingue reluctantly
                                     issues a royal decree ordering all French *flibustiers*
                                     to cease depredations against the Spanish.

April 20, 1687   Having stealthily rowed upriver for five days,
                                     Grogniet and Dew surprise Guayaquil with 260
                                     rovers, subduing resistance by 11:00 A.M. and
                                     herding 700 prisoners into its main church. Rich
                                     citizens are terrorized into raising ransoms,
                                     buildings are ransacked, and the pirates depart
                                     by April 23, with much booty and 250 captives,

	to reunite with their waiting ships off Puná. Grogniet dies of his wounds shortly thereafter, being succeeded in command of the *flibustiers* by Pierre Le Picard.
May 1687	In Veracruz, Armada de Barlovento crewmen riot and desert because of lack of pay and the arrival of competing Biscayan privateers.
August 30, 1687	Picard's five *flibustier* vessels materialize off Tehuantepec, briefly occupying it with 180 men.
January 2, 1688	After skirmishing against some Peruvian privateers in the Gulf of Fonseca, Picard scuttles his ships and leads 260 *flibustiers* up into the central highlands, gliding down the Coco River to emerge at Cape Gracias a Dios by March 9.
August 1688	A buccaneer sloop and piragua drop anchor off Tabasco, Mexico, being defeated after sending 20 men upriver to raid Chontalpa.
September 27, 1688	Louis XIV of France invades contested areas of the Palatinate in the Rhineland, escalating continental tensions.
November 15, 1688	Because of Protestant fears that James II will impose his Catholic faith on England, Willem of Orange and his English-born wife, Mary, disembark at Torbay from a huge Dutch expedition, sweeping uncontested into London before Christmas, while James flees into exile in France.
November 26, 1688	France declares war against Holland.

KING WILLIAM'S WAR, THE RED SEA, AND MADAGASCAR (1689–1694)

Noteworthy commanders: Adam Baldridge, John Phillip Beare, Jean de Bernanos, Jean-Baptiste Ducasse, Pierre-Paul Tarin de Cussy, George Dew, Henry Every, Thomas Griffin, Nathaniel Grubbing, Louis de Harismendy, Thomas Hewetson, John Hoar or Hore, George Reiner, and Thomas Tew

April 3, 1689	Seventeen French West Indian vessels and 1,200 volunteers take the Dutch island of Sint Eustatius.
April 18, 1689 (O.S.)	News of James II's deposal reaches Boston, and his unpopular royal governor for New England is seized and deported to London.

May 6, 1689	Captain Jean-Baptiste Ducasse, his four royal vessels reinforced at Cayenne by a large merchantman, the 40-gun privateer *Dauphin* of Dunkirk, plus hundreds of local volunteers steers into the Surinam River, only to be repulsed by its Dutch defenders.
July 27, 1689	Governor-General de Blénac sails from Martinique with 14 merchantmen and 23 island sloops, plus Ducasse's naval squadron, to lead the French residents of Saint Kitts in a preemptive strike against their English neighbors. After two weeks' fruitless siege of Fort Charles, Ducasse's 120 *flibustiers* install six heavy pieces atop a commanding hill, compelling the English to surrender the next morning.
Early December 1689	De Graaf sorties from Saint-Domingue with a *flibustier* flotilla, snapping up prizes off Jamaica's north shore and plundering plantations.
December 26, 1689	Sir Timothy Thornhill sails from Nevis with 500 troops aboard 10 vessels, subduing Saint Barthélemy by January 4, 1690.
Early 1690	An expedition of 300 Mexicans aboard four vessels attacks the logwood cutters in the Laguna of Términos, capturing two sloops before vigorous resistance by the Baymen oblige them to withdraw.
January 9, 1690	The English rover Hewetson arrives off Marie-Galante with 400 Antiguan volunteers, plundering this tiny French outpost before returning to Nevis. Scottish-born captain William Kidd commands the 20-gun *Blessed William* in this expedition.
January 29, 1690	Thornhill makes a two-pronged assault on Saint Martin, checked when Ducasse counters with 700 men aboard five vessels. Thornhill's small army is rescued by Hewetson and Kidd, but their freebooters are unhappy at being engaged at such high risk and little profit, so that when Kidd goes ashore on February 12, his men steal *Blessed William*. Hewetson also quits Crown service shortly thereafter.
March 1690	James II lands in Ireland at the head of a French army, hoping to reclaim his throne from William

	and Mary, until defeated at the Battle of the Boyne on July 11 and forced back to France.
May 3, 1690	New England's provost-marshal, Sir William Phips, presses three private ships and five vessels, leading 700 men to seize French Acadia (modern Nova Scotia).
Early June 1690	In the Caymans, de Graaf captures a Jamaican coast guard sloop, learning that the English are contemplating a joint operation with the Spaniards of Hispaniola against French Saint-Domingue.
June 30, 1690	A dozen Royal Navy warships under Commodore Lawrence Wright, plus 20 brigantines and sloops bearing 3,000 militiamen under Governor-General Codrington, land and retake Saint Kitts from the French by July 26.
July 5, 1690	Governor de Cussy's 400 riders, 450 buccaneers, and 150 black fighters are checked a mile and a half short of the Dominican frontier town of Santiago de los Caballeros, suffering more than 40 killed before burning it down and retiring.
Summer 1690	A second expedition sorties from Veracruz against the logging camps in the Laguna of Términos, surprising its Baymen and burning 80 vessels.
July 22, 1690	Picard's flotilla plunders Block Island and threatens Newport, Rhode Island, in retaliation for English strikes against Canada. His raiders are chased off by the retired privateer Thomas Paine with a pair of sloops.
July 29, 1690	Codrington detaches Thornhill to recoup Sint Eustatius.
August 19, 1690	Phips sails northeast from Hull with 32 vessels and 2,000 colonial militiamen to assault Quebec City. His expedition does not crawl within sight of this objective until October 15, and, despite landing 1,300 men, cannot puncture the French defenses before winter sets in.
January 21, 1691	An army of 700 Dominican raiders and 2,600 militiamen who have circled around from Santo Domingo aboard five warships of the Armada de

	Barlovento overwhelm 1,000 French defenders at Savane de la Limonade; Governor de Cussy and more than 400 of his followers are slaughtered, leaving the victors to sack Cap-François (modern Cap-Haïtien).
April 6, 1691	Codrington and Commodore Wright, with 3,000 men aboard 19 vessels (including three Brandenburg privateers), seize Marie-Galante, and one week later storm ashore on Guadeloupe. Yet sickness soon saps their ranks, so that when Ducasse arrives on May 23 with 11 vessels bearing two infantry companies and 600 *flibustiers* from Martinique, the demoralized English withdraw without a fight.
February 27, 1692 (O.S.)	In the Bahamas, a mob of "desperate rogues, pirates, and others" free rough-hewn Colonel Cadwallader Jones from prison, restoring him into office as governor.
June 7, 1692 (O.S.)	At 11:40 A.M., Port Royal is devastated by an earthquake.
June 30, 1692	Seven corsair vessels appear 18 miles northeast of Campeche, occupying its satellite port of Jaina.
July 1692	Santa Marta, Colombia, is sacked by French *flibustiers*.
April 11, 1693	Rear Admiral Sir Francis Wheeler's 32 ships and 15 lesser vessels sweep down the west coast of Martinique, depositing 2,300 troops plus 1,500 privateers and sailors. Codrington follows one week later with another 1,300 volunteers, but the English cannot quell French resistance, so they reembark by April 30—having suffered 800 killed, wounded, or captured.
June 27, 1694	Ducasse attacks Jamaica with 3 royal warships and 19 *flibustier* vessels bearing 3,200 men. Forewarned by the escaped privateer Captain Stephen Elliott, the outnumbered English refuse to be drawn out of Port Royal so that the French remain ashore for four weeks, devastating the island's eastern shores.
	Ducasse then reembarks his men under cover of darkness and sends all but his three largest ships to assault Carlisle Bay, farther west. Some

1,400 to 1,500 *flibustiers* land under de Graaf on the night of July 29, clashing against 250 English defenders and scouring its plantations until the French expedition weighs.

QUEEN ANNE'S WAR (1702–1713)

Noteworthy commanders: Jean du Buc, William Dampier, Benjamin Hornigold, Henry Jennings, Claude de Lachasney, Peter Lawrence, James Martel, Pierre Morpain, Blas Moreno Mondragón, and Woodes Rogers

November 14, 1701	Vice Admiral John Benbow reaches Barbados with 10 Royal Navy warships to winter at Jamaica in expectation of hostilities next spring.
January 2, 1702	The French vice admiral François Louis de Rousselet, Comte de Château Renault, reaches Martinique with 30 warships and 7 auxiliaries, being authorized three weeks later to launch a preemptive strike against Barbados—but he demurs, instead sailing for Puerto Rico to plan joint operations with the Spaniards.
May 15, 1702	England and Holland declare war against France and Spain.
July 14, 1702	Christopher Codrington, governor-general of the English Leeward Islands, leads 1,200 militiamen and privateers in a descent upon the shared island of Saint Kitts, expelling its French settlers.
July 21, 1702	War is proclaimed on Jamaica, and the next day Governor Peter Beckford begins issuing tightly restricted privateering licenses.
July 22, 1702	Benbow sorties from Port Royal with part of his fleet, burning a half dozen French vessels off Léogâne before blockading Cartagena.
August 30, 1702	Benbow begins a five-day fight against a Franco-Spanish convoy, emerging fatally wounded.
December 1702	In London, the Council of Trade and Plantations complains that England's Dutch allies are not campaigning vigorously against Spanish America but are instead trading clandestinely.
March 19, 1703	An English expedition under Commodore Hovenden Walker, reinforced by more than 1,000 militiamen and privateers from the Leeward

	Islands, assaults Guadeloupe. Two weeks later, this French colony is rescued by 3 warships and 12 lesser vessels bearing 820 men from Martinique, half of whom are *flibustiers*.
July 1703	Some 600 *flibustiers* descend on the Dutch half of Sint Maarten, forcing many inhabitants to flee.
October 1703	A joint expedition out of Santiago de Cuba—150 Spanish corsairs and a large number of French *flibustiers* aboard two frigates under Blas Moreno Mondragón and Claude Le Chesnaye—surprise Nassau in the Bahamas, slaughtering more than 100 residents and throwing down its defenses.
February 1704	Having rounded Cape Horn, the former buccaneer William Dampier reaches the Juan Fernández Islands with his 26-gun *Saint George* and 16-gun galley *Cinque Ports,* to unsuccessfully prowl the Pacific.
July 16, 1704	A force out of Campeche surprises the English logwood camps in the Laguna de Términos, capturing 135 interlopers over the next two weeks, plus 20 vessels.
February 17, 1706	A recently arrived French squadron under Commodore Henri, Comte de Chavagnac, plus two dozen vessels from Martinique and Guadeloupe bearing 1,200 *flibustiers,* are repulsed at Nevis, so instead devastate Saint Kitts.
April 2, 1706	A second squadron having reached Martinique under Commodore Pierre Le Moyne d'Iberville, a dozen French men-of-war, and two-dozen *flibustier* craft bearing 2,000 volunteers overwhelm Nevis, stripping it of 4,600 slaves and much booty.
August 16, 1706	Six French privateers under Captain Jacques Lefebvre depart Havana with 200 Cuban troops and two field pieces, being reinforced at Saint Augustine and mounting an unsuccessful assault on Charleston, South Carolina, by September 9.
May 1, 1707 (O.S.)	England and Scotland are united into a single nation, Great Britain.
August 13, 1707	The youthful French privateer Captain Pierre Morpain brings a captured English slaver and

merchant frigate loaded with food into Annapolis Royal, Nova Scotia, refreshing its tiny garrison recently besieged by New Englander forces. One week later, Morpain helps defeat a second attempt to overrun this outpost.

January 18, 1708

In a rare land assault by English privateers, four vessels sack and burn Lerma, near Campeche.

June 8, 1708

Three Royal Navy warships under Commodore Charles Wager engage a Spanish silver convoy off Cartagena, destroying its flagship and taking a prize.

January 1709

The English privateer Captain Woodes Rogers rounds Cape Horn with his 30-gun frigate *Duke* and Captain Stephen Courtney's 26-gun *Duchess* (the latter piloted by Dampier), assaulting Guayaquil in May and capturing a Manila galleon off Baja California by year's end.

August 16, 1710

A privately financed expedition of six hired French warships and two consorts manned by 1,500 freebooters appears outside Rio de Janeiro under Jean-François du Clerc, disembarking and marching overland to attempt to storm the city, only to become surrounded and captured.

October 1710

An expedition of 3,500 New England troops aboard 31 transports escorted by a Royal Navy squadron capture Annapolis Royal, Nova Scotia.

Late April 1711

A flotilla bearing 200 Spanish volunteers sweeps through the English logwood camps in the Laguna de Términos, carrying a half dozen prizes back to Campeche.

June 1711

The Martinican *flibustier* and militia lieutenant-colonel Jean du Buc l'Étang descend on Antigua and Montserrat with 2 privateer ships and 11 lesser vessels, only to suffer some 60 casualties and be driven off by the 50-gun HMS *Newcastle.*

August 7, 1711

Rear Admiral James Littleton's five two-deckers and a sloop intercept two vessels of a Spanish plate fleet entering Cartagena.

September 12, 1711

The famed Saint Malo privateer René Duguay-Trouin appears outside Rio de Janeiro with a large fleet loaned by the French Crown and financed by private investors. Masked by mist, he bursts past its defenses, disembarking a force that captures this city nine days later. However, his shareholders will complain bitterly over the lack of returns once he regains Brest.

October 1711	Great Britain and France sign peace preliminaries, terms for a broader cessation of hostilities to be worked out among other powers at Utrecht.
June 1712	The veteran privateer Jacques Cassard of Nantes arrives off Surinam with 10 warships loaned by the French navy, expenses underwritten by private subscribers, to seize Dutch prizes before peace can be finalized. Unable to breach Surinam's river defenses, he heads to Martinique for reinforcement.
July 16, 1712	Bolstered by 1,500 volunteers, Cassard fails to land on Antigua, so four days later, he storms Montserrat, wreaking destruction and securing immense booty. When a quartet of English relief ships appears with 600 men from Antigua, Cassard's engorged formation scatters toward Guadeloupe.
October 10, 1712	Cassard attacks Surinam again, advancing upriver with 1,100 men paralleling his ships on land, until checked by the Dutch defenses outside its capital. A 16-gun French frigate and some troops nonetheless slip into the unprotected hinterland, so that the Dutch pay for their plantations to be spared. The same happens next month at Berbice.
January 25, 1713	Cassard's fleet and nine freebooter vessels attack Sint Eustatius, scattering its Dutch inhabitants into the jungle, then invade Curaçao with 560 soldiers, 320 *flibustiers,* and 180 sailors on February 18. The Dutch pay 115,000 Spanish pesos for Cassard to depart.
April 11, 1713	The Treaty of Utrecht is signed, ending 11 years of warfare.

PIRATES' LAST HURRAH (1713–1718)

Noteworthy commanders: Sam Bellamy, Stede Bonnet, Francis Fernando, Henry Jennings, Louis La Buze, James Martel, Edward Thatch or "Blackbeard"

April 17, 1713   English buccaneers strike north out of Belize to oc-
                              cupy Cozumel, then sack Chubulná on August 5.

April 30, 1714   Annoyed by persistent raids into Nicaragua
                              and Costa Rica by Miskito Indians and their for-
                              eign allies, Madrid orders the "extermination or
                              enslavement" of these tribespeople by means of
                              a 1,200-man sweep.

August 1, 1714 (O.S.)   Queen Anne dies without an heir; she is suc-
                              ceeded by her German-born second cousin
                              George I, Elector of Hanover.

January 1715   Concerned about possible Spanish retaliation for
                              rogue privateers operating out of the Bahamas,
                              Captain Thomas Walker—holder of an outdated
                              commission as judge of Nassau's defunct vice-
                              admiralty court and self-anointed deputy gov-
                              ernor—visits Havana, fielding angry complaints
                              from the Cuban governor. Upon his return,
                              Walker makes eight arrests but cannot send his
                              prisoners to Jamaica for trial.

July 30–31, 1715   Overnight, a plate fleet bound from Havana
                              toward Spain is wrecked by a storm on Flori-
                              da's barrier reefs, leaving a dozen rich galleons
                              strewn along 40 miles of uninhabited coastline
                              near Cape Canaveral. Survivors limp back into
                              the Cuban capital by mid-August, so that a sal-
                              vage flotilla with divers is dispatched, who raise
                              5 million of an estimated 7 million pieces of eight
                              in lost royal bullion before worsening weather
                              causes operations to cease by late October 1715.

                              Yet the immense amount of treasure still left lures
                              an onrush of fortune seekers, idled West Indian
                              rovers, and other desperadoes into these waters
                              to scavenge among the debris.

November 1715   The pirate captain Benjamin Hornigold brings a
                              Spanish prize into New Providence in the Baha-
                              mas and angrily releases his colleague Daniel Still-
                              well from jail, threatening to burn down Judge
                              Walker's home for interfering in such affairs.

February 19, 1716   Spanish salvors return to the Florida coast from
                              Havana, setting up camp at Cape Canaveral to
                              resume working the wrecked galleons and chas-
                              ing off smaller groups of foreign scavengers.

Late May 1716

Off Saint-Domingue, Hornigold is voted out as captain by his pirates in favor of Samuel Bellamy, because he "refused to take and plunder English vessels." Hornigold departs with 26 loyal hands aboard a small prize sloop, and Bellamy retains 90 men aboard the flagship *Mary Anne.*

Early July 1716

Allegedly seeking to avenge heavy-handed actions by the Spanish salvors, the Jamaican rover Henry Jennings lands 300 freebooters from five vessels at their Cape Canaveral base camp, dispersing its 50 occupants (most of the Spaniards being at the wreck sites), then plundering 350,000 pesos' worth of salvaged coin before departing.

Upon learning of this attack, Cuba's authorities will retaliate by issuing letters of reprisal against all British vessels, thereby heightening tensions throughout this region.

November 9, 1716 (O.S.)

The pirate sloops *Mary Anne* of Captain Samuel Bellamy of Cape Cod and *Postillion* of the French *flibustier* Louis La Buze make a number of interceptions in the Virgin Islands, inaugurating a three-month reign of terror in the Lesser Antilles.

November 30, 1716 (O.S.)

In London, the British government informs the Council of Trade and Plantations that measures must be taken "to dislodge those profligate fellows or pirates that may have possessed themselves of the island of Providence," capital of the Bahamas. A solution is proposed by next summer to be enacted in three steps: first, a proclamation granting a general pardon to any and all pirates who surrender before a specific date; second, dispatch of a recolonizing expedition to reclaim Nassau as a lawful port; third, enough Royal Navy support in the Caribbean to not only hunt down renegades in the Bahamas but the entire region as well.

December 11, 1716

Some 100 Spanish soldiers and 500 Mexican volunteers aboard 11 vessels from Campeche and Tabasco sweep into the Laguna de Términos to uproot its English logwood camps, seizing almost 20 foreign craft. Only Captain Thomas Porter continues to resist, melting into the jungle

	with 150 followers, but the other captured trespassers are allowed to depart—for the Spaniards intend to stay, beginning to erect a redoubt to bar the Laguna entrance.
January 17, 1717 (O.S.)	The 30-gun, 140-man Royal Navy frigate *Scarborough* of Captain Francis Hume catches James Martel careening his pirate flotilla inside a shallow bay on the northwestern coast of Saint Croix in the Virgin Islands, destroying almost all of them over the next few days.
Late February 1717	Bellamy intercepts the rich 300-ton, two-year-old English slaver *Whydah* in the Windward Passage, retaining it as his new flagship and increasing its armament to 28 guns.
April 1717	The wealthy Barbadian Stede Bonnet slips out of Carlisle Bay aboard his custom-built, six-gun sloop *Revenge,* to inexplicably launch himself into a piratical career.
April 26, 1717 (O.S.)	Near Cape Cod, Bellamy seizes a small pink bound from Nantasket toward New York City—the 53rd and final prize of his career—before his damaged flagship *Whydah* is driven ashore by a storm that night and destroyed with all hands.
July 15, 1717	At nightfall, 335 buccaneers who have landed from a trio of sloops at the northeastern tip of Tris Island, storm the newly installed Spanish fort's eastern ramparts, as its presence prevents their reentry into the Laguna de Términos. Despite being pressed back into their compound, the defenders are able to withstand this assault and drive the English back to their ships, never to return.
September 5, 1717 (O.S.)	British proclamations of a royal pardon for pirates are sent across the Atlantic, offering amnesty to any renegades who submit before the end of June 1718.
September 29, 1717 (O.S.)	Having prowled north from the Bahamas to prey upon the peacetime maritime traffic off Virginia, Blackbeard begins making numerous captures off Cape Charles over the ensuing three weeks, converting three of these prizes into pirate consorts and recruiting more followers. After two

	last seizures within Delaware Bay on October 22 (O.S.), Thatch disappears southward.
November 28, 1717	Blackbeard's two sloops capture the 300-ton French slaver *Concorde* near Martinique, sailing it to Bequia in the Grenadines to convert it into his new 32-gun flagship, *Queen Anne's Revenge.* Thatch attacks Guadeloupe 10 days later, and many more interceptions ensue as his flotilla works west into the Windward Passage.
December 1717	An emissary from Bermuda brings a copy of the royal amnesty for pirates to lawless Nassau, where it is at first received with hostility, before a delegation agrees to seek out confirmation.
Early February 1718	Blackbeard reaches Roatán Island with two prizes, anchoring in Coxen's Hole to careen *Queen Anne's Revenge.*
Mid-March 1718	Thatch quits Roatán with his flagship and a sloop, attacking a foreign logwood fleet off Turneffe Atoll in early April. Roaming past the Cayman Islands, Cuba, and Nassau, he heads up the Atlantic seaboard, repeatedly ransacking vessels.
May 22, 1718 (O.S.)	Blackbeard arrives off South Carolina with *Queen Anne's Revenge* and three sloops manned by almost 400 pirates. Hoping to obtain pardons and disappear ashore with their booty, the rovers are rebuffed by the local authorities, so Thatch angrily blockades Charleston's entrance as of June 4 (O.S.), intercepting numerous vessels and exchanging his captives for a chest of expensive medicines.
	Six days later, Blackbeard grounds his flagship and a sloop in Beaufort Inlet, escaping upriver to Bath, North Carolina, with all the booty and 20 loyal hands.
August 1718	Despite having purchased a home and married, Blackbeard resumes pirating.
September 26, 1718 (O.S.)	Two eight-gun sloops manned by 130 South Carolinians sight Bonnet's 46-man *Royal James* at anchor with two prizes inside the Cape Fear River, beating it into submission the next day.
November 22, 1718 (O.S.)	Blackbeard is defeated and slain in Ocracoke Inlet by two armed sloops out of Virginia.

November 23, 1718 (O.S.)	In the Windward Passage, Charles Vane's 12-gun brigantine pursues a sail, only to turn tail when it proves to be a 24-gun French warship. Next day, 75 of his crewmen vote Vane out in favor of his quartermaster, John "Calico Jack" Rackham.
December 5, 1718 (O.S.)	Having made a string of captures off West Africa, the pirate Edward Seegar or "Edward England" arrives off Barbados with a brigantine and sloop.
December 10, 1718 (O.S.)	Bonnet is executed on the waterfront of Charleston, South Carolina.

WAR OF THE QUADRUPLE ALLIANCE (1719–1720)

Noteworthy commanders: Edward England, Louis La Buze, "Calico Jack" Rackham, Bartholomew Roberts, and Charles Vane

February 1719	Having refreshed in the Bay of Honduras, Vane and his first mate, Robert Deal, put out to sea, only to lose their small sloops in a storm and become marooned.
March 1719	Having recrossed the Atlantic, Edward England begins another summer-long campaign off West Africa.
April 19, 1719	A French warship reaches Biloxi with orders for Louisiana's governor to attack Spanish Pensacola. Less than a month later, four French ships and 600 volunteers surprise its garrison, deporting the Spaniards to Havana.
August 4, 1719	A Cuban counterexpedition of 1,600 corsairs, two companies of Spanish regulars, 900 volunteers, and 300 displaced Pensacolans appears off the lost West Florida outpost, compelling its 260 French occupiers to surrender three days later. A trio of Cuban corsair vessels then proceeds to blockade Mobile.
September 1, 1719	Three French royal warships and two auxiliaries reach Dauphine Island with almost 2,000 men, chasing away its Cuban blockaders. Two weeks afterward, the French again advance on Pensacola by sea and land, driving out its reinstalled Spanish garrison and razing the town.

September 1719	Having traversed the Atlantic from West Africa, Bartholomew Roberts's 32-gun *Royal Rover* cuts a merchantman out of a Portuguese convoy and plunders it at Cayenne of a reputed 400,000 gold *moidores*.
December 13, 1719	A few hundred English buccaneers march inland to assault Sancti Spíritus, Cuba, only to be spotted and repelled.
January 27, 1720	Spain and France temporarily patch up relations.
February 18, 1720	A Royal Navy snow from Jamaica delivers a formal complaint to Cuba's authorities about the privateering activities of Christopher Winter and Nicholas Brown, two English Catholic rovers serving under Spanish colors.
February 24, 1720 (O.S.)	A dozen vessels bearing 1,200 to 1,300 Cuban corsairs surprise Nassau in the Bahamas, making off with 100 slaves and considerable booty.
February 1720	Roberts makes a string of captures in the Lesser Antilles, then abandons his flagship *Royal Rover* at Danish Saint Thomas to steer for North America.
March 22, 1720 (O.S.)	Having been carried prisoner into Jamaica aboard a merchantman, Vane is sentenced to death.
May 15, 1720	Having rounded Cape Horn and plundered Paita, Peru, George Shelvocke's *Speedwell* is wrecked on the Juan Fernández Islands.
June 1720	Roberts ransacks 22 British ships in Newfoundland's Trepassey Bay, then seizes a half dozen French vessels off the Grand Banks, selecting one as his new flagship.
August 17, 1720 (O.S.)	Edward England's 34-gun *Fancy* and John Taylor's 36-gun *Victory* engage three East Indiamen resting at Johanna Island, near Madagascar. Captain James Macrae's *Cassandra* resists desperately before surrendering, reducing *Fancy* to a hulk. Its disgusted pirates vote England out as captain.
August 1720	Roberts makes a series of captures off New England before steering for the West Indies.
September 4, 1720 (O.S.)	Roberts arrives at Carriacou in the Grenadines to careen, then three weeks later attacks Saint Kitts's principal anchorage of Basseterre.

Late October 1720   Having failed to reach Africa, Roberts takes up
                             station on Saint Lucia, intercepting many English
                             and French merchantmen off Barbados and Mar-
                             tinique until next spring, when he again quits
                             this hunting ground.

**Early November   A Jamaican privateer captures the pirate vessel of
1720 (O.S.)**   "Calico Jack" Rackham, bringing him into Kings-
                             ton to be hanged.

1

INTRODUCTION: GENERAL HISTORY OF THE GOLDEN AGE OF PIRACY

They are desperate people, the greater part having been men o'
war for twenty years.

—Governor Sir Thomas Modyford's opinion
on Jamaica's restive privateers, 1664

Ever since people first ventured out onto the open oceans, there have
been instances of robbery and murder upon the high seas, the strong
preying upon the weak. Merchants, sailors, and passengers have all
traveled warily since the beginning of time, the very word *pirate* having originally derived from the ancient Greek term *peirates* or "brig-
and" and its Latinized version of *pirata*. The tale has oft been told of
how a 21-year-old Julius Caesar was captured while sailing through
the Aegean Sea almost two millennia ago by Cilician pirates—at
least once, and possibly even twice—who held him for ransom at the
Dodecanese islet of Pharmacusa. His family allegedly paid 25 talents of silver to secure his release, weighing roughly the equivalent of
1,500 pounds or three-quarters of a ton of this precious metal.

Four years afterward, around 75 BCE, Caesar was seemingly intercepted for a second time, and his Greek biographer Plutarch would
record a couple of centuries later how, when this second Cilician
band had

demanded a ransom of twenty talents, Caesar burst out laughing: they
did not know, he said, who it was that they had captured, and he volunteered to pay fifty. Then, when he had sent his followers to the various
cities in order to raise the money, and was left with one friend and two
servants among these Cilicians (among the most bloodthirsty people in
the world), he treated them so highhandedly that whenever he wanted
to sleep, he would send to them to tell them to stop talking.[1]

This second ransom was apparently delivered to his hostage-takers
within 38 days, from the seaport of Miletus in modern Turkey, so that
the young Roman aristocrat was once again released. But on this occasion, Caesar quickly assembled a flotilla of vessels, cornered most of
these pirates before they could disperse, and—as he had often cheerily
informed them during his captivity, according to Plutarch—brought
them into Pergamon to be crucified, supposedly granting those who
had treated him best while he had been their hostage the favor of having their throats slit in a small gesture intended to ease their dying
agonies.

Piracy would remain a recurrent problem in almost every corner of
the globe for the next 2,000 years, flaring up as virulently in Asian
or Arabic waters as in the Mediterranean or North Atlantic. A 14th-
century treatise penned by the Chinese writer Lung-Ya-Men described
the dangers lurking in the Strait of Malacca during his own day, when
this channel was more commonly known by the ominous name of
Dragon-Teeth Strait. Junks carrying bulk commercial cargoes from east
to west, he noted, would be allowed to pass through unmolested by
any of its seashore tribesmen, so as to proceed freely out into the Indian
Ocean and trade along its far reaches. Yet upon the Chinese junks'
return passage through the strait, rich and heavy with their accrued
profits and bartered goods,

> some two or three hundred pirate *praus* will put out to attack them.
> Sometimes [the junks] are fortunate enough to escape with a favorable
> wind; otherwise the crews are butchered, and the merchandise made off
> with in quick time.[2]

Virtually every narrow waterway in the world has endured similar
bouts of piracy during its history. Given the profit motivation driv-
ing such criminal activity, even in the most ancient of times, rovers
typically ventured out to sea on swift hit-and-run forays, combing
nearby sea lanes during peak traffic periods to increase their chances
of quickly locating a victim, then retiring into a safe anchorage or sanc-

tuary ashore to plunder their prize at leisure and extort ransoms for their captives before melting back into civilian life.

The Aegean Archipelago, Strait of Messina, and other Mediterranean chokepoints have been prowled by marauders ever since the dawn of written history, while the English Channel and Scandinavian Kattegat were controlled throughout much of the Middle Ages by seaside warlords. The dread Barbary corsairs preyed for centuries upon the streams of merchantmen funneling through the Strait of Gibraltar, plundering cargoes and enslaving their crews, as did many impoverished clansmen clustered along the distant Horn of Africa—whose villages overlooked the sea lanes that brought all coastal traffic from India, Arabia, and East Africa down into the Gulf of Aden and headed into the mouth of the Red Sea, whose 20-mile-wide channel is still known today as Bab-el-Mandeb or the Gate of Tears. This sun-baked strait would provide such abundant prey that it was even hunted during the 1690s by such far-ranging freebooters as Thomas Tew of Newport, Rhode Island, and Captain William Kidd of New York City, as well as modern-day teenage Somali gunmen.

CARIBBEAN BREEDING GROUND

Nevertheless, what is popularly known today as the golden age of piracy had its origins in an entirely new hunting ground, first penetrated during the 16th century by West European rovers stealing across the Atlantic in pursuit of Spanish prizes: the Antilles. After this region's initial Spanish colonizers had carved out a few hard-scrabble outposts in this vast arena, most of its residents had subsequently been lured away onto the American mainland—enticed by the prospects of subduing the immensely wealthy native kingdoms of Mexico and Peru, where rolling estates and rich mines could be secured by the conquistadors, to be tended by millions of docile vassals.

Consequently, seamen from rival European nations found long, lonely stretches of empty coastline once they, too, gained the West Indies. At first, they merely paused on a few of these isles in passing to refresh their water and provisions before pressing deeper into the archipelagos—being wartime privateers bent upon intercepting galleons and sacking Spain's vulnerable American holdings. Inevitably, though, some of these transients began returning into the Caribbean during the rare intervals of peace back in Europe to barter for exotic produce from its coastal tribespeople, many of whom remained hostile to the Spaniards concentrated around highland cities deeper inside the continent. The rare tropical goods that they had to offer commanded fantastic prices in Old World markets, so that by the late 16th century, private companies were already multiplying in many West European seaports, intent on securing permanent toeholds in the tropics so as to harvest their own commercial cash crops of tobacco or sugar.

Crown ministers in Madrid angrily denounced all such seaborne visitors (many of whom were Protestants) as criminal trespassers and heretical pirates, subject to the harshest penalties under their laws, even if engaged in nothing more than peaceful commerce. However, many Spanish American coastal residents themselves—who were obliged to pay top prices for the trickle of legally allowed imports that reached them out of Seville or Cadiz thanks to Spain's rigidly controlled trade monopolies—proved much more welcoming, and a brisk clandestine trade soon began between foreign smugglers and local purchasers, these transactions usually conducted in quiet inlets far from official supervision. The shoreline of northwestern Hispaniola and the Gardens of the Queen Archipelago off southeastern Cuba became such notorious hotbeds for smuggling that Spain ordered them entirely denuded of Spanish residents as of 1605 in a vain attempt to stem this traffic.

A pattern had nonetheless taken root, whereby merchantmen would clear their European home ports with cargoes of manufactures, pausing off West Africa to barter some of these items for slaves. Highly coveted as laborers, these captives would, in turn, attract eager Spanish American buyers once the traders' ships dropped anchor off any of a dozen friendly, sparsely inhabited coves in the Antilles; these Spanish purchasing agents moreover usually bought European wares out of the holds as well, paying for everything with fine silver coins that were difficult to obtain elsewhere. Masters would then reload their vessels with some locally abundant produce to sail home and sell this cargo for an additional healthy profit—having gained a handsome return at each successive stage of their transatlantic voyage.

Veteran captains and seamen who participated in such smuggling operations repeatedly would come to

- familiarize themselves with extensive stretches of unclaimed West Indian shorelines, discovering hidden inlets and anchorages along their length in which to set up transient shore camps to make repairs, careen, and refresh (some of these havens would eventually evolve into unassailable strongholds for future generations of pirates, such as Tortuga Island off Haiti, Abraham's Cay on the pestilential Mosquito Coast, the Bocas del Toro maze, and Roatán Island);

- befriend coastal tribesmen and runaway black slaves, from whom they would learn how to feed themselves in the West Indies, soon provisioning entire flotillas of visiting vessels through hunting wild cattle, pigs, and turtles, as well as gathering regional staples such as maize and tropical fruits;

- develop immunity to many regional diseases, which would decimate future colonizing expeditions and royal warships sent out from Europe (leaving Caribbean privateers as the sole reliable means of defense for the earliest private commercial outposts that would come to be established); and

- gain detailed intelligence about habitual Spanish movements and military strengths from captives, deserters, and escaped colleagues, plus firsthand experience of the best lookout spots and chokepoint hunting grounds for intercepting prizes, such as the Mona and Windward Passages, Île à Vache, Isla de Pinos, and Cape Corrientes at the western tip of Cuba.

As Spain's decay worsened during the 17th century, the volume of this transatlantic traffic steadily increased, until foreign enclaves began dotting more and more of the Windward and Leeward Islands, as well as South America's Wild Coast, with their vessels probing ever deeper and more confidently into the maze of Caribbean islands. Earliest among these trespassing pioneers had been the Dutch—tough, shrewd traders, whose West Indische Compagnie would dominate traffic in these waters for decades to come—as well as a few utopian outposts created on islands such as Tortuga and Providencia by English Puritans. Then in December 1654, a major expedition had also burst into the region, specifically dispatched by England's lord protector Oliver Cromwell to conquer a new stronghold in the West Indies, in contemptuous violation of the indifferent truce that was then prevailing between London and Madrid.

Although this major endeavor failed in its initial objective of capturing Santo Domingo, smaller Jamaica was overrun and retained instead. Hardy French Huguenot settlers reoccupied nearby Tortuga Island in the wake of this same conquest, so that 10 years of simmering warfare would grip the entire region as the enfeebled Spanish Crown vainly tried to drive out these stubborn footholds—in the process, merely inciting a wave of devastating counterstrikes against its own American colonies. All of these factors would combine to transform the Caribbean into an ideal breeding ground for piracy, as—in the absence of any supportive royal squadrons—its fledgling private outposts began commissioning freebooters of every nationality to bolster their precarious state of defense, thereby creating an unruly body of freelance men-of-war who would come to flourish over the next three decades, yet always remain prone to

- seeking employment under any flag of convenience (some, such as Dutch-born Jelles de Lecat and the Englishman John Philip Beare, even taking service with the Spaniards);
- regularly combining into large multinational groups for joint strikes against Spanish America, regardless of whatever Crown policy was being upheld back in Europe and often bolstered by ships visiting in the theater seasonally out of frozen Europe or North America during their winter months (who were even more inclined to lawlessness than local residents, as they could disappear over the horizon with any ill-gotten gains, far from the scene of their depredations);
- finding a wide variety of welcoming ports in which to sell their booty and squander their loot, especially since Spanish coinage and mainland produce remained prized commodities among the earliest European outposts;
- enjoying inexhaustible excuses to supplement their wartime forays by obtaining individual letters of reprisal to continue operating even during peacetime, thanks to Madrid's entrenched antagonism against any and all foreigners beyond the line (their heavy-handed *guardacosta* patrols furnishing a steady stream of complaints of abuse and mistreatment, which, in turn, allowed these mercenaries to secure additional commissions); and
- operating throughout this era against virtually no serious naval opposition, as Spain's bankrupt Crown could not afford any significant countermeasures, freeing rovers to act strictly in their own narrow self-interest—always on the offensive, in hit-and-run raids directed against targets chosen simply for their wealth and vulnerability rather than any strategic military importance.

RISE OF THE BUCCANEERS (1654–1679)

The Commonwealth authorities who had been installed to garrison newly conquered Jamaica, found their position notably weakened within the very first year of their occupation by the return of most State warships to England, plus a wave of epidemics that quickly claimed 4,500 of their 7,000 soldiers' lives. Acutely aware of their defensive debility, they sought to compensate for this weakness by freely issuing commissions to any freebooters who chanced to call. Among the earliest rovers to prowl the Caribbean with Jamaican licenses would be Puritan coreligionists who had sailed down from North America as well as foreign mercenaries such as the Dutch-born brothers Abraham and Willem Blauveldt or "Bluefield," Kempo Sibata of "Pequott" (modern New London, Connecticut), Laurens Prins or "Lawrence Prince," the Belgian-born Adriaen van Diemen Swart, and the Danish privateer Jon Petersen or "John Peterson."

On nearby Hispaniola, French hunters known as *boucaniers*—from their practice of curing meat in extemporized smokehouses called *boucans*—also began probing ever deeper inland from its western and northern shorelines, clashing with the few Spanish plantation owners who were clustered farther to its southeast around the city of Santo Domingo, thereby adding to the surly undertone that was already coming to characterize this entire troubled theater. Out of such frictions, a distinct class of irregular French privateers called the *flibustiers* would emerge, their ranks often consisting of Huguenot settlers who were willing to make seasonal forays against their Spanish foes under any flag of convenience, being motivated principally by personal animosity and a need for money.

Larger European conflicts would also contribute to this ceaseless round of turmoil in the West Indies, each new outbreak being seized upon as excuses whenever they happened to flare up on the far side of

Pirates fighting their way aboard a ship during the early 18th century; a painting by Frederick J. Waugh, 1910. (Library of Congress)

the Atlantic—although the freewheeling corsairs would often reinter-
pret these distant disputes to suit their own particular purposes, such
as when Jamaica's licensed privateers flatly refused to attack their
country's nominal Dutch enemies during the Second Anglo-Dutch War
of 1665–1667, instead openly declaring that "there was more profit with
less hazard" to be gotten against the neutral Spaniards and thus con-
fining most of their subsequent operations against that traditional
opponent. Their French colleagues did exactly the same, such as when
Jean-David Nau l'Olonnais swept through the hapless Laguna de
Maracaibo during the summer of 1666, in direct contravention of the
peaceful relations supposedly existing between Paris and Madrid.

Soon, the freebooters' propensity for such unauthorized depredations began to exasperate their home governments, as well as the
emerging class of merchant traders and large-scale planters who were
beginning to expand their commercial interests and influence in the
West Indies and wished for some measure of peace and stability in
order for these ventures to prosper. Such growing intolerance would
lead to the arrest of Henry Morgan and Governor Sir Thomas Modyford of Jamaica, after the spectacular peacetime raid they had engi-
neered against Panama in January 1671. Yet the protracted European
struggle that almost immediately thereafter ensued, pitting France
against Spain and Holland for the remainder of the 1670s, continued
to provide ample employment for a whole new generation of piratical
mercenaries—including such men as Thomas Paine of Martha's Vine-
yard, who would enrich himself so handsomely during his years of
renegade service as a cohort of French *flibustiers* that he was eventually
able to settle down as a wealthy and well-respected citizen of Newport, Rhode Island, where he died at the ripe old age of 87 in 1715.

Meanwhile, the ungovernable privateers would continue making
assaults in the Antilles, even after a general peace had been temporarily patched up back in Europe with the signing of the Treaty of Nijme-
gen in the spring of 1679. Notwithstanding, a citizen of the Spanish
American port of Cartagena would lament three years after this particular transatlantic ceremony had been concluded that, during the
ensuing interlude of supposed "peace" in the West Indies,

> Trinidad has been robbed once; Margarita and Guayana burnt once
> and sacked twice; La Guaira sacked once and its inhabitants sold, the
> ransom for its women and children amounting to more than 100,000
> pesos, in addition to the 300,000 which [the pirates] seized in the city
> and other damages. [These raiders also] entered Puerto Caballos and

A West Indian corsair, as depicted amid his booty by Howard Pyle. Note his musket, pistol, and cutlass, as well as how a ship's yard and canvas have been used to erect the tent, a common practice whenever resting in a deserted bay. (Merle Johnson, comp., *Howard Pyle's Book of Pirates* [New York: Harper & Brothers, ca. 1921])

sacked Valencia, which is more than twenty leagues inland. Maracaibo has been robbed many times, and in the occupation of 1678, the enemy remained more than six months, reaching Trujillo, which is more than sixteen days' journey inland . . . and causing such heavy damage to its farms, that whereas before they provided twenty shiploads of cacao [a year], today they produce no more than four. The city of Riohacha has been abandoned, the city and garrison of Santa Marta sacked more than three times and burnt once, from which its citizens have yet to recover. And here in Cartagena, which formerly had more than twenty ship-owners, today not a single one remains.[3]

Still worse was to follow, for over the next few years, the buccaneers would grow in boldness and attain the zenith of their cruel power under such gifted leaders as Laurens de Graaf and the Sieur de Grammont, seizing major port cities such as Veracruz and Campeche and holding them with contemptuous impunity. Their strength even awed Captain David Mitchell of the 48-gun frigate HMS *Ruby*—the most powerful Royal Navy warship stationed in the West Indies—when he chanced upon a pirate assembly anchored off Cuba's Isla de Pinos in April 1685. Espying the renegade Captain Joseph Bannister's *Golden Fleece* riding in their midst, he went aboard Grammont's flagship to demand this outlaw's arrest for illegally serving under a foreign commission; yet when the *flibustier* chieftain piously assured the Royal Navy officer that Bannister had not actually entered French service yet, Mitchell "thought it best not to insist further."

EXPANSION AND DECLINE (1680–1688)

Ironically, such unchallengeable power would also contribute to the pirates' growing disillusionment and the first probes outside their traditional theater of operations during the 1680s, after they found that individual ship prizes were becoming ever more scarce in the Caribbean, while a growing number of Spanish American coastal towns were being abandoned altogether—thereby providing fewer easy targets for smaller bands of freebooters. Simultaneously, major strongholds were becoming better fortified and Spanish riches more prudently guarded deeper inland, all at a time when rover gatherings for any contemplated strike were attracting record numbers of expectant volunteers from throughout the entire region and beyond—so many, in fact, that no target except the very richest city could possibly satisfy all such participants when its booty would have to be split up among such a host of contentious campaigners.

Therefore, in response to the declining prospects brought on by their success in the West Indies, some of the more aggressive captains took to anchoring their ships in hidden bays on Golden Island and trudging their crews through steamy jungles with native guides across the narrow Isthmus of Panama to seize coastal craft on its far shores and use these to initiate a whole new reign of terror against Spanish shipping in the hapless Pacific. A decade of such far-flung marauding would ensue, with commanders such as Bartholomew Sharpe, George Dew, and Pierre le Picard eventually struggling back around Cape Horn or fighting their way across Central America with considerable booty and immediately decamping from the West Indies to avoid prosecution on any charges of piracy because of a lack of material witnesses to such distant crimes.

For during their absence, piracy and privateering had continued to undergo notable changes in the Caribbean. Simple questions of supply and rearmament were becoming a greater worry for those commanders who had chosen to remain behind there, while the number of safe havens where rovers might dispose of their plunder and effect repairs was contracting as commercial and plantation interests had at last begun enacting laws designed to rein in and regulate such unbridled conduct. Gone were the days when any booty-laden flotilla of whatever nationality might find a rollicking welcome at Jamaica, and, although less developed harbors might still beckon such independent operators, their establishments and resources were inferior. A few veteran captains—seasoned campaigners such as Michiel Andrieszoon and Jan Willems—had even taken to traveling as far north as Boston or Rhode Island to find temporary sanctuaries, until these venues, too, would become closed to them by royal decrees.

For on November 16, 1686, an agreement was signed between James II of England and Louis XIV of France aimed at restricting the lawless rampages of each nation's buccaneers in the New World. And such an arrangement had sprung from a much broader 20-year truce crafted two years previously between Europe's war-weary powers at Ratisbonne or Regensburg, whose very first article called for a complete cessation of hostilities "within Europe and without, both on this side of and beyond the Line."

In such a changed and evolving diplomatic environment, the French governor of Saint-Domingue—Pierre-Paul Tarin, Sieur de Cussy, long an ardent champion of its pugnacious *flibustiers*—was directed to publish a royal proclamation on March 9, 1687, which commanded all French freebooters to cease their depredations against Spanish American targets and embrace an amnesty, "on conditions that they return into ports and cease their piratical acts and become inhabitants, or give themselves to the business of the sea." The high-water mark of Caribbean privateering and its piratical offshoots had crested and was at last starting to recede.

FALL FROM GRACE (1689–1713)

A mere two years later, when the War of the League of Augsburg or King William's War exploded in Europe—with France being ranged against the combined might of England, Holland, and Spain— Governor de Cussy would complain bitterly to Paris that his concerns about disbanding the *flibustiers* of Saint-Domingue had been amply vindicated. "I destroyed privateering here because the court so willed it," he wrote from Port de Paix that same August 1689, adding that if he had not been commanded to do so by the Crown ministry, "there would be ten or twelve stout ships on this coast, with many brave people aboard to preserve this colony and its commerce."

Moreover, many rovers who did remain active and found renewed employment as wartime privateers during the ensuing eight years of conflict would find considerable disappointments. Those who served during King William's War under English or Dutch colors were prevented from attacking their traditional Spanish targets, while legitimate prizes soon grew scarce as the outnumbered French merchant shipping was swept from the seas. On the other side, *flibustiers* fared better in their independent cruises, but their participation in major enterprises such as the invasion of Jamaica in 1694 netted only meager rewards, as more than a thousand freebooters took part as unsalaried auxiliaries for relatively little gain because of their large numbers.

West Indian mercenaries in general, once so crucial to any successful operation in that theater, now found their roles reduced to a mere secondary status in expeditions spearheaded by royal squadrons or regiments. Their self-serving attitude toward military duty made privateers seem like unreliable, mercurial scavengers to senior European officers when compared to the more sternly disciplined naval seamen and regular troops being brought out across the ocean. The 1,000 illdisciplined French buccaneers, for example, who—motivated largely by greed—volunteered to join Admiral de Pointis's final assault against Cartagena in the spring of 1697, were treated with outright contempt by this haughty, blue-blooded commander: assigned the worst quarters, barred from entering the conquered city, and cheated of their lowly share in its booty, much to their fury. They even sued Pointis in a Parisian court, eventually obtaining a slightly larger payout.

Significantly, the richest hauls made during King William's War by privateers were to come from small independent forays, such as Thomas Tew's or William Mayes's lone-wolf forays far around the world into the neutral Indian Ocean and Red Sea—illicit campaigns that contributed nothing to Crown strategy or the actual conduct of naval operations yet proved so spectacularly profitable for these few-score participants that they would spawn dozens of imitators. Lonely harbors along Madagascar's extensive coastline provided temporary way stations for such lawless rovers as they circled around the Cape of Good Hope to exploit this vulnerable new hunting ground.

But the great heyday of Caribbean privateering was clearly fading, a fact that would be underscored during the War of the Spanish Succession or Queen Anne's War, which erupted in 1702 and lasted for a dozen years. During this struggle, the alliance between the French and Spanish Crowns meant that it would now be the *flibustiers* who would have to refrain from attacking Spanish targets, although British and Dutch rovers scarcely fared any better. Notwithstanding an early flurry of captures of merchantmen, their land assaults proved dismal failures, and their old freewheeling tactics were being much more tightly monitored by the Crown authorities. Respectable letter-of-marque vessels enjoyed precedence in securing licenses, their good conduct being enforced through the posting of bonds, while the more roguish freebooters were reduced to supplementing their limited prize earnings through smuggling, blockade running, and even salvage work.

LAST ANGRY HURRAH (1714–1725)

By the time Queen Anne's War finally ceased in the spring of 1713, most people welcomed a return to peace after a generation of unremitting conflict. Only the now-unemployed privateers—already disappointed by their slender pickings during this recently concluded conflict—were reluctant to resume eking out a meager living as low-paid merchant sailors. Long gone were the days when such veteran rovers might have been needed in most major colonies, treaties having long since resolved most territorial disputes with Spain, while royal garrisons and naval patrols were becoming permanent fixtures in Antillean waters, providing a much more reliable means of defense throughout that entire theater. Moreover, most West Indian economies were now expanding and increasingly dominated by large-scale plantations and their ancillary services. As the 18th century advanced, merchant vessels would continue to arrive with thousands more African slaves and depart with ever-larger commercial shipments of sugar and tobacco.

Freebooters, already viewed with distrust by Crown officials and leading citizens because of their propensity for unsanctioned and disruptive actions, found no place in this new economy. Several hundred of the wilder spirits consequently drifted into the Bahamas, whose archipelago had been left depopulated by repeated wartime raids by Cuban corsairs, and since the peace was being neglected by its bankrupt private owners back in London. The deserted anchorage of Nassau on New Providence Island became virtually an open port, where wayward rovers might gather and operate completely without restraint. The influx of such ruffians and free spirits accelerated after a Spanish plate fleet was wrecked on the nearby Florida coast in late July 1715, sparking an onrush of fortune seekers and other desperadoes into these waters who transformed idle Nassau into a thriving pirate lair.

With its colonial administration eradicated years earlier, renegades such as Charles Vane and Benjamin Hornigold began venturing in and

The Spaniards painstakingly built dozens of forts during the 17th century to protect themselves from Caribbean pirates. This is El Castillo, a stronghold overlooking the Devil's Torrent rapids on the San Juan River, erected during 1673–1675 so as to prevent any more raids upstream into the interior of Nicaragua. (Corbis)

out of its harbor with impunity, disposing of illicit prizes and even emplacing guns in Fort Nassau's crudely reconstructed embrasures so as to control the harbor and the tattered remnants of its town. Marauders could act there as they pleased, bringing in vessels of every nationality and clearing for any destination without any pretense at legality. At the same time, a Spanish sweep along the remote Mosquito Coast and the erection of a permanent fort at the mouth of Mexico's Bay of Campeche in December 1716 had reduced the available number of sanctuaries elsewhere for such outlaws.

Fearful that the Bahamas were becoming "another Madagascar," worried Crown ministers in London informed the Council of Trade and Plantations that measures would have to be taken "to dislodge those profligate fellows or pirates that may have possessed themselves of the island of Providence." In September 1717, a transatlantic proclamation was sent out, offering a general pardon to any and all such rogues who surrendered by next summer, when a recolonizing expedition was scheduled to arrive and reclaim Nassau as a lawfully constituted port under a Crown-appointed governor—furthermore backed by a deployment of peacetime Royal Navy patrols that were not only to hunt down any diehards in the Bahamas but throughout the Caribbean as well.

Despite blustering defiance, the last great generation of pirates would not contest this reclamation of Nassau. Instead, the most recalcitrant either dispersed beforehand so as to continue roving freely—such as Blackbeard, Stede Bonnet, Edward England, Richard Noland, and others—while the more calculating remained in that port to swear fealty to the arriving governor, to test what service they might find as loyal privateers, a course chosen by such hard-bitten captains as Benjamin Hornigold and John Auger. Only Charles Vane directly challenged the entry into Nassau's anchorage by Woodes Rogers's expedition on the morning of July 27, 1718 (O.S.), before grudgingly making way and escaping via its eastern channel.

The new royal governor stepped ashore that same afternoon, to be greeted by an honor guard of 300 boozy pirates under Hornigold and several lesser commanders. Yet none of these leaders would be appointed to any posts in Nassau's new administration, nor would they be employed in helping reconstitute its militia companies or in repairing its decrepit fortress or in any other civic improvement such as erecting a new barracks and eastern battery. The disappointed rovers soon began drifting away, and Rogers informed his superiors in London later that same summer: "We have scarce half of those who have been pirates left, for they soon became weary of living under

The pirate Capt. Stede Bonnet being brought before his captor, Col. William Rhett, in September 1718; scene off the Cape Fear River mouth of North Carolina, as imagined by Howard Pyle. (Merle Johnson, comp., *Howard Pyle's Book of Pirates* [New York: Harper & Brothers, ca. 1921])

restraint, and are either gone to several parts of North America, or engaged themselves on services at sea, which I was willing to promote, for they are not the people I ought to think will make any land improvements, and I wish they may be faithful at sea."

Bereft of their last major refuge, the pirates scattered, some disappearing back into civilian life in the Carolinas or Rhode Island. However, their most defiant leaders—those who had preferred to remain roaming the seas, deriding any proffered royal amnesty—now conducted themselves as wanton criminals, preying without qualms upon merchantmen sailing even under their own national flag and abusing their hapless victims in brutal fits of anger. "I am a free prince," one such diehard leader—Sam Bellamy—had supposedly roared at the master of a Boston merchant ship that he had captured off South Carolina, "and I have as much authority to make war on the whole world as he who has a hundred sail of ships at sea, and an army of one hundred thousand men in the field!"

Yet such a boast masked hidden fears due to the rovers' clearly faded strength and grim prospects. Homeless except for a few impoverished bolt-holes sweltering in remote, unwanted corners of the world, they would restlessly and maliciously prowl the oceans to Africa and Madagascar, then back to Brazil and the Antilles, and up to North America—all without finding any release except impoverished retirement, or death.

NOTES

1. Plutarch, *Life of Julius Caesar*, chapter 2.
2. Donald B. Freeman, *The Straits of Malacca: Gateway or Gauntlet?* (Montreal: McGill-Queen's University Press, 2003), 175.
3. David F. Marley, *Pirates and Privateers of the Americas* (Santa Barbara, CA: ABC-CLIO, 1994), x.

2

DAILY LIFE IN THE PIRATE WORLD

This cursed trade has been so long followed, and there is so many of it, that like weeds or Hydras they spring up as fast as we can cut them down.

—Jamaica's governor, Sir Thomas Lynch, January 1673

What we know today as the golden age of piracy first flared up in the Caribbean, spread into the Pacific, and eventually seared the distant shores of West Africa, the Indian Ocean, and Brazil, before finally being tamped back down by the expansion of royal rule and global commerce. During the brief 75-year reign of these restless nomads—scarcely three generations—a unique lifestyle would evolve, still recognizable to modern eyes.

The first buccaneers had begun as impoverished West Indian settlers who, once their simple planting was done and the cyclical hurricane season had ended, would take to small boats and assemble into armed bands to attack Spanish American shipping and towns. They were already steeped in the Antillean lifestyle and diet, indifferent to any diplomatic niceties back in Europe, and accepted orders from no one except their chosen leaders—charismatic rogues such as Henry Morgan or Jean-David Nau l'Olonnais, who knew how to lead such mercurial men in their raw thirst for booty. And upon the successful conclusion of any campaign, most of these buccaneers would simply fade away with their loot, vanishing into tiny settlements hidden around tropical bays—to sortie once again several months later as the spirit or need moved them.

The success of such early raiders, along with the conquest of colonial footholds on both Jamaica and Saint-Domingue (Haiti), would spawn a distinct new class of seagoing mercenaries in the Caribbean who would likewise soon master these piratical tactics. Giving themselves over completely to freebooting and pillage as a profession, these privateers or *flibustiers* would raid Spaniards for supplies and then strike at a choice target—selected strictly for its profitability—under any flag of convenience. At first, colonial administrators had welcomed these lawless operators into their ports, especially to dispose of prizes that notably stimulated their local economies, while the very presence of such marauders furthermore reassured honest settlers and scared away Spanish corsairs. Seasoned commanders such as Laurens de Graaf even came to be wooed with knighthoods and lands during the 1680s, before Crown ministers in London and Paris finally decided to curtail all support for such wanton depredations, because they adversely affected the plantation-based sugar trade that was beginning to surge in importance.

More and more seaports were closed to the most blatant offenders, and returning to civilian life became perilously complicated for unrestrained mavericks. Some defiant captains had already penetrated into the Pacific, learning that crimes committed in those distant waters were difficult to prosecute at home. Many North American adventurers consequently began making forays halfway around the world during the lean years of King William's War, winning fortunes through piratical interceptions in the Red Sea and covert disposal of their booty with corrupt accomplices at home. Yet once peace was officially restored, Captain William Kidd found himself run to ground in Boston as an outlaw in 1699 and hanged for just such an illegal escapade.

After another disappointing decade spent serving as privateers during Queen Anne's War from 1702 to 1713, the last generation of rovers exploded into a wave of angry aggression under such unrepentant pirates as Sam Bellamy and Blackbeard, attacking vessels of every nationality—including their own—with a reckless fury, scornful of any proffered royal pardons or humanitarian appeals.

HOW DID PIRATES LIVE?

Throughout these various stages in their evolution, pirates had tended to retain certain practices that had originated with their Caribbean roots—such as a predilection for rum and spicy West Indian dishes—as well as other observances that were more widely commonplace to that age. For example, like most people living during the late 17th and early 18th centuries, prior to the invention of electric lighting,

- pirates usually worked from sunup to sunset, rising shortly before daybreak and sleeping in only on Sundays;
- they ate two meals a day, once in the morning and again in mid- to late afternoon, in gatherings around a communal kettle; and
- they frequently smoked tobacco, a habit often acquired in childhood.

Lacking any regular supply system, pirates furthermore had to steal provisions whenever they could find them and thus often endured real want, thirst, or need during their far-flung wanderings—fueling their heartless pillaging of many vessels and towns that had the misfortune to fall into their hands.

At Sea

No vessel or crew during this era could operate for more than a few months on the open ocean before their crudely preserved food and

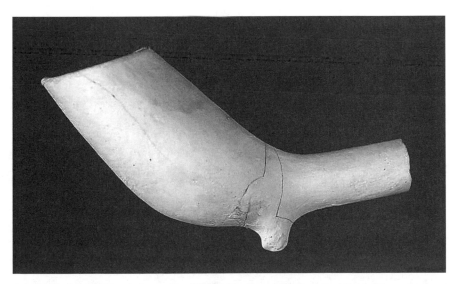

Pipe bowl recovered from Blackbeard's flagship *Queen Anne's Revenge*, lost while trying to work its way into Beaufort Inlet, North Carolina, in June 1718. Smoking was very widespread during the 17th and 18th centuries, starting at a very early age. (Karen Browning/North Carolina Department of Cultural Resources)

drink began to grow foul, firewood for cooking meals began to run low, and the wooden ships themselves required maintenance. This was especially true of pirate vessels, which frequently crammed as many men aboard as possible in order to overwhelm and carry off prizes or even assault towns. Typically, pirate ships sailed much more heavily manned than merchant vessels, while lacking the ready resources of food, drink, and supplies available to royal warships of a comparable size.

For this reason, pirates normally remained at sea for only short intervals, prowling a rich hunting ground for prizes before making a few captures, then retiring into a lonely anchorage to recuperate. The capture of any vessel transporting provisions might facilitate such a retreat. Voyages to distant destinations such as the Red Sea would have to be done in stages, and shipboard life for rovers tended to mirror those aboard other contemporary vessels. Pirates

- slept in hammocks;
- ate twice a day in small groups known as messes, meals being cooked in a central galley;
- received an equal portion of whatever rations were available to the crew;
- manned the sails and rigging to work their vessel;
- helped maintain the ship's equipment and armaments;
- and sometimes held drills.

Prisoners or slaves were often forced to perform the heaviest or dirtiest duties aboard ship, while discipline among the pirates was not as heavy handed as on contemporary warships or merchantmen—although they were sufficiently organized to properly work their vessel. Orders still had to be obeyed at sea, because any inattention or drunkenness could result in disastrous consequences for a wooden ship under sail. Not even a fearsome captain as Blackbeard could have navigated for thousands of miles of open ocean and through perilous West Indian shoals without a competent crew.

On Land

The earliest buccaneers had been most dangerous when operating ashore, many being ex-soldiers. They were also capable of skillfully using boats to steal along jungle coastlines or to push scores of miles up winding, tropical rivers, to surprise their Spanish American victims. Buccaneer armies even marched in loose battle lines and unleashed ferocious volleys upon their opponents, sometimes after having trekked for many miles through steamy wilderness. Yet their military prowess was eventually superseded and rendered redundant by royal regiments sent out to the Antilles from Europe, plus the erection of powerful fortified garrisons throughout the Americas, which reduced buccaneers to the status of unwanted and unreliable auxiliaries to the professional generals who henceforth commanded during time of war.

Therefore, by the early 18th century, pirates would mostly venture onto land to rest, resupply, careen their ships, and ride out stormy weather. They proved adept at setting up shore camps everywhere in the world—as far abroad as the Galapagos Islands, California, and Madagascar—in which they could live for weeks, even months on end. After exploring and securing a sheltered anchorage, pirates would proceed to lighten their ship in preparation for being warped up close to the beach and tilted over so as to begin cleaning its hull, by first

- ferrying all guns, powder barrels, and heavy rounds ashore, to be installed into defensive batteries;
- unslinging the sails, yardarms, blocks, and rigging to be used to erect large pavilions ashore, the largest usually reserved as a mess hall and others to protect general stores;
- transferring shipboard machinery to be used to operate the wooden hoists on land;
- occupying the highest point of land around as a lookout spot to be kept manned around the clock; and
- clearing a rough campground.

Pirates normally claimed spots to sling their hammocks between trees, a short distance away from the main campfire. A normal routine would be as follows:

- At dawn, the night watch would be relieved and any prisoners released from confinement.
- After breakfast, work on the ship or its equipment would resume.
- Labors would ease as the tropical heat built up in the afternoon, before a halt was finally called for supper.
- After this main meal had been consumed, pirates often broke up into groups and entertained themselves with target shooting, competitions, music, gambling, and plays.
- At sundown, prisoners would be confined once again for the night and a watch set.
- Most captains allowed individual pirates to remain unsupervised around the campfire after lights-out.

If any stay proved protracted, fresh food could become a problem, so foraging parties might be sent out to hunt, fish, or rustle livestock or raid nearby villages. The entire pirate encampment might be relocated if local stocks of fish, game, or fruit became too depleted, while detachments might split away from the group altogether.

Leadership

It was often while at rest that changes in command might occur, such as one captain being voted out in favor of another. For example, after cruising around Cuba, Benjamin Hornigold and his French consort, Louis La Buze, dropped anchor off a quiet Haitian harbor in late May 1716, where the former was surprised to be voted out in favor of crewman Samuel Bellamy "upon a difference arising amongst the English pirates because Hornygold [sic] refused to take and plunder English vessels."[1] The proportion of this vote was reflected when Hornigold departed for South Carolina with only 26 loyal hands aboard a small prize sloop, leaving Bellamy in command of 90 pirates aboard the flagship *Mary Anne*.

To modern eyes, the marauders' adherence to democratic principles in electing their leaders seems admirable and enlightened—especially during an era when inherited titles, royal appointments, and a rigid hierarchy ruled almost every other aspect of society. But pirates believed in expressing their will and in adhering to their ancient right of putting important matters to a vote. Some gatherings had proven truly memorable. On April 7, 1683, a multinational throng of buccaneers had met on a beach at Roatán to debate a proposed assault against Veracruz. This large Mexican seaport had never been threatened in living memory, yet doubters among the crowd were swayed when the *flibustier* chieftain Grammont allegedly bellowed out over their heads: "I would believe it almost impossible, except for the experience and valor of those who hear my words."[2] Enflamed, the pirates had endorsed this plan with a roar of acclamation, 1,300 to 1,400 thereupon setting sail to carry out this bold attack.

Yet their democratic ideals could also prove mean-spirited and vindictive. Bellamy himself, after intercepting and plundering a harmless merchant sloop out of Boston in April 1717, intended to restore this vessel to its master—but his company instead voted to sink it. "Damn my blood," Bellamy swore, as he told the unfortunate master of their decision, "I'm sorry they won't let you have your sloop again, for I scorn to do anyone a mischief, when it is not for my advantage."[3] The merchant skipper had to watch his sloop slide beneath the waves, and some time afterward, he was set ashore on Block Island, regaining his home at Newport, Rhode Island, by May 1, 1717 (O.S.)—four days after Bellamy and most of his pirate crew had perished in a storm.

Rules

Early buccaneer expeditions had often been preceded by the signing of a charter party, a document specifying how booty was to be divided, losses compensated, and so forth. The expression had originally been a French commercial term, used whenever two or more merchants had shared a hired vessel. If only a single individual were involved, the question of assigning cargo space would not be a pressing concern; yet in the case of a *charte-partie*—literally, a "split charter"—each consignor's portion had to be carefully allotted. Seventeenth-century French *flibustiers,* many of whom were ex–merchant sailors, adopted this phrase to their own usage by agreeing in writing on a proportional distribution of "purchase" before any cruise, with special provisos for compensating the wounded, senior commanders, and so on. Such documents could be submitted to a court of law for arbitration.

For pirates, many of whom were illiterate, such written agreements held special significance. By the second decade of the 18th century, with piracy on the decline, new members joined by signing the written articles of a particular crew. By then, though, such documents had become more like secret covenants, the outlaws themselves going to great pains to destroy such papers whenever in danger of capture, as they realized that they could be presented against them as evidence. The untimely death of Bartholomew Roberts off the West African coast in February 1722 resulted in the discovery of just such a set of papers in his cabin, which read in its entirety:

I. Every man shall have an equal vote in affairs of moment. He shall have an equal title to the fresh provisions or strong liquors at any time seized, and shall use them at pleasure, unless a scarcity may make it necessary for the common good that a retrenchment may be voted.

II. Every man shall be called fairly in turn by the list on board of prizes, because over and above their proper share, they are allowed a shift of clothes. But if they defraud the company to the value of even one dollar in plate, jewels, or money, they shall be marooned. If any man rob another, he shall have his nose and ears slit, and be put ashore where he shall be sure to encounter hardships.

III. None shall game for money, either with dice or cards.

IV. The lights and candles should be put out at eight at night, and if any of the crew desire to drink after that hour, they shall sit upon the open deck without lights.

V. Each man shall keep his piece, cutlass, and pistols at all times clean and ready for action.

VI. No boy or woman to be allowed amongst them. If any man shall be found seducing any of the latter sex and carrying her to sea in disguise, he shall suffer death.

VII. He that shall desert the ship or his quarters in time of battle, shall be punished by death or marooning.

VIII. None shall strike another on board the ship, but every man's quarrel shall be ended on shore by sword or pistol, in this manner: at the word of command from the quartermaster, each man being previously placed back to back, shall turn and fire immediately. If any man do not, the quartermaster shall knock the piece out of his hand. If both miss their aim, they shall take to their cutlasses, and he that draws first blood shall be declared the victor.

IX. No man shall talk of breaking up their way of living, till each has a share of £1,000. Every man who shall become a cripple or lose a limb in the service, shall have eight hundred pieces-of-eight from the common stock, and for lesser hurts proportionately.

X. The captain and the quartermaster shall each receive two shares of a prize; the master, gunner, and boatswain, one and one half shares; all other officers, one and one quarter, and private gentlemen of fortune [i.e., ordinary hands] one share each.

XI. The musicians shall have rest on the Sabbath Day only, by right; on all other days, by favor only.

These rules were typical of those enforced on other contemporary pirate ships.

WHERE DID PIRATES COME FROM?

The vast majority of freebooters did not aspire to spend their life as outlaws, or even to serve a particularly long time at sea. If anything, they entertained rather vague notions about enriching themselves through a few bold and lucrative captures so as to someday retire from seafaring in comfort. Few succeeded. It was almost impossible to win enough money through captures alone, since long-term investments were beyond the reach of most low-born people during the 17th and 18th centuries. And in any event, the younger rovers often squandered their booty on reckless sprees, while seasoned commanders could seldom amass enough money to sustain their families and retinues for any extended period of time.

Even pirate chieftains who happened to make spectacular hauls had to persist for years in their rough calling. The great Laurens de Graaf would enjoy repeated successes against the Spaniards, taking many ships and sometimes entire cities, yet he would spend a quarter century roving, well into his middle age. Thomas Tew slipped back into his home port of Newport, Rhode Island, in April 1694 with a dazzling fortune—only to ship out again that same November and be killed within a year while attempting another capture in the Indian Ocean. The brutish Blackbeard betrayed hundreds of his colleagues and disappeared up a North Carolina river with the bulk of their combined booty in June 1718 to purchase a pardon and a house at Bath and even marry a local girl—yet he had resumed his sea robberies by that same August and was hacked and shot to death in a bloody confrontation with a naval force before the year was out.

Despite such discouraging fates, the ranks of West Indian pirate crews would be continuously replenished for many decades, principally from the callings that follow.

Wartime Privateers

Fighting men who operated as mercenaries during wartime usually did not enjoy any return to peacetime employment. Many freebooters preferred to continue roving, even under different flags or with the flimsiest of authorizations, rather than submit to their only other alternative: low-paid jobs as merchant sailors. Since the earliest days of buccaneering, independent-minded adventurers had found outlets to continue with their calling, sometimes conducting themselves so marginally as to drift over into a legal definition of piracy.

For example, the licensed privateer Willem Albertszoon Blauveldt regained his home port of New Amsterdam—modern New York City—in the spring of 1649 with his six-gun, 50-man ship *La Garce*, bringing in a Spanish bark captured off Tabasco, only to be informed that a quarter-century of hostility between The Netherlands and Spain had at last ceased back in Europe. To retain this prize, Blauveldt and his crew had to swear that at the time of its seizure, they had "heard nothing of a peace with Spain,"[4] so this bark was eventually awarded to them by the autumn of 1651. Yet Blauveldt—a veteran West Indian campaigner who knew no other life than roving—would nonetheless continue making forays south into the Antilles, even though he could no longer bring home his prizes as a licensed Dutch rover. Rather, it is believed that he operated as of 1652 under a French commission obtained from an obliging West Indian governor, as that country remained at war

Pirate recruits paraded before Capt. Henry Morgan for admission into his ranks; although an imagined scene by Howard Pyle, commanders did indeed seek additional followers when embarking on major enterprises. (Merle Johnson, comp., *Howard Pyle's Book of Pirates* [New York: Harper & Brothers, ca. 1921])

against Spain—authorization that caused some unease among New Amsterdam's officials whenever Blauveldt and his rough-hewn crew happened to return home to relax between cruises.

When another Dutch captain, Pieter de Graeff, arrived to sell off his own Spanish prize in July 1656—seized while likewise sailing under a French letter of marque issued to him by the governor of Guadeloupe—he was required to post a hefty security "to prove the legality of his commission and the lawfulness of the prize."[5] And perhaps not coincidentally, this was to be the last year that Blauveldt's name also appeared in New Amsterdam's records, having presumably emigrated to resettle among the English Puritans on recently conquered Jamaica, where his Frisian-born friend and colleague Remco Siebada was already serving as a welcome auxiliary.

Over the next 60 years, thousands of private captains would secure licenses from a wide array of countries—England, France, Holland, Portugal, Denmark, Spain, and Germany—to conduct diverse hostilities in the West Indies, hundreds becoming so accustomed to such employment as to follow it for years. The last generation that emerged as outright pirates during the early 18th century had also just spent a decade or more fighting as privateers during Queen Anne's War from 1702 to 1713, and continued roving on their own account.

Resident Buccaneers

One of the earliest sources of 17th-century pirate crewmen were the small bands of hunters who roamed along the jungle shores of Hispaniola, Cuba, and Central America. They were crack shots, inured to the climate, answered to no one, traveled easily aboard dugout canoes, and hated the Spaniards. As long ago as 1620, when the French privateer Charles Fleury had first visited Plateforme in Haiti, he and his crew had met a pair of such hunters ashore—one mulatto and one black, slaves who had escaped from Baracoa in Cuba—roaming with their pack of 10 large dogs. They had offered to supply the Frenchmen's vessel with meat from the cattle and pigs that were running wild on Hispaniola. When Fleury accepted, the hunters killed 18 cows within two days and cured the meat by smoking rather than salting it. They had furthermore told Fleury "that if he had a larger ship, in less than fifteen days or three weeks, they could have filled it with hides."[6]

Pockets of such tough, seminomadic woodsmen could be encountered along various stretches of coastline, most having adopted the Arawak style for curing meat. Wherever a large cow was slain, a wooden *boucan* or smokehouse would be erected near the carcass to cure choice cuts inside with a slow fire to be retrieved later. Such men were consequently called *boucaniers* in French, *bucaneros* in Spanish, and buccaneers in English. In many ways, they were similar to the mountain men who would later open the American West: pathfinders who had adapted to local conditions and customs, coming to excel in the wilderness.

To the Spanish, these buccaneers—whose ranks included many runaway slaves, hostile tribesmen, and heretical castaways—were a threat to lonely estates as rustlers, poachers of game, slave stealers, trespassers, and in general a pestilential nuisance to be hunted down like vermin. A prolonged and pitiless guerrilla struggle would be well under way by the mid-17th century, particularly on Hispaniola, where the buccaneers had grown so numerous and strong as to gather together seasonally for seaborne counterattacks against Spanish targets. Leadership among such rugged individualists, who referred to themselves as the Frères de la Cote or Brethren of the Coast, would be by popular acclaim and be retained as the rough form of democracy observed in piratical ranks for generations to come.

A typical mid-17th-century buccaneer in the West Indies, with his musket and dogs for hunting wild cattle or pigs, whose meat could then be cured over a slow fire as in the background; from a 1686 edition of the work of Alexandre-Olivier Exquemelin. (Art Media/StockphotoPro)

The initial private French settlements on Tortuga and northwestern Hispaniola relied on *boucaniers* for their survival and defense, and so tolerated for many years their unilateral depredations against the local Spaniards, regardless of whatever royal policy might be prevailing back in Paris. As a result, many of the most famous pirate offensives of the 1660s and 1670s—including large-scale joint enterprises with English allies such as Edward Mansfield or Henry Morgan—featured significant participation by *boucaniers*. It would not be until the late 1680s, when the French Crown at last began reining in unauthorized West Indian strikes, that buccaneer involvement would wane.

Religious Refugees

Rather surprisingly, some of the earliest West Indian rovers were members of various Protestant sects, who, wishing to escape official constraints in Europe on their nontraditional observances, had financed expeditions across the Atlantic to create their own utopian communities amid the freedoms of the New World.

Puritans

One such group was the Puritans, who during the 1630s had sent parties to occupy various West Indian outposts. First they had reached Santa Catarina, which they renamed Providence Island; then San Andrés, which they renamed Henrietta Island in honor of the English queen; and Tortuga Island off Hispaniola, which they called Association Island. These colonists' intent had been to support themselves by growing tobacco and cotton as well as by raiding the nearby shipping lanes of their Catholic foes, the Spaniards.

The Puritans' agricultural endeavors failed, yet they proved surprisingly effective rovers. When an English Catholic priest, Thomas Gage, traveled through these same waters as a passenger aboard a plate fleet bound toward Mexico, he later recorded:

> The greatest fear that I perceived possessed the Spaniards in this voyage, was about the island of Providence, called by them Santa Catarina, from whence they feared lest some English ships should come out against them with great strength. They cursed the English in it, and called the island the den of thieves and pirates.

Spanish counteroffensives had massacred the settlers on Tortuga Island and eliminated the last of these Puritan enclaves by 1641; yet smaller lairs survived on Roatán Island and the Mosquito Coast, while coreligionists back in England thirsted for revenge.

Eventually, the Commonwealth of Oliver Cromwell would dispatch a full-blown naval expedition late in 1654—without any declaration of war—to conquer a major new colony among Spain's West Indian possessions, failing to carry Santo Domingo but capturing Jamaica instead. Cromwell then called upon the Puritans in New England to support this new Antillean foothold, so that many of its earliest visitors were Puritan seafarers.

Huguenots

In France ever since the early 1680s, the Sun King, Louis XIV, had moved to exert absolute power. Already victorious in war, with a rich treasury, servile nobility, and a flourishing economy and arts, he had taken on its organized religions. An assembly of Catholic clergymen had been called in November 1681 to curtail the prerogatives of the pope. Henceforth, French bishops could not leave, papal legates could not arrive, royal ministers could not be excommunicated, and ecclesiastical laws could not be made without the king's consent.

And because Louis held that, to truly unite his nation, religious unanimity was required, he had also moved that same year against its Huguenots or Protestants. In a brutal measure, rough *dragons* or royal dragoons had been quartered in Protestant homes and encouraged to mistreat residents until they converted to Catholicism. Hundreds of thousands had begun to flee into Switzerland, The Netherlands, England, and German principalities.

In March 1685, the Sun King had issued an edict expelling all Jews from France's colonies. Then he had announced the Edict of Fontainebleau in October, which revoked the religious tolerance enshrined in the 1598 Edict of Nantes. Protestant rites were to be completely banned, their ministers were ordered to leave, and Huguenot newborns were to be baptized as Catholics "under penalty of a fine of five hundred *livres*, to be increased as circumstances may demand." Most Protestants who had not already fled made a grudging conversion. By January 17, 1686, Louis could boast that of his 800,000 to 900,000 Huguenot subjects, only 1,000 to 1,500 remained.

Yet a large percentage of France's most skilled craftsmen had been driven away as a result. Silk weavers, glaziers, silversmiths, clock makers, cabinetmakers, and many others were lost. In the West Indies, experienced planters and refiners would leave, and the French Royal Navy would lose some of its most able officers. And even those who remained as Catholic converts would often serve under a cloud of suspicion, with slim chances of promotion.

Indentured Servants

Although it is generally conceded that French *engagés* enjoyed better terms of service than their English counterparts—signing up for only three to four years' servitude, for example, as opposed to seven—it was nonetheless a deeply resented position that fed a steady stream of disillusioned recruits into freebooter ranks. Alexandre-Olivier Exquemelin and Ravenau de Lussan were only two of many young adventurers who began their privateering careers by fleeing West Indian masters to go a-roving. Henry Morgan was another young man who served an indenture, of which he remained very ashamed throughout the remainder of his life, eventually denying it had ever occurred.

Many became runaways simply because they despised manual labor, although there were also frequent instances of ill usage. The written instructions issued by Governor Bertrand d'Ogeron to the captain of his ship *Nativité* in August 1665 "for the preservation of *engagés* and their health"[7] reveals a host of potential abuses. The transportees were not to be struck by the seamen, D'Ogeron wrote, but only by "the captain, pilot, or quarter-master";[8] they were to be allowed ashore once land was reached, not kept on board where "sadness might make them fall ill, as I have often witnessed."[9] They were to be provided adequate sleeping and storage space during their passage, their belongings being well protected from sailors "who are ordinarily very given to thieving."[10] Fresh food and drink were also to be supplied, not some "wretched, rotten meal"[11] that would make them sicken and die; and they were not to be overcharged for their provisions. From such mistreatment would emerge many runaways to swell the ranks of the early *flibustiers*.

ESCAPE BACK INTO CIVILIAN LIFE

No rover intended to live at sea all his life or to retire into loneliness in a remote and primitive tropical bay. Like most seafarers, pirates aspired to return home—or at least back into civilized society—preferably to pass their days easily, rich with booty. Yet such an escape would prove increasingly difficult to achieve as the 17th century ended and the 18th began, with Crown policy growing more restrictive and the attention of officials more alert. As early as June 1688, for example, Captain Edward Davis and a few of his cutthroats had tried to slip peaceably

into Virginia after a three-year campaign against neutral Spanish merchantmen in the Pacific, only to be arrested upon arrival by Captain
Simon Rowe of HMS *Dumbarton*—on suspicion of piracy because of
the £1,500 of battered silver they had brought with them.

Davis and his men piously insisted that this booty had been procured in the South Sea to help them "spend the remainder of their days
honestly and quietly"; yet they were nevertheless thrown into irons.
When Rowe questioned a black slave who they had also captured and
brought along with them from the Pacific, the Royal Navy officer concluded that the rovers should have been hanged as multiple murder-
ers. Instead, Davis and the rest of his men were allowed to travel to
England aboard the merchantman *Effingham* late in 1690 to stand trial
(their appearance in court guaranteed by dispatching their treasure
separately). Although eventually cleared of all charges, these ruffians
were constrained in March 1693 to cede £300 of their booty toward
building a college in Virginia, which became William and Mary.

By the time King William's War concluded a few years afterward,
royal officers were becoming increasingly effective at running down
renegades wherever they might try to slip ashore. Even well-connected
Captain William Kidd found no escape, and a like fate befell one of his
crewmen.

Hunting Down a Pirate (Boston 1699)

On the chilly Saturday evening of November 11, 1699 (O.S.), a special messenger from the admiralty judge in Rhode Island reached
Governor Richard, Earl of Bellomont, with news that a wanted mutineer, murderer, and Red Sea pirate named James Gillam had traveled
toward Boston 10 days previously with the intent of shipping "himself
for some of the Islands, Jamaica or Barbados,"[12] beyond reach of the
law. Since this particular messenger could also recognize the mare on
which this renegade had been mounted, Bellomont sent him with a
constable

> to search all the inns in town for the mare, and at the first inn they went
> to they found her tied up in the yard. The people of the inn reported that
> the man that brought her thither had lighted off her about a quarter of
> an hour before, had then tied her, but went away without saying any-
> thing. I gave orders to the master of the inn that if anybody came to look
> after the mare, he should be sure to seize him; but nobody came for her.[13]

The governor therefore published a reward of 200 pieces of eight the
next morning for information on Gillam, "whereupon there was the

strictest search made all that day and the next that was ever made in this part of the world, but we had missed of him."[14] However, knowing that an old rover in Boston named Captain Andrew Knott was friendly with the outlaw, Bellomont questioned both him and his wife separately, learning that Gillam was traveling under the pseudonym James Kelly and had gone across the Charles River to stay in Charlestown with another acquaintance, Captain Francis Dole.

Consequently, the governor

> sent half a dozen men immediately over the water to Charlestown and Knot with 'em; they beset the house and searched it, but found not the man, Dole affirming he was not there, neither knew he any such man. Two of the men went through a field behind Dole's house, and passing through a second field they met a man in the dark (for it was 10 o'clock at night) whom they seized at all adventures, and it happened as oddly as luckily to be Gillam; he had been treating two young women some few miles off in the country, and was returning at night to his landlord Dole's house.
>
> I examined him, but he denied everything, even that he came with Kidd from Madagascar, or ever saw him in his life; but Capt. Davies who came thence with Kidd, and Kidd's men, are positive he is the man and that he went by his true name Gillam all the while he was on the voyage with 'em, and Mr. Campbell, Postmaster of this town, whom I sent to treat with Kidd, offers to swear this is the man he saw on board Kidd's sloop under the name of James Gillam. He is the most impudent, hardened villain I ever saw.[15]

Nevertheless, even Bellomont felt moved to acknowledge in his report to the Council of Trade and Plantations in London how: "My taking of Gillam was so very accidental, one would believe there was a strange fatality in that man's stars."[16]

NOTES

1. John Franklin Jameson, *Privateering and Piracy in the Colonial Period: Illustrative Documents* (New York: Macmillan, 1923), 294.

2. David F. Marley, *Sack of Veracruz: The Great Pirate Raid of 1683* (Windsor, Ontario: Netherlandic Press, 1993), 13.

3. George Francis Dow and John Henry Edmonds, *The Pirates of the New England Coast, 1630–1730* (Salem, MA: Marine Research Society, 1923), 121; quoted from Johnson's *History of the Pirates* (1727).

4. Jameson, *Privateering and Piracy*, 14.

5. E. B. O'Callaghan, ed., *Calendar of Historical Manuscripts in the Office of the Secretary of State, Albany, N. Y., Part I: Dutch Manuscripts, 1630-1664* (Albany, NY: Weed, Parsons, 1865), 170.

6. David F. Marley, *Wars of the Americas: A Chronology of Armed Conflict in the Western Hemisphere*, vol. 1 (Santa Barbara, CA: ABC-CLIO, 2008), 215.

7. Philippe de Vaissière, *Saint-Domingue* (Paris: Perrin, 1909), 27.

8. Ibid.

9. Ibid.

10. Ibid.

11. Ibid.

12. *Calendar of State Papers, Colonial: America and West Indies*, vol. 17 (London: Her Majesty's Stationery Office, 1908), 553.

13. Ibid.

14. Ibid.

15. Ibid., 554.

16. Ibid.

3

FOOD

The poorer people must have starved, if the shipping had not brought more provisions than usual. Many of them have been forced to leave Barbados and go to Jamaica and other places, merely from want of food.

—Governor-General Francis, Lord Willoughby, reporting on the aftermath of a plague of locusts, February 1664

Even amid the lush tropical beauty of the Caribbean, without any deep seasonal plunge into winters, hunger was frequently experienced during the late 17th and early 18th centuries. Fresh provisions would remain a constant source of worry for most ship commanders, including captains of very belligerent pirate crews. Foodstuffs in general were difficult to preserve in such warm climes, while supplementary supplies were imported only fitfully from overseas, and many local resources were either viewed with suspicion or ignored altogether. Crabmeat, for example, while delicious to eat and enjoyed by many slaves and among the poor, was rumored to cause temporary blindness, so it was avoided on many occasions.

All of these factors—difficulties in preservation, scarcities of supplementary foods, overlooked local resources—would combine to produce many hardships for residents and seafarers alike. As early as October 1656, Captain William Powell had reported on the deplorable straits in which the protectorate's victorious soldiers had been abandoned on newly conquered Jamaica:

> They have had a very sad dispensation, and have wanted that comfort that the State allowed them. Most of the provisions sent were laid on shore and rotted and spoiled, while many poor souls perished for want. Has seen many a poor soul languish and die of hunger by the wayside.[1]

A half-century later, starvation still haunted the West Indies, adding a fearsome twist to the cruel piratical practice of marooning their victims on desert isles. In a letter sent by Colonel William Rhett from South Carolina to his wife in November 1709, he described how a certain Captain Williams had been captured by enemy corsairs during Queen Anne's War, who had given him a cast-off sloop to carry him and his survivors home; but in traversing the Bahamas,

> the French and Spaniards took them again and stripped them, took their sloop away and put them on a maroon island, where they lived upon conches and whelks several weeks, till Capt. Joyce by chance found them and took them on board, else must have perished.[2]

BASIC CARIBBEAN STAPLES

Before joining the ranks of the buccaneers himself during the late 1660s, their future chronicler, Alexandre-Olivier Exquemelin, had listed the food crops that were then being harvested on French Hispaniola as beans, sweet potatoes, cassava, and corn. The beans, he stated, would be baked with meat, and then made into a pottage with eggs. Sweet potatoes were commonly prepared for breakfast by being

> cooked in a big pan with a little water, covered closely with a cloth, and in half an hour they are ready and as dry as chestnuts. They are served with butter and a sauce made of lemon juice, lard, and red peppers.[3]

The wealthier classes emulated the custom practiced throughout Spanish America, where breakfast often consisted of a cup of hot chocolate and some sweetbreads.

Any leftover cooked sweet potatoes, according to Exquemelin, would be cut into slices and put into a crock, then have hot water poured over them. This liquid would be strained through a cloth into a cauldron and left to ferment for a few days, resulting in a drink called *mobby*, which was considered to be "very good and nourishing."

A Royal Navy cook, boiling salt beef or pork in a cauldron. Incapacitated seamen were often assigned to such duties, whether aboard naval, commercial, privateer, or pirate vessels. (Art Media/StockphotoPro)

Cassava was mass produced throughout the West Indies to provide sustenance for its large and ever-expanding numbers of indentured servants and slaves. The plants were extracted from the manioc shrub, which was native to tropical America. The tuberous roots were dug up and scraped with graters of copper or tin; the shavings were put into coarse sacks to have all their moisture pressed out, then were sifted, resulting in a fine meal with the texture of sawdust. This fine meal would then in turn be baked on a hot iron griddle into a sort of cake, and these put on the rooftops to dry in the sun. Any remaining coarse residue that could not pass through the sieve would be used to make cakes five or six inches thick, which were then piled on top of each other and left to ferment into a beerlike drink. A type of tapioca could also be prepared from this meal; yet, because of cassava's lowly association with the servile classes, all such variants—the cakes, the drink, the tapioca—held a negative connotation among European emigrants.

In a letter dated November 19, 1681, the Comte de Blénac, governor-general of the French Antilles, would deplore the heartless exploitation of newly arrived indentured servants, narrating how a typical settler treated his *engagé*:

> He usually puts him on a diet of cassava, water, and three pounds of stinking beef a week. The *engagé,* who is unaccustomed to such a life, falls prey to colic, swelling of the legs, fever, and stomach-ache. The settler believes his money lost, as the agreed indenture continues to expire, so no matter how sick, will beat him to make him work.[4]

From such ill treatment would emerge many embittered runaways to swell the ranks of the *flibustiers*—and most with a lifelong distaste for cassava.

Corn was another staple widely grown throughout the Antilles, as well as on the American mainland. A young piratical deserter named Jean Villebon (a contemporary of Exquemelin) would tell his Costa Rican interrogators in April 1669 how he and 25 companions had been roaming along that province's Caribbean shoreline, crammed aboard two piraguas in search of a larger ship that they might join or seize. Upon reaching Portete—an open anchorage two miles west of what is today Puerto Limón—a detachment of 16 of these marauders had raided the inland Spanish farms around Matina for food, returning with a mule bearing corn and five others loaded with bananas. After feasting on this crude fare, including three of the mules, the young Frenchman had decided that he had enjoyed *flibustier* life long enough and slipped away from their company to give himself up to the Spaniards.

A mere three years previously, the English buccaneer Edward Mansfield had led 700 to 800 pirates up into Costa Rica's central highlands to surprise its capital of Cartago, only to be undone by hunger, thirst, and fatigue. The Spaniards had been inspired to resist this advance when they learned that their enemy had chanced upon some natives transporting bags of ground meal and, fallen to fighting among themselves over this meager spoil, they had been reduced to such desperate straits.

In contrast, when the pirate captains George Wright and Jan Willems would intercept some coastal traders a decade and a half later amid the San Blas Islands, laden with "corn, hog, and fowls," this humble bounty would prove enough to allow both crews to retire contentedly ashore into encampments near Darien and careen their vessels.

Naturally, permanent foreign colonists throughout the Antilles would learn to adapt to local resources over time, although the regional diet and cuisine remained quite simple and straightforward. For example, pigeons migrated through Tortuga Island every year, according to Exquemelin,

> in such multitudes the inhabitants could live on them alone, without using other meat. But when this season is past, they are no longer good to eat. They become thin and bitter to the taste.[5]

In May 1717, Captain Benjamin Candler of HMS *Winchelsea* conducted an antipiracy sweep through the unclaimed Virgin Islands, finding that their few hundred scattered residents subsisted mostly on "Indian corn, yams, and potatoes"—leading such an impoverished existence that he felt certain these people "can never be otherwise than a nest for pirates as they are now, for they caressed them, and gave them money."[6] Likewise, two years afterward, the recently arrived governor of the Bahamas, Woodes Rogers, would complain to London about the apparent laziness of his new subjects, commenting that, with regard to work,

> they mortally hate it, for when they have clear'd a patch that will supply them with potatoes and yams, and very little else, fish being so plenty and either turtle or goanas [*sic:* iguanas] on the neighboring islands, they eat them instead of meat, and covet no stock of cattle, but thus live poorly and indolently with a seeming content, and pray for nothing but wrecks or the pirates.[7]

EARLY BUCCANEER CUISINE

West Indian rovers often cooked bananas with their meat or fermented this fruit into a liquor, although Exquemelin warned that such drink was "as strong as wine, and if you take too much, makes you drunk and gives you a severe headache." And in any event, he furthermore noted that such fare was not regularly consumed by freebooters on a campaign, for upon mustering to put out to sea,

> they first discuss where to go and get food supplies. This means meat— for they eat nothing else on their voyages, unless they capture other food-stuffs from the Spaniards. The meat is either pork or turtle, which is also salted.[8]

Indeed, the more lengthy and numerous the contemplated pirate expedition, the greater the need for ample supplies.

When Jamaica's governor, Sir Thomas Modyford, addressed a gathering of 600 privateers in Bluefields Bay in November 1665, who had been specifically recalled to remind them where their proper duty lay during the Second Anglo-Dutch War—which was to attack the Dutch rather than the neutral Spaniards, as they had been doing—these captains responded positively to his exhortations for assaulting Curaçao, then promptly steered in the complete opposite direction, instead crossing over to the south coast of Cuba to push 42 miles inland and torch the town of Sancti Spíritus before Christmas, holding its citizenry as hostages against a ransom of 300 head of cattle. These ill-disciplined rovers would later try to justify this deviation by arguing that some among their ranks held outdated Portuguese commissions, issued by the French governor of Tortuga, who independently authorized such attacks against the Spanish.

But the fact was that pillaging Spaniards or other victims was the freebooters' accustomed method for replenishing their provisions on a large scale. And once a buccaneer ship was fully stocked with meat,

A piece of pewter flatware recovered from Blackbeard's lost flagship, *Queen Anne's Revenge*. Most such items have been salvaged from near its wrecked stern, where the senior officers would have normally eaten their meals. (Wendy Welsh/North Carolina Department of Cultural Resources)

Exquemelin went on to explain, two meals would be prepared every day, by boiling a portion to be shared equally:

> When it is boiled, the fat is skimmed off the cauldron and put into little calabashes, for dipping the meat in. The meal consists of only one course, and often it tastes better than the food to be found on a gentleman's table. The captain is allowed no better fare than the meanest on board.[9]

The customary eating practice at the time was to hold one's food down on a plate with a double-tined fork, cutting and passing portions of it into the mouth on the tip of a sharp knife. Spoons were also used for soups or stews, each individual's set of utensils being designed to fold up or nestle into a portable kit carried on their person. A refinement that began to become more commonplace toward the end of the 17th century meant using the fork to lift portions of food into one's mouth, so that three tines became the norm for forks, with round-tipped knives for cutting. Plates carried aboard most ships were usually squares made out of wood, and pewter mugs were used for drinking—although pirate crews that had been successful in looting rich merchants often dined incongruously off China or even silverware.

BEEF

The first foreign interlopers to reside on Hispaniola had hunted the wild livestock left behind when its Spanish settlers had been withdrawn on Madrid's orders, curing the meat from their largest kills directly where the beasts fell in extemporized smokehouses called *boucans*—so that these hunters came to be known as *boucaniers* or buccaneers. Naturally, cattle provided the most bountiful game for large groups of men, and beef became a choice staple among the earliest rovers. This predilection is amply borne out by historical records, which confirm that freebooter crews repeatedly extorted or stole large amounts of cattle from Spanish America, as in the following examples:

- During the summer of 1666, Jean-David Nau l'Olonnais demanded 20,000 pesos and 500 head of cattle to leave Maracaibo intact, upon the withdrawal of his booty-laden throng of *flibustiers*.
- Late in March 1668, Henry Morgan marched a large force of his mercenaries into central Cuba, storming the city of Puerto del Príncipe

and demanding 50,000 pieces of eight, plus 500 cattle, which were shipped so as to supply his subsequent strike against Portobelo.

- Toward the end of 1671, when Jelles de Lecat forsook Jamaican service altogether, he first rustled cattle along the coast of southern Cuba to restock his ships' provisions before venturing into the Gulf of Mexico—ironically, to obtain a commission to the Spanish out of Campeche.

- In August 1682, the *flibustier* Captain Jean Toccard seized the tiny and impoverished Mexican port of Tampico, simply to slaughter a large quantity of its local cattle before decamping with his reprovisioned flotilla.

- In December 1685, Laurens de Graaf was spotted going ashore at Cuba to steal cattle as supplies for his crews, who were about to careen five of his vessels.

Indeed, the quest for meat remained such a constant preoccupation for many 17th-century seafarers that Beef Island became a not uncommon name in the Caribbean—one of the most famous variants being Ile-à-Vache or Cow Island off southwestern Haiti. Another such Beef Island was not an island at all but rather a long, narrow strip of land more properly called Xicalango Point, connected to the Mexican mainland due west of Isla del Carmen. This low strip encloses the western portion of the vast Laguna de Términos or Bay of Campeche, a popular destination for early renegades and adventurers forging out of Jamaica. To these interlopers, Beef Island was a particular stretch where cattle had been routinely rustled or slaughtered over the years. In November 1681, an Englishman named Jonas Clough described how a year and a half previously he had been aboard one of three New England sloops when a Spanish expedition under Felipe de la Barreda had suddenly appeared and "took two of the sloops and forced the third ashore on Beef Island, called by the Spaniards *Jica Lanoga* [sic: Xicalango]."[10] More than 80 poachers had, as a result, been marooned there, he added, until they agreed to surrender more than a month later. And although these Englishmen thought that they had been promised safe conduct to the Cayman Islands or Jamaica, they were instead carried off as prisoners to Mexico City, where they were very harshly treated.

Another Beef Island was to be found off the eastern extremity of Tortola in the Virgin Islands and still bears this name today. Early in 1684, one of pirate captain George Bond's prizes—a Dutch ship that he had seized at Surinam—was reported by the Jamaican authorities to have been recaptured "at Beef Island, near Saint Thomas."[11] And while on an inspection tour through these same sparsely populated and by then pirate-infested waters in mid-November 1717 (O.S.), Governor Walter Hamilton of the English Leeward Islands would describe the scant resources available on Tortola, then go on to laconically add: "another little island called Beef Island lies just joining to it, the channel not above a mile broad, only fit for boats to go through; has but two families upon it."[12]

Cattle rustling had become a regular feature of West Indian warfare by the time that English, French, and Dutch colonies had begun fighting amongst themselves as part of broader European conflicts. During the French assault against Jamaica in June 1694, for instance, France's 54-gun flagship *Téméraire* was driven by foul weather into Bluefields Bay, where the *flibustier* chief Jean Bernanos led 60 of his men ashore— who were serving aboard this royal warship as auxiliaries—to loot a nearby plantation and forage for provisions. Surprised by a unit of Jamaican militia, these pillagers had to be recalled by a round shot fired over their heads from the anchored warship, and the defenders afterward noted how "they ran aboard in such haste that they left their meat they had killed, and some cattle they had tied up to carry aboard, and their bread and salt, and sailed away as soon as they could get up their anchors."[13]

TURTLE

Along with cattle, turtle was another great source of meat protein for people living in the West Indies during the 17th and 18th centuries. Aside from the fact that these creatures were plentiful and could be freely caught in sheltered shallows or along many lonely beaches, they could also be kept alive in a ship's hold—thus ensuring freshness in an era when smoking, salting, and pickling were the only means of preservation. English seamen had discovered this ready resource shortly after their conquest of Jamaica: Captain Christopher Myngs, for example, on his homeward passage with a three-ship Commonwealth convoy early in 1657, reported to London how he had made a brief stopover in the Bahamas before clearing for the open Atlantic to buy 8,560 pounds of turtle meat as food for the crew of his flagship *Marston Moor.* And Captain John Francis of the 40-gun frigate HMS *Diamond* would inform the navy commissioners upon his return home in July 1662 how

> according to orders from Col. D'Oyley, Governor of Jamaica, set sail thence on April 24th to the Caiman Isles for turtle to victual home, but coming too soon for it [i.e., prior to the seasonal appearance of any large numbers of turtles], stayed till May 29th, and then set sail for England, being forced to take turtle of a Frenchman.[14]

The French chronicler Exquemelin would also describe in considerable detail how the *flibustiers* of the 1660s often ventured across to the south cays of Cuba, the so-called Gardens of the Queen, to obtain turtle meat:

> Here they drag the ship up the beach to careen her. Everyone goes ashore and sets up his tent, and they take turns to go on marauding expeditions in their canoes. They take prisoner the turtle-fishers of Bayamo—poor men who catch and sell turtles for a living, to provide for their wives and children. Once captured, these men have to catch turtle for the rovers as long as they remain on the island. Should the rovers intend to cruise along a coast where turtles abound, they take the fishermen along with them. The poor fellows may be compelled to stay away from their wives and families four or five years, with no news whether they are alive or dead.[15]

Such heartless exploitation was to be practiced by pirates elsewhere for many decades to come. When an expedition of 500 *flibustiers* under Jean-David Nau—better known as Nau l'Olonnais, *le Capitaine François*, or the French Captain—reached Abraham's Cay (modern Bluefields in Nicaragua) with three Spanish prizes in May 1667, intending to prepare a raid up the San Juan River, he first sent out boat parties to procure supplies. These pirate bands combed the shorelines of the Mosquito Coast and seized native fishermen, forcing them to help hunt turtles and manatees in the Bocas del Toro Archipelago for months thereafter.

Exquemelin explained how green turtles were the buccaneers' preferred choice, being of medium size (and thus easy to hoist aboard and maintain alive in a ship's hold), to say nothing of being "extremely good to eat—the flesh very sweet, and the fat green and delicious." This picture was marred when he went on to describe how this fat was also

> so penetrating that when you have eaten nothing but turtle flesh for three or four weeks, your shirt becomes so greasy from sweat you can squeeze the oil out, and your limbs are weighed down with it.[16]

Turtles were widely hunted and sold throughout the West Indies, and their consumption was hardly limited to seafarers. In a letter written from Jamaica on November 15, 1684 (O.S.), its acting governor, Hender Molesworth, declared that turtle meat "is what masters of ships chiefly feed their men in port, and I believe that nearly 2,000 people, black and white, feed on it daily at [Palisadoes] Point, to say nothing of what is sent inland."[17]

Because of such widespread demand, numerous places still bear this name in the Antilles today, usually in its Spanish or French variants: the Dry Tortugas off the Florida Keys—so called because meat was dried there in the sun as opposed to being salted, as at the Salt Tortugas off Venezuela; Île de la Tortue or Tortuga Island, north of Haiti; Green Turtle Cay in the Bahamas; Tortola in the Virgin Islands; and Tortuguero in Costa Rica.

As noted, hungry pirate crews would frequently prey upon the small craft that were engaged in this trade. One poor turtler complained to Governor Peter Heywood of Jamaica in late December 1716 of being robbed of "what little he had" by a pirate sloop, whose ruffianly crew had then furthermore burdened him with three outcast members and a young boy that they were expelling from their ship. And on September 4, 1720 (O.S.), Captain Bartholomew Roberts's pirate ship and sloop suddenly materialized at Carriacou in the Grenadines, capturing the tiny sloop *Relief* of Bermuda as it lay there turtling. Its frightened master, Robert Dunn, would later recount how he was compelled to feed these 130 ravenous cutthroats, before finally being lucky enough to be let go—with merely "some bundles of old rigging and cloth, in return for his tending them."[18]

PORK

Like wild cattle, the earliest *boucaniers* had also hunted wild pigs on French Hispaniola, and pork was to remain a favorite meat among Antillean residents and visitors alike, despite being somewhat less abundant than turtle or beef. Sir Charles Lyttleton, deputy governor of Jamaica, referred to it in an October 1663 report to London as "the planters' food,"[19] but demand would so far outstrip supply throughout the islands that it soon had to be imported in large quantities from North America and Ireland, preserved with salt.

Beef might be rustled from nearby Spanish territories, turtle was widely and freely available along many shorelines, yet there was never enough fresh pork to satisfy all, so that its importation into the region had begun early on, along with other European-style products such as flour and butter. A gentleman wrote from Barbados in November 1669 how there was "a place much cried up of late, taken from the Dutch now called New York, and one of its governments called New Jersey, of which Mr. Carteret of Jersey is Governor; yields store of beef, pork, peas, flour, butter, and horses," for which the West Indies returned "strong liquors, sugar, cotton, molasses, and ginger."[20]

An early buccaneer on Saint-Domingue or Haiti, roasting a pig on a spit; from a 19th-century reedition of Exquemelin. (Samuel Hazard, *Santo Domingo: Past and Present* [New York: S. Low, Marston, Low, & Searle, 1873])

As a result of increased traffic, ship-borne consignments of salt pork soon became more commonplace. When Captain Edward Collier had joined Henry Morgan's anchored privateer fleet off Ile-à-Vache on October 29, 1668 (O.S.), he found lying amid this formation "the *Cerf Volant* of [La] Rochelle, Captain La Vivien commander, that robbed Isaac Rush of Virginia, Master of the *Commonwealth*, of 12 barrels of pork, a barrel of butter, and another of flour."[21] This paltry theft would prove to be the French commander's undoing, for when Collier further pressed to see Vivien's privateering commission, he

> made several evasions, but subsequently produced one from Monsieur de Beaufort to La Vivien; but on his taking Rush's provisions, he went by the name of Captain La Roche of Toulon, and Rush coming into the Isle of Vacour [*sic:* Ile-à-Vache] the next day, maintained that he was the same man, whereupon Captain Collier, believing he was no other than a pirate, had him brought aboard his ship "in order to his trial" at Jamaica.[22]

Salt pork would remain a basic staple aboard all vessels of this era—
for pirates, merchant sailors, and Royal Navy personnel alike—yet the
nutritional deficiencies of salted provisions would become equally self-
evident to those involved in seaborne life, although the exact causes
and solutions remained beyond their scientific grasp. For example,
Jamaica's merchants and supply agents would offer a series of proposals to the Crown in October 1696 toward improving that island's maritime traffic, which included the suggestion

> that all the men on the King's ships be fed during their stay in these parts
> with fresh provisions. This may be done (and the Island will undertake
> it) for the King's usual allowance of bread and beer, and sixpence a head
> per day (which is the cost to the King of salt provisions), that is to say: on
> three days a week they may have fresh beef, turtle, etc., and on the other
> days, peas, pulp, plantains, and other wholesome food. But this cannot
> be done unless a competent person be appointed as Commissary of Pro-
> visions, who might also act as Commissary of Musters.[23]

That very next month, a naval captain also addressed this same issue
separately, when, in the wake of horrific losses endured due to disease
during a recent expedition against Hispaniola, he pointed out that
seamen employed

> in these voyages commonly feed much on salt provisions, which makes
> them more subject to fevers and leads them to drink great quantities of
> liquor, which—when the water grows bad—causes fluxes and other dis-
> eases. I wish that instead of the greatest part of the salt provisions, there
> could be carried a great many sorts of vegetable products, which in my
> opinion could be as cheaply and easily carried, and being wholesome
> cooling food, would be better fitted for those climates.[24]

Ironically, pirates—who were never issued regular rations of salt
provisions, except perhaps after capturing a well-stocked prize, and
instead had to scrounge for their sustenance on a day-to-day basis—
unwittingly ended up eating more fresh meat, vegetables, and fruits,
because these foods were what they could most readily steal or extort
locally.

PIRATES AND HUNGER

More than most other seafarers, freebooters often had to inure themselves to want, for they lacked any reliable supply system throughout
their history, or even unimpeded access to major seaports. Typically,
the provisioning of a large warship during this era was exemplified as

when the Council of Barbados voted in May 1673 to restock the 54-gun HMS *St. David*, a fourth-rate Royal Navy vessel with a nominal complement of 200 men, with "13,000 lb. bread, 5,000 lb. beef, 1,374 lb. pork, 30 bushels of peas, 1,000 gallons rum, and 2,500 lb. fish for her voyage to England."[25] Such ready availability of an assortment of foodstuffs was completely beyond the reach of almost every freebooter flotilla that ever sailed, except perhaps occasionally after a large-scale rustling sweep or the looting of a large town or commercial fleet. Captains as solvent or well organized as Laurens de Graaf were extremely rare, who—while blockading Cartagena—calmly placed an order with a visiting Dutch-born Jewish trader named Diego Maquet for a consignment of wine and meat to be delivered from Port Royal a few weeks hence to his next intended destination, Roatán Island.

Much more usual was the plight of the 330 raiders whom John Coxon led overland through Panama's northern jungles in February 1680, trudging afoot for three days and nights down the Cascajal River Valley to avoid Spanish coastal lookouts, "without any food, and their feet cut with the rocks for want of shoes."[26] After surprising Portobelo and ransacking its dwellings and warehouses, these footsore rovers were rejoined by their vessels 10 miles northeast of this gutted city at a coastal hamlet named Bastimentos. They thereupon proceeded to impose a brief sea blockade on Portobelo as well, which netted an additional pair of Spanish merchantmen, before finally distributing their booty and dispersing into the Bocas del Toro archipelago—there to feast and effect repairs, "being the best place to careen our ships, by reason there is good store of turtle and manatee and fish."

Consequently, accounts of piratical rapacity in their desperate quest for food were to be repeated all too often over the ensuing decades, making them impossible to ignore. For instance:

- When the Armada de Barlovento captured the *flibustier* vessel *Prophète Daniel* of Captain Antoine Bernard at the Cayman Islands on August 4, 1683, as it was escaping after having participated in Laurens de Graaf's and the Sieur de Grammont's sack of Veracruz, a written Spanish report later described this prize as being a 35-ton sloop "with a crew of seventeen men, two guns, two swivel-guns, a blunderbuss, two carbines, three cutlasses, 80 pounds of gunpowder,"[27] and a cargo comprised of 30 tons of stolen cheese.
- Master Richard Burgess of the ship *Maryland Merchant* out of Bristol, after having his merchandise rifled and vandalized in Lynnhaven Bay in late July 1699 by John James's pirate galley *Alexander*, personally witnessed how eagerly his captors had then "seized the cargo of corn and pork from a North Carolina sloop,"[28] indicative of their hun-

ger. Previously, this same pirate captain had politely told Burgess that "he designed no prejudice to the English nation as to their persons, but particular wants would be supplied."

- During that same winter of 1699–1700, the Jamaican privateer John Breholt was detained and investigated at length by the authorities at Charleston, South Carolina, and eventually cleared to depart next spring, all charges against him having been dropped. Yet embittered by his treatment and at the exhaustion of his provisions because of such a lengthy layover, Breholt belligerently sailed his 36-gun, 120-man frigate *Carlisle*

  out of Ashley River about March 26 [1700 O.S.], came to an anchor without the bar, landed on Sullivan's Island and there killed a great many cows, hogs, and goats, the best of which they carried on board. He told Captain Clay he designed either to sail for Smith's Island in Virginia to get more provisions, or else to Cape de Verd [*sic:* Cape Verde].[29]

The last great outburst of piracy, which erupted during the peaceful autumn of 1716, was likewise to be characterized by numerous and blatantly criminal seizures of supplies from innocent merchantmen by outlaw bands:

- The West Indian renegade James Martel used his single vessel to capture a string of minor island traders—insignificant prizes, except for their cargoes of foodstuffs, which in turn allowed him over the next few months to assemble and sustain a pirate flotilla consisting of two 20-gun ships, two sloops, plus a prize.
- The sloop *Bonetta* of Antigua was overhauled between St. Thomas and St. Croix on November 9, 1716 (O.S.) and plundered by two pirate sloops under Captains Black Sam Bellamy and Louis La Buze. Its frightened merchant master, Abijah Savage, was released and later declared that his attackers "only wanted provisions, and a ship to make a voyage."[30]
- Less than a month after that incident, Blackbeard's own *Queen Anne's Revenge* and an accompanying pirate sloop bore down on the tiny *Margaret* of Saint Kitts while it was lying off Vieques Island, near the eastern tip of Puerto Rico. Its shaken master, Henry Bostock, would later relate how he "was ordered on board and Captain Tach [*sic:* Thatch] took his cargo of cattle and hogs, his arms, books, and instruments."[31]

After Blackbeard betrayed, cheated, and abandoned his unwilling subordinate Stede Bonnet in North Carolina's Beaufort Inlet in early July 1718, the latter rescued two dozen pirates who had also been left to starve by Thatch on a nearby sandbank and prepared to clear for the Lesser Antilles. Yet with only 10 or 11 barrels of provisions left aboard his sloop *Revenge,* Bonnet realized that it would be impossible to reach the Danish West Indian island of Saint Thomas and purchase a privateering commission against the Spaniards, as had been his intent. Instead, he and his crew were constrained to attempt to reprovision *Revenge* first, before initiating this voyage, by preying upon the coastal traffic off Cape Henry. Soon, reports would begin to multiply as to how this desperate gang had intercepted

> a small sloop from Virginia bound to Bermuda, from which they took twenty barrels of pork and gave her in return two barrels of rice, and as much molasses. The next day, they took another Virginia-man bound to Glasgow, out of which they took two men and a few small things, and gave her a barrel of pork and another of bread. . . . The 29th of July [1718 O.S.], they took a sloop of fifty tons, bound from Philadelphia to Barbados laden with provisions, which they kept; as also another of sixty tons from Antigua to Philadelphia having on board rum, molasses, sugar, cotton, and indigo to the value of five hundred pounds, all of which they kept.[32]

These latter two supply vessels allowed Bonnet to put into the Cape Fear River estuary and set his prisoners to work on careening and repairing *Revenge* for his lengthy passage. However, this expedient of lingering in those waters was clearly so dangerous that he had even altered his sloop's name into *Royal James* and personally adopted the pseudonym of Captain Thomas, yet to no avail: Bonnet was trapped inside this anchorage and captured along with his 46 pirates in late September 1718 by a pair of South Carolinian sloops and taken to Charleston to be executed two weeks before Christmas.

And in one final, yet revealing commentary on the importance of food to pirate bands, it should be noted that the very first article of the covenant signed in 1721 by Captain Bartholomew Roberts's cutthroat crew stated that every member "shall have an equal title to the fresh provisions or strong liquors at any time seized, and shall use them at pleasure, unless a scarcity may make it necessary for the common good that a retrenchment may be voted."

PIRATES' DELIGHT: SALMAGUNDI

As pirates expanded their depredations out of the Caribbean during the late 17th and early 18th centuries into the distant Pacific Ocean, Red Sea, and Indian Ocean, they carried with them many of the exotic tastes and customs brought from the Antilles, including a predilection for rum punches and flip—as well as a communal stew or ragout made with a mixture of meats, to which vegetables and other ingredients could be added in random profusion by each individual partaker, the whole then being highly seasoned and known as salmagundi.

This dish remained especially popular among West Indian buccaneers, not least because it entailed a shared contribution to a general pot, from which all could draw—in true brotherhood fashion. Its preparation also reflected the extraordinary measures to which crews often had to resort to render shipboard meals more palatable. In times of plenty, though, such meals could make for hearty eating. One such elaborate concoction began with whatever meats were available being

> roasted, chopped into chunks, and marinated in spiced wine, then combined with cabbage, anchovies, pickled herring, mangoes, hardboiled eggs, palm hearts, onions, olives, grapes, and any other pickled vegetables that were available. The whole would then be highly seasoned with garlic, salt, pepper, and mustard seed, and doused with oil and vinegar—and served with drafts of beer and rum.[33]

Reputedly, Bartholomew Roberts was breakfasting on salmagundi in his great cabin aboard his anchored flagship *Royal Fortune* when he was surprised and killed off the West African coast on the morning of February 10, 1722 (O.S.), by HMS *Swallow*.

NOTES

1. *Calendar of State Papers: Colonial, America and West Indies*, vol. 9, 1674–1675 and Supplementary Addenda (London: Her Majesty's Stationery Office, 1893), 116.

2. *Calendar of State Papers: Colonial, America and West Indies*, vol. 24 (London: Her Majesty's Stationery Office, 1922), 531.

3. Alexandre-Olivier Exquemelin, *The Buccaneers of America*, trans. Alexis Brown, intro. Jack Beeching (London: Penguin, 1969), 60.

4. André Baudrit, *Charles de Courbon, Comte de Blénac, 1622–1696* (Fort de France: Société d'Histoire de la Martinique, 1967).

5. Exquemelin, *The Buccaneers of America*, 30.

6. *Calendar of State Papers, Colonial: America and West Indies*, vol. 29 (London: Her Majesty's Stationery Office, 1930), 340.

7. *Calendar of State Papers, Colonial: America and West Indies*, vol. 31 (London: Her Majesty's Stationery Office, 1933), 100.

8. Exquemelin, *The Buccaneers of America*, 70.

9. Ibid.

10. *Calendar of State Papers, Colonial: America and West Indies*, vol. 11 (London: Her Majesty's Stationery Office, 1898), 142.

11. Ibid., 574.

12. *Calendar of State Papers: Colonial, America and West Indies*, vol. 30 (London: Her Majesty's Stationery Office, 1930), 148.

13. *Interesting Tracts Relating to the Island of Jamaica, Consisting of Curious State Papers, Councils of War, Letters, Petitions, Narratives, etc., Which Throw Great Light on the History of That Island from Its Conquest down to the Year 1702* (St. Jago de la Vega, Jamaica: Lewis, Lunan and Jones, 1800), 256.

14. *Calendar of State Papers, Colonial: America and West Indies*, vol. 5 (London: Her Majesty's Stationery Office, 1880), 100.

15. Exquemelin, *The Buccaneers of America*, 72.

16. Ibid., 73.

17. *Calendar of State Papers*, vol. 11, 719.

18. *Calendar of State Papers*, vol. 29, 212.

19. *Calendar of State Papers*, vol. 5, 164.

20. *Calendar of State Papers, Colonial: America and West Indies*, vol. 7 (London: Her Majesty's Stationery Office, 1889), 45.

21. *Calendar of State Papers, Colonial*, vol. 9: 1674–1675 and Supplementary Addenda, 116.

22. *Calendar of State Papers: Colonial, America and West Indies*, vol. 9, 520.

23. *Calendar of State Papers: Colonial, America and West Indies*, vol. 15 (London: Her Majesty's Stationery Office, 1904), 181.

24. Ibid., 209.

25. *Calendar of State Papers*, vol. 7, 487.

26. Dr. Philip Henry George Gosse, *The Pirates' Who's Who* (New York: Dulau, 1924), 43.

27. David F. Marley, *Pirates of the Americas* (Santa Barbara, CA: ABC-CLIO, 2008), 520.

28. *Calendar of State Papers, Colonial: America and West Indies*, vol. 17 (London: Her Majesty's Stationery Office, 1908), 390.

29. *Calendar of State Papers: Colonial, America and West Indies*, vol. 18 (London: Her Majesty's Stationery Office, 1910), Page 315.

30. *Calendar of State Papers*, vol. 29, 231.

31. *Calendar of State Papers*, vol. 30, 150.

32. C. Lovat Fraser, *Lives and Adventures of Sundry Notorious Pirates* (New York: McBride, 1922), 105.

33. Douglas Botting, *The Pirates* (Alexandria, VA: Time-Life Books, 1978).

4

DRINK

He fancied the gods had got drunk over their tipple, and were
gone together by the ears.
          —Captain Black Sam Bellamy, joking to his crew during
                              a thunderstorm at sea in the spring of 1717

Piracy has long been associated with strong drink, particularly rum,
and there is ample documentary evidence to confirm such an affinity.
Yet the whole issue of finding potables that were safe enough to drink
was a tricky one throughout this era and concerned people of virtually
every walk of life because of the negligible health standards that were
then observed, to say nothing of the many hazards that still lurked
undetected by the scientists of that day, such as amoebas or bacteria.

WATER

Clean drinking water was particularly difficult to obtain or transport
across any significant distances during the 17th and early 18th centuries,
even for major cities. Port Royal, for instance—with several thousand
people crammed onto the western tip of its narrow spit of land—was
utterly dependent on boatmen who ferried fresh water across from the
clear Río Cobre on Jamaica's mainland, in casks aboard wherries, to be
sold from canoes to individual establishments or homes.

Conveying large amounts of water aboard sailing ships at sea was also problematic, and even more complicated in warm climes such as the Caribbean tropics. Wooden casks were heavy and awkward to maneuver in the close confines below decks or to row ashore for replenishment and then to be manhandled back into storage. They often leaked out on the ocean because of the constant movement from the waves. Plus their contents could soon turn brackish in the stifling West Indian heat, although ship-borne water supplies were principally destined for cooking purposes, not so much for drinking. And given the unreliable quality of open-water sources everywhere, it was common practice in Europe and the Americas to consume this liquid mixed with other potables: small beer, for example—beer diluted with water—was routinely drunk at breakfast or with light meals by people of all ages and at every level of society.

IMPORTED EUROPEAN BEVERAGES

Traditionally, sailing ships had carried cider, beer, or brandy for their crews' daily consumption while operating in the cooler home waters of the North Atlantic, but it was found that these first two spirits quickly spoiled once brought into the tropics. As early as July 24, 1655 (O.S.), Vice Admiral William Goodson had written from newly conquered Jamaica to the commissioners of the navy in London, directing "that no drink be sent but brandy in very substantial casks, and a little vinegar, for the cider wholly decays, and the beer grows flat or sour."[1] The practice of substituting local West Indian stimulants would soon begin to gain widespread acceptance among inhabitants, although the importation of European spirits also continued throughout the entire colonial era, often being regarded as a luxury item. Pirates, of course, usually only tasted such finer drinks after looting a prize.

Wines and Brandies

Wines and their derivatives were not native to the Antilles but remained a frequent import throughout much of the colonial period. They were transported from various places—such as Madeira or the Canary Islands and sherry from Xeréz in Spain—and in varying strengths, some of which spoiled more quickly than others and all commanding relatively high prices. As such, wines constituted rare yet disposable booty for many rovers, such as in the following instances:

- In 1672, the Dutch-born Jamaican renegade privateer John Peterson was charged with piracy for—among other things—having violently seized off Cuba "a great ship laden with wines from the Canaries, killing a Governor, two captains, and eighteen men."[2]

- Four years later, the privateer John Deane, while in command of the *Saint David* out of Port Royal, was accused by John Yardley of having intercepted his merchant ship *John Adventure* on the high seas, and "drunk out several pipes of wine and taken away a cable value £100,"[3] for which Deane was criminally charged (although eventually reprieved).

- Late in the summer of 1680, when the newly created squadron of Brandenburg privateers slipped into the quiet South American anchorage of Santa Marta and emerged with the hired English merchantman *William and Anne* as their prize, they were delighted to discover that it was loaded with Canary wine and brandy.

- And two years afterward, an angry band of English buccaneers (including Lionel Wafer) stole a ship recently arrived at Saint-Domingue from France, which was bearing a rich cargo of wines. They sailed to Virginia and sold the wine to finance their return for another rampage in the Pacific Ocean.

Wines were normally only available in or near major seaports. An inventory taken of a typical Port Royal tavern in 1685, listed its stock of alcoholic beverages as consisting of 52 gallons of brandy, one and a half pipes of wine, and two and a half dozen bottles of "bad clarrett." Five years later, this same establishment would boast 60 gallons of rum and "one and twenty gallons wine."[4] Very seldom would a freebooter be as solvent or well organized as Laurens de Graaf, who—while blockading Cartagena—placed an order with a visiting Dutch-born Jewish trader named Diego Maquet for a consignment of wine and meat to be delivered within the next few weeks from Port Royal to de Graaf's next intended destination of Roatán Island.

The fortified wines produced on Portugal's Madeira Islands held a special allure for all sailors during the age of piracy, as they had neutral grape spirits blended into them during their preparation to minimize spoilage. This technique had apparently been first discovered by chance, when a Portuguese ship had returned to Madeira with an unsold cargo of wine after a lengthy sea voyage. Its flavor had actually been enhanced during its travels by the ship's movements and the heat in its hold, plus the wine itself remained drinkable long after being opened—both esteemed qualities in an era long before any kind of effective preservatives could be developed. Little wonder, then, that

Dark-green wine bottle recovered from
Blackbeard's sunken flagship *Queen Anne's
Revenge*, deliberately created in a squat
shape so as to prevent tipping—a profile
ungallantly known during that era as the
"Queen Anne shape." Most wines degraded
aboard heaving ships or in tropical heat,
except Madeira. (Wendy Welsh/North Carolina Department of Cultural Resources)

- with one of the final acts of his lurid piratical career, Sam Bellamy
  sent four cutthroats across in a boat from his flagship *Whydah* to re-
  move some choice Madeira wine from a small pink that he intercepted
  on April 26, 1717 (O.S.), although they could then not extract any crates
  of this delicacy from its cramped hold—and that night almost all
  hands perished on Cape Cod in a dreadful storm; or that

- a mere five months afterward, Blackbeard would make the first recorded capture of his own nefarious career by pillaging the 40-ton
  merchant sloop *Betty* "of certain pipes of Madeira wine" off Virginia's
  Cape Charles, before removing its crew and then scuttling this gutted
  vessel.

Beers and Ciders

As noted, beers and ciders tended to spoil rather quickly when brought
into the warm tropics, so they figured much less often in historical records and were not commonly consumed among freebooters. The few

occasions on which beer was mentioned usually referred to a recently arrived consignment: for example, the privateer John Morris escorted the merchant sloop *Blue Dove* into Port Royal harbor in January 1664, having intercepted it while this sloop was steering from Amsterdam toward Cuba. But the Jamaican admiralty court ruled that this prize had to be released, so that Morris afterward grumbled that all he had got for his troubles was "an English ensign and a hogshead of strong beer."

Not surprisingly, beer tended to fare somewhat better in colder, northern climes. When the English merchant captain William Holman successfully defended the fishing port of Ferryland in Newfoundland against a French attack during the summer of 1694—the fifth year of King William's War—a grateful government in London later offered to compensate him for his expenses. Holman's claim included a sum for "one hogshead of sherry wine, twenty gallons of brandy, and a barrel of strong beer which I gave the men to encourage them in time of fight."[5]

And given beer's short-lived properties, the French Dominican priest Jean-Baptiste Labat must have been flattered when, during a peacetime visit to Barbados in September 1700, he was hospitably greeted at the English governor's palace with "beer, pipes, and various wines" for his entertainment.

WEST INDIAN BEVERAGES

The practice of substituting local stimulants for European imports had begun during the earliest phases of foreign occupation in the Antilles, those spirits derived from the sugarcane industry proving to be especially hardy—and popular, their consumption eventually spread all around the world. Juices, spices, and other additives were used in experimental measures, each individual choosing blends to suit his or her tastes.

Punch

Sweetening beverages with sugar or molasses and flavoring drinks with lime or other fruits to make them more palatable was already a well-established practice in the 17th-century Caribbean, resulting in a wide range of combinations or blends generally known as punches. One particular type of mixed drink that was to gain great favor among all West Indian seafarers—pirates included—was called flip; it was made chiefly with "hot small beer and brandy, sweetened and spiced" to suit each individual palate.

A gentleman at Port Royal wrote to his friends back in England, describing some other, more moderate blends that were also available there for consumers: "our drink is chiefly Madeira wine, lemonades, punch, and brandy; for cool drinks, mobby we have, made of potatoes, cacao-drink, sugar-drink, and rappé made of molasses." Still more genteel concoctions could be found in better establishments, such as the "silabubus [*sic*], cream tarts and other quelque choses" sold at fashionable Barré's Tavern—syllabubs being drinks or dishes made by curdling cream or milk with an admixture of wine, cider, or some other acid, producing a soft curd, which was then whipped or solidified with gelatin and sweetened or flavored to taste.

Yet such light fare was hardly to the taste of hearty seamen, or to the working class in general. Much more frequent were communal punches mixed in a large bowl for all to partake from during any convivial gathering. More sober members of society often lamented the excesses resulting from such drinking bouts: Governor-General Lord Willoughby of the English Leeward Islands, for instance—while writing to London in early April 1668 during a wartime inspection tour of Nevis—joked that one of his militia subordinates was "a man of good reason, and at a bowl of punch I dare turn him loose to any Monsieur in the Indies."[6] A more angry complaint was lodged by Governor Daniel Parke early in May 1709, deploring the cavalier proceedings that were produced in the Assembly of Antigua:

> One thing shall be put to the vote, and carried one way; if some of the cunning men don't like it, two or three hours afterwards, they will continue to get some of the members out of the House with a bowl of punch, or some other way, and put the same question and have it carried quite contrary; and then adjourn the House, and so it must stand.[7]

Lieutenant-Governor Daniel Hope voiced a similar opinion of the uncouth, hard-drinking membership of Bermuda's government in March 1724: "It is fitter to be imagin'd, than for me to tell your Lordships, the effects which rum punch produces in an Assembly of 36 men."[8]

For indeed, rum was the preeminent liquor mixed into most West Indian punches. The expression *puncheon rum* is still used to this day on Trinidad and Tobago to describe an exceptionally high-proof variant distilled on those islands, with the express aim of being blended or diluted into smoother drinks.

Rum

This alcoholic beverage is made by distilling a liquid by-product of sugarcane, such as molasses—a resource that was to become ever more abundant and cheaply available throughout the West Indies as the output from its plantations multiplied. The origins of the very name *rum* are unknown, some believing that it was a garbling of a term native to the Antilles, others asserting that it came from an old English adjective meaning anything that was considered excellent, valuable, or handsome—as in the expression "rum booze," which was recorded as early as the mid-16th century in England to describe any fine wine, while "rum mort" meant the queen, and "rum blower" denoted a beautiful woman. Whatever the case, the word rum soon came to be applied to the sugar-based spirits being distilled, consumed, and exported from the Caribbean isles.

Its potency was often masked by the sweeteners and fruit juices mixed into punches, yet the effects of overindulgence were impossible to ignore. Governor Sir Thomas Modyford of Jamaica wryly observed in November 1665: "The Spaniards wondered much at the sickness of our people, until they knew of the strength of their drinks, but then wondered more that they were not all dead."[9] Ravages brought on by the excessive consumption of rum would trouble the authorities for decades to come, their symptoms often being confused with those of other diseases whose causes remained scientifically undetected, such as dysentery or yellow fever. Jamaica's merchants and chandlers, for example, offered a broad series of proposals in October 1696 to the Crown in London that were intended to improve that island's maritime traffic—and which included the suggestion that Royal Navy pursers

> be restrained from supplying the seamen with rum and strong waters. The pursers, for an unreasonable gain, supply the men upon tick [i.e., on credit] with rum, whereof they make punch, wherewith being heated they expose themselves to the night-dews, which in that part of the world are generally fatal.[10]

This policy of procuring rum for Royal Navy warships in the West Indies was still less than a decade old, having apparently begun after Admiral Sir John Narborough—the commissioner of the navy responsible for its Victualling Department—had visited Barbados in November 1687 aboard his 48-gun HMS *Foresight* and bought "600 odd gallons of rum to be served to our ship's company in lieu of brandy," thus recommending this practice for the entire service.

In open acknowledgement of rum's potency, its Dutch euphemism was *kilduijvel*, a racy term that translated literally means "kill-devil." When, during the Third Anglo-Dutch War, the 30-gun *Schaeckerloo* of Captain Passchier de Witte captured a large English merchant yawl in May 1673, outward-bound from Barbados toward Maryland, this captor gleefully reported to his superior, Commodore Cornelis Evertsen, that it was transporting a cargo of "*kilduijvel* and molasses."

And beyond the immediate deleterious consequences from overindulgence, prolonged consumption of rum could also result in an acute medical condition known as the dry gripes—a stomach malady so closely associated with the Antilles that it was more commonly called the West-India dry gripes and was actually a low-grade form of lead poisoning resulting from the distillation of this alcohol through lead piping. The gradual buildup of lead in any habitual drinker's body could climax in extremely painful intestinal cramps—being "dry" in that they were not relieved by diarrhea but continued to escalate into an excruciating constipation. Yet for such as the Brethren of the Coast, even this fate could not fully curb their thirst for rum.

DRINKING ESTABLISHMENTS

It was an oft-repeated joke among 17th-century Englishmen that the first institution the Spaniards established in any new colony was a church, while the Dutch always started with a fort—in contrast to the English, who invariably began with a drinking house. As with many jests, it contained a kernel of truth, for seaports frequented by English seamen certainly abounded in drinking establishments. Yet it was also an age in which virtually everyone drank, many to excess, regardless of nationality. The Dutch included some legendary imbibers, the chronicler Alexandre-Olivier Exquemelin having left us the following hair-raising description of Captain Gerrit Gerritszoon, better known on Jamaica as Rok Brasiliano, during one of his memorable benders ashore at Port Royal:

> When he was drunk, he would roam the town like a madman. The first person he came across, he would chop off his arm or leg, without anyone daring to intervene, for he was like a maniac.[11]

Rough-hewn French *flibustiers* could be just as guilty of overindulging. Exquemelin recorded the wild behavior of his very own master, the deputy-governor of Tortuga Island, who

> often used to buy a butt of wine and set it in the middle of the street with the barrel-head knocked in, and stand barring the way. Every passer-by had to drink with him, or he'd have shot them dead with a gun he kept handy. Once he bought a cask of butter and threw the stuff at everyone who came by, bedaubing their clothes or their head, wherever he best could reach.[12]

Because of their nomadic existence, pirates especially enjoyed marking their rare returns into a major port with a rollicking celebration in its dockyard haunts. Yet such places served as gathering spots in general for all segments of society, not just returning sailors. Generally speaking, English establishments of this era were categorized into the larger, more prestigious taverns—which offered meals and rented rooms, in addition to selling liquors—and the more lowly punch houses, whose amenities were fewer and meaner.

Taverns

In January 1670, a well-educated young Christian named John Style wrote from Port Royal to Lord Arlington, a collegiate friend who had gone on to become secretary of state, describing the many vices he had encountered among the rough-and-tumble frontier society that was just then emerging on Jamaica, including his observation that

> the number of tippling houses is now doubly increased, so that "there is not now resident upon this place ten men to every house that selleth strong liquors." There are more than 100 licensed houses, besides sugar and rum works that sell without license; and what can that bring but ruin, for many sell their plantations, and either go out for privateers, or drinking themselves into debt, sell their bodies or are sold for prison fees.[13]

A handful of more genteel establishments catered to a better class of clientele, but the vast majority sought to appeal to resident tradesmen and workers as well as visiting seamen. Some of the better-known names among the scores of taverns that lined Port Royal's narrow and twisting tropical streets, prior to that city's spectacular destruction by an earthquake in June 1692, were such colorful ones as the Sign of Bacchus, Black Dog, Blue Anchor, Cat and Fiddle, Cheshire Cheese, The Feathers, The George, The Green Dragon, Jamaica Arms, King's Arms, Mermaid, The Salutaçon (Salutation), The Ship, Sugar Loaf, Three Crowns, Three Mariners, Three Tunns, and The Windmill.

However rustic in design, taverns were at least minimally regulated by the urban authorities, and most offered some form of meals, entertainment, and lodging in addition to their sale of beverages. Several even enticed customers with billiards rooms, which seem to have been situated in the yard or otherwise removed from the barroom, so as to minimize drink-fueled frictions among the patrons. The George, for instance—which "fronted to the old market place," according to a contemporary report—had built a special room for players; the same was true at The Feathers, whose billiard room was situated above another room overlooking its courtyard. Darts constituted another popular pastime, as well as backgammon and gambling in general—that "enchanting witchery," according Charles Cotton's 1709 edition of *The Compleat Gamester.*

Taverns were usually crowded with customers around the midday hour, and again every weekday evening after 6:00 P.M., and especially on Saturdays or before holidays, when people could sleep in the next morning. Not surprisingly, the gregarious Henry Morgan was a frequent and welcome patron, never losing the common touch despite having been knighted and elevated to the position of Jamaica's deputy-governor. After his superior, Governor Lord Vaughan, had condemned a popular freebooter to death in April 1676, public opinion quickly rose against this verdict, and Vaughan was soon tellingly writing to Lon-

Pirates plotting in a seaside tavern at night, as imagined by Howard Pyle—the wall behind them adorned with crude graffiti, depicting the hanging of "Capt. Tech." (Merle Johnson, comp., *Howard Pyle's Book of Pirates* [New York: Harper & Brothers, ca. 1921])

don how, "since the trial, Sir Harry has been so impudent and unfaithful at the taverns and in his own house, to speak some things which seemed to reflect upon my justice, and to vindicate the pirate."[14] The condemned rover was duly reprieved, and Morgan would continue his habits until he died of dropsy a dozen years later—a direct result, according to his physician, of being "much given to drinking and sitting up late."[15]

Punch Houses

Much lower in prestige were the punch houses, establishments that simply sold alcoholic stimulants, without offering many of the other services or amenities provided at proper taverns. Punch houses were usually smaller and meaner in design and often contained gambling dens or brothels. One appalled visitor to 17th-century Port Royal would describe its punch houses as dives full of "such a crew of vile strumpets and common prostitutes, that 'tis almost impossible to civilize" the town. Unwary patrons might be robbed, while drunken customers might have their bills inflated into astronomical sums. The chronicler Exquemelin, himself familiar with Port Royal during its bawdy heyday, would later remember how

> the tavern-keepers let [buccaneers] have a good deal of credit, but in Jamaica one ought not to put much trust in these people, for often they will sell you for debt, a thing I have seen happen many a time.[16]

Such swindles were commonplace in other Caribbean ports as well. In September 1678, the assembly on Saint Kitts passed an act enjoining its "tavern-keepers and rum punch-house keepers, not to trust any person upon account for above 200 pounds of sugar, before taking a note for the same."[17] In other words—since sugar substituted for currency on that particular island—a customer was not to be allowed to run up a high bill without at least providing written confirmation before exceeding this preset limit of 200 pounds of sugar.

Throughout the great age of piracy, denizens of punch houses would be regarded as the dregs of society. A vivid example of this disdain was contained in the spiteful report submitted to London by Jamaica's lieutenant-governor Hender Molesworth in August 1687, after learning that the English privateer John Philip Beare had switched allegiance in peacetime to become a hated Cuban *guardacosta*. Molesworth had angrily related how this turncoat had even married upon reaching Havana, allegedly informing his new Spanish employers that his wife was a noblewoman, who ran away with him, and they actually fired the guns of the castle as a salute to her, while the Governor and most of the chief men of the town were present at the wedding. The nobleman's daughter is a strumpet that he used to carry with him [aboard ship] in man's apparel, and is the daughter of a rum-punch woman of Port Royal.[18]

PIRATES AND DRINK

Throughout their short but bloody reign, tales would frequently be told of the freebooters' predilection for heavy drinking—significantly enough, most often in binges. Certainly, there was a great deal of truth behind this image, yet many people of every walk of life drank to excess during that era. Pirates might have been more greedily unrestrained than most individuals in the amounts they consumed, yet this wildness may have been attributable to the more informal discipline observed among their ranks—plus the fact that they were so often drinking freely from someone else's liquor.

A Hard-Drinking Age

Virtually every public or private celebration held during the 17th or early 17th centuries entailed some amount of alcoholic consumption. For instance, the jolly and earthy archbishop of York, Lancelot Blackburne (who had allegedly served aboard buccaneer ships as a young man in the West Indies during the early 1680s), would be remembered years afterward for having ordered—during an ecclesiastical visit to Nottingham—that pipes with tobacco and liquor be brought into the vestry "for his refreshment after the fatigue of confirmation."[19]

As for specific examples of heavy communal drinking by other Caribbean seafarers in general, such a list would be endless and would reveal the great extent of excess in public life during those days, as illustrated by the following tales:

- In December 1661, the Jamaican privateers James Risby and George Freebourne met the merchant ship *Sint Pieter* of Amsterdam off the Cuban coast, whose captain, Henry Hambrouck, had secured permission from the Spanish authorities to take on wood and water—and was using this excuse to make repeated stops along that coastline, illegally selling goods to its inhabitants. Wishing to careen, Hambrouck asked advice from the two privateer veterans, who recommended a quiet bay and joined him there at anchor. The Dutch unloaded their cargo in anticipation of careening, and as Christmas 1661 was approaching, all three crews sat down on the beach, eating and drinking together throughout that day—until the Dutch had become so hopelessly drunk by evening that Risby and Freebourne helped themselves to their finest goods and sailed away before their fellow revelers could regain consciousness.

- When the Dutch-born rover Jan Erasmus Reyning returned into Jamaica's Montego Bay early in 1671—fresh from having taken part in Henry Morgan's sack of Panama—he found his brother-in-law riding at anchor aboard the merchantman *Witte Lam* of Zeeland, with a letter from home. Nostalgic for his family, Reyning had thereupon arranged passage home aboard this Dutch vessel—but his piratical colleagues then held such riotous, drunken, violent parties aboard their own ships that *Witte Lam*'s master grew alarmed and preferred to slip away without him.

- On December 8, 1671 (O.S.), Acting Captain John Wilgress was dismissed from command of the largest Royal Navy warship then stationed in the Caribbean—the 40-gun frigate HMS *Assistance* at Port Royal, Jamaica—for his "wicked, drunken behavior."[20]

- Two and a half years later, the great Dutch admiral Michiel de Ruyter materialized off Martinique with a huge battle fleet in July 1674, disgorging 1,000 troops to storm its lightly defended stronghold of Fort-Royal (modern Fort-de-France); yet this assault column became bogged down in crossfires, and their discipline collapsed after a rum warehouse was breached, fueling such rampant drunkenness that the troops stumbled back to their boats in considerable disarray. Delighted by this unexpected triumph, the French garrison would long remember this battle as the *Victoire du Rhum* or the Victory of Rum.

- That same Christmas Day 1674 (O.S.), Colonel Philip Warner— England's deputy-governor on Antigua—landed with 300 men on the island of Dominica, to meet his illegitimate half-brother Thomas Warner, head of one of the local tribes, and ask his assistance in a retaliatory strike against some hostile natives. This request proved to be merely a treacherous ruse, though, for once Thomas's followers had assembled, the colonel "made them very drunk with rum, gave a signal," and had them all slaughtered—presumably to eradicate all traces of his unwanted sibling and nephews, who were an embarrassment to the official family.

- During Queen Anne's War, 200 Cuban corsairs were able to wade ashore unchallenged into the streets of Nassau one dawn in September 1703, taking its defenders utterly by surprise, because the acting governor of the Bahamas, Ellis Lightwood—"a gentleman of considerable estate in that island"—had hosted a raucous party the previous night to celebrate the birth of his son, so that every able-bodied Englishman had gone to bed very late, and very drunk.

Not surprisingly, even the most convivial social gathering involving pirates could explode into violence whenever such copious amounts of liquor were being served to such mercurial outlaws. One spectacular instance of a party spinning recklessly out of control occurred when the Dutch-born rover Otto van Tuyl—a Red Sea veteran who had moved his family from New York City to the lawless island of Madagascar during the 1690s—invited Captain Thomas Howard and some 70 of his ruffians from the 36-gun *Prosperous*, after their ship had put into the marauder anchorage at Saint Mary's Bay,

> to visit his plantation in the mainland and attend a celebration held in honor of the christening of two of his children. The company accepted and were hospitably entertained. [But] word having been passed around by someone envious of his prosperity, that Van Tuyl had once killed some pirates, the fickle rascals—without any facts to justify the fancy— pillaged his house, and in violation of all laws of hospitality took him prisoner. Such goods as they could not transport in cases, they burned or threw into the river, and it was decided to take Van Tuyl to the ship and hang him from the yardarm.[21]

Fortunately, one friendly rover cut Van Tuyl's restraints during this drunken chaos so that he was able to escape into the woods. Rallying a body of native allies, he then lay in ambush for Howard's pinnace and canoe as they returned downriver toward Saint Mary's Bay. This ingrate pirate captain was wounded in an arm with a gunshot in passing, and the canoe overset near the river bar, so that Van Tuyl was at least able to recuperate his hostage women and seize two of his recent guests before returning to his destroyed home. Shortly thereafter, he and his entire traumatized family moved back to New York.

Restraint at Sea

Yet despite their reputation for excessive drinking, which was to be frequently reaffirmed over ensuing decades, no rovers—indeed, no sailors of any kind during the age of sail, whether ill-disciplined freebooters or privateers, honest merchantmen, or naval professionals— could afford to become inebriated while their vessels were under way. There were difficulties enough in simply keeping a wooden warship under control at all times out on the ocean, to say nothing of closer inshore, as well as being prepared to meet any sudden call to action, so that even the wildest young pirates had—of necessity—to curtail their self-indulgent sprees until after their vessels had safely dropped anchor. Otherwise, so many shipboard duties—such as going aloft or handling heavy gear and equipment—could kill or maim unwary sailors, while any mistake might damage or imperil the ship.

Inattention through drunkenness could also have other unforeseeable consequences. For example, the veteran captain Robert Searle served in Morgan's push across the isthmus to assault Panama City in January 1671, then immediately thereafter was given command of a tiny flotilla of commandeered coastal craft with instructions to pursue Spanish civilians and noncombatants who had fled across to hide among its offshore islands. Yet upon reaching Taboga, Searle and his men came upon a large cache of abandoned wine, which, by evening, they were well on their way to consuming. Deep into their cups, they failed to post lookouts, and so did not notice that the 400-ton *Santísima Trinidad* of Captain Francisco de Peralta had appeared off that same island from farther out in the gulf. This galleon had departed Panama earlier, along with *San Felipe Neri*, carrying away the bulk of the Spaniards' valuables prior to the buccaneer assault.

Unaware that the pirates had spread out so quickly from the Panamanian mainland, De Peralta set a seven-man party ashore on Taboga to secure water for his suffering passengers. This party was instead captured and brought before Searle, who questioned them and thus belatedly discovered the presence of such a wealthy prize nearby—but by the time he and his befuddled men could react, De Peralta had become suspicious at the disappearance of his watering party, so that the galleon vanished back into the night. When the main army of buccaneers learned of Searle's missed opportunity a few days later, they were outraged, threatening violence. Even writing years after this mischance, the chronicler Exquemelin—who had apparently been among Morgan's piratical followers at Panama—could still not keep his scorn out of the account, as he related how, when the captive watering party had been brought before Searle, the old wine-soaked rover "had been more inclined to sit drinking and sporting with a group of Spanish women he had taken prisoner, than to go at once in pursuit of the treasure ship."[22]

To avert such consequences, outright drunkenness was discouraged aboard pirate ships. The covenant signed by Captain Thomas Tew's following of select, hard-bitten mercenaries, for instance—even prior to clearing Bermuda for their criminal Red Sea foray in January 1693 aboard the eight-gun, 70-ton sloop *Amity*—contained the following article: "That if any man of the said company shall in time of service, be so drunk and incapable that he does not fight and withstand the enemy, then he or they shall be cut off or punished according as the Captain and the major part of the company thinks meet."[23]

Given the poor quality of nonalcoholic beverages available to all crews serving at sea during this era, the daily consumption of a certain amount of spirits was inevitable, although seldom allowed to any great excess. Even a commander who was personally a heavy drinker—such as Blackbeard—might allow his cutthroats some leeway as to when and how deeply they might imbibe, but no dereliction of duty would be tolerated through drunkenness. Otherwise, it would have been literally impossible to work the large and cumbersome *Queen Anne's Revenge* for thousands of miles, past reef-lined West Indian isles and along the perilous lee shores of Florida and the Carolinas, with an impaired crew. And, of course, every commander furthermore knew that excessive drinking aboard any small vessel crammed with heavily armed young desperadoes could explode into murderous fights—to say nothing of mutinies.

Celebratory Returns into Port

Perhaps even more than their naval or merchant counterparts, most freebooters yearned to put into a welcoming port, where they might relax and squander their money in liquor-fueled indulgences. Typically, naval officers and merchant masters would carefully regulate their crews' consumption of spirits while at sea, then discharge them with full pay upon reaching port, turning a blind eye to their wanton sprees. Pirates likewise aspired to swarm ashore with any booty that they might have won, and with a similar objective in mind.

The earliest buccaneers were more freely able to act out such fancies, as they were officially welcome by the authorities at Port Royal and most other major West Indian harbors. Exquemelin would later describe how Rok Brasiliano returned to Jamaica during the late 1660s with a wealthy Mexican prize

> and lorded it there with his mates, until all was gone. For that is the way with these buccaneers—whenever they have got hold of something, they don't keep it for long. They are busy dicing, whoring, and drinking so long as they have anything to spend. Some of them will get through a good two or three thousand pieces of eight in a day—and next day not have a shirt to their back.[24]

Shortly thereafter, a band of 400 English buccaneers were known to have refused Morgan's proposal for joining his campaign against Maracaibo, instead following Captain Charles Hadsell in a competing attack against Cumaná—which ended in failure. Returning into Port

Royal, these defeated rovers found Morgan's men already crowded triumphantly into its taverns, who "ceased not to mock and jeer at them for their ill success at Comana,"[25] further rubbing it in by asking: "Let us see what money you brought from Comana, and if it be as good silver as that which we bring from Maracaibo."

Such unbridled celebrations would slowly decline in number throughout most major Caribbean seaports, as official disapproval gradually built up against hosting or entertaining such unlicensed raiders. For example, despite England's neutrality during the ongoing Franco-Spanish hostilities, Port Royal's authorities nonetheless greeted a squadron of French *flibustiers* and their English colleagues in July 1677 as they returned from their sack of Santa Marta. Its captive Spanish bishop and a friar were released to Jamaica's new governor, Lord Vaughan, and he furthermore sent some of his royal officers aboard the pirate flagship to attempt to also "procure the liberty of the [Spanish] Governor and others"—only to have these officials report back that they had found "the privateers all drunk, [so that] it was impossible to persuade them to do anything by fair means." When Vaughan subsequently informed the English freebooters that it was now against the law for them to serve under foreign colors, the French became "damnably enraged" and sailed off—without releasing any more captives—to spend their plunder elsewhere.[26]

As fewer Antillean ports became available to them, some mercenaries would begin venturing as far north as New England, in quest of welcoming outlets to enjoy their binges. In 1684, excited Massachusetts officials would use extraordinary means to attract a visit by a pair of wandering, booty-laden pirate ships—Michiel Andrieszoon's *Mutine* and Jan Willems's *Dauphine*—as they moved up the Atlantic seaboard, after having stolen a fortune in Spanish money from two Dutch West Indiamen off of Cuba. Governor Edward Cranfield of neighboring New Hampshire would complain to London that he had been

> credibly informed that they [the pirates] share £700 a man. The Bostoners no sooner heard of her off the coast than they dispatched a messenger and pilot to convoy her into port, in defiance of the King's proclamation [of March 1684, prohibiting aid and abetment to rovers]. The pirates are likely to leave the greatest part of their plate behind them, having bought up most of the choice goods in Boston.[27]

Eventually, royal decrees would begin to restrict access into North American ports as well, particularly by such blatant lawbreakers during peacetime.

Too extravagant a celebration could attract unwanted attention. Early in 1720, Captain Bartholomew Roberts discharged four of his piratical minions with their share of the spoils aboard a boat, as his *Royal Roger* prowled past Virginia, to proceed inshore and disappear back into civilian life. They rowed deep into Chesapeake Bay and up the Black River, until all four stepped ashore and soon found a tavern nearby, "where they might ease themselves of their Golden Luggage," according to the account later published in the newspaper *American Weekly Mercury*. But this quartet spent their money so lavishly—one even purchasing the freedom of several indentured English women servants, for the princely sum of £30—that this drunken display of wealth brought them to the attention of the county authorities, who committed them to jail on suspicion of piracy, and they were hanged.

Yet such was the tenor of these times, that such binges continued. The conduct of many legitimate privateers returning into port between wartime forays would remain equally unrestrained, and seemingly among all nationalities. The French rover Étienne Montauban, for instance, regained Bordeaux after a lengthy absence in September 1694, his 34-gun *Trois Frères* bringing in three rich prizes. However, this French captain soon became alarmed when his 170 *flibustiers*—"finding themselves in a large city where pleasure and abundance reign"—began running up enormous expenses on his credit. He lamented,

> Every night was passed in amusements, every day in running in masks throughout the city; they had themselves carried in chaises, with torchbearers even at high noon, while a few died of their debauches, and four others deserted me.[28]

Fearful of seeing all his profits evaporate, Montauban could only pray for an early departure of his man-of-war and its unruly crew next spring.

Unwinding in Lonely Anchorages

Dropping anchor in a lovely tropical harbor to temporarily ease the strain of crowded shipboard life and cares of round-the-clock watch duties was also a cause worth celebrating for many a nomadic pirate crew. Even the loneliest of anchorages could become a festive spot, given a refreshment of foods and sufficient liquor to drink. William Dampier recorded how the isolated English loggers in the Bay of Campeche, among whom he lived during the years 1676 to 1678, would joyfully welcome visiting vessels and prove that

they had not forgot their old drinking-bouts, and would still spend £30
or £40 at a sitting on board the ships that came hither from Jamaica,
carousing and firing of guns three or four days together.[29]

It was during just such a festivity while lying at anchor off Ile-à-
Vache, at the southwestern tip of Haiti in January 1669, that Henry
Morgan was almost killed. Having gathered seven corsair captains
aboard his flagship *Oxford,* they had agreed to sail under his command
to attack the great port of Cartagena on the Spanish Main, after which
"they began on board the great ship to feast one another for joy of
their new voyage." Dining heartily on the quarterdeck while their
crewmen roistered on the forecastle, they "drank the health of the King
of England and toasted their good success, and fired off salvoes"[30]—
until suddenly as the tropical darkness was falling, *Oxford*'s magazine
exploded through neglect by the drunken gunner. Only six men and
four boys survived out of a company of more than 200, including
Morgan himself, plus the lucky few sitting beside him on the quarterdeck.

Yet given the limited entertainments available to sailors visiting the
remotest corners of the world during that age, drinking would continue unabated whenever pirates happened to congregate to enjoy a bit
of respite—be that in unrefined bolt-holes such as Madagascar, lawless Nassau, along the Mosquito Coast, or even wherever two ships
chanced to meet at sea. When the Jamaican pirate hunter Jonathan
Barnet slipped out of Port Royal in early November 1720 (O.S.) to surprise "Calico Jack" Rackham, he later reported to the governor that
he had found this outlaw relaxing at the western tip of that island,
having just

met near the Negril Point a small pettiauger [*sic:* piragua], which upon
sight of him, ran ashore and landed her men; but Rackham hailing them,
desired the pettiauger's men to come aboard him and drink a bowl of
punch, swearing they were all friends and would do no harm. Hereupon
they agreed to his request, and went aboard him, though it proved fatal
to every one of them, they being nine in all.

For they were no sooner got aboard, and had laid down their muskets and cutlasses in order to take up their pipes, and make themselves
merry with their new acquaintance over a can of flip, but Captain Barnet's
sloop was in sight, which soon put a damp to all their merriment.[31]

Drink-Fueled Excesses

In light of the general proclivity toward overindulging in alcohol
throughout this era, especially to mark any auspicious occasion, it is

hardly surprising to learn that many pirate crews could explode into wild abandon at the plundering of a rich prize, or sacking of a town, or triumphant entry into a welcoming harbor. Although not necessarily subject to the same harsh discipline as other contemporary sailors, their hand-to-mouth existence as nomadic renegades nonetheless meant that the daily lives of pirates were fraught with very real hunger, thirst, and want. Denied access into major seaports so as to legally replenish their shipboard stocks of potables and perishable foods, freebooters fell upon any spoils with a ravenous appetite.

Many stories would be recorded of drink-fueled binges, in which pirates crudely ransacked civilian homes in towns they had seized or delighted in vandalizing hapless merchant vessels they had captured. In just one of countless examples of such wanton outbursts, eyewitnesses described how Captain Louis Guittard's 28-gun flagship *La Paix* and an accompanying pirate sloop had entered Chesapeake Bay with two prizes in late April 1700, further seizing the merchantman *Nicholson* of Master Robert Lurting before this entire flotilla dropped anchor in Lynnhaven Bay. Having been at sea continuously for several weeks, Guittard allowed his 140 cutthroats liberty to relax while they pillaged their prizes at leisure, indulging themselves in a drunken party. Lurting noted that "about 100 hogsheads of tobacco, besides bulk tobacco, clothing, and several materials of the ship" were deliberately tossed overboard from his fully loaded ship during this rampage. His only consolation was that the hungover pirates were in no condition to resist the next morning, when the Royal Navy frigate HMS *Shoreham* of Captain William Passenger bore down and captured them.

NOTES

1. *Calendar of State Papers, Colonial: America and West Indies,* vol. 9 (London: Her Majesty's Stationery Office, 1893), 93.

2. *Calendar of State Papers, Colonial: America and West Indies,* vol. 7 (London: Her Majesty's Stationery Office, 1889), 420.

3. *Calendar of State Papers,* vol. 9, 429.

4. Diana Vida Thornton, "The Probate Inventories of Port Royal, Jamaica" (master's thesis, Anthropology Department, Texas A&M University, August 1992), 45.

5. *Calendar of State Papers, Colonial: America and West Indies,* vol. 14 (London: Her Majesty's Stationery Office, 1903), 592.

6. *Calendar of State Papers, Colonial: America and West Indies,* vol. 5 (London: Her Majesty's Stationery Office, 1880), 558.

7. *Calendar of State Papers, Colonial: America and West Indies,* vol. 24 (London: Her Majesty's Stationery Office, 1922), 292.

8. *Calendar of State Papers, Colonial: America and West Indies*, vol. 34 (London: Her Majesty's Stationery Office, 1936), 69.

9. *Calendar of State Papers*, vol. 5, 332.

10. *Calendar of State Papers, Colonial: America and West Indies*, vol. 15 (London: Her Majesty's Stationery Office, 1904), 181.

11. Alexandre-Olivier Exquemelin, *The Buccaneers of America*, trans. Alexis Brown, introd. Jack Beeching (London: Penguin, 1969), 80.

12. Ibid., 82.

13. *Calendar of State Papers*, vol. 7, 49.

14. *Calendar of State Papers*, vol. 9, 390.

15. G.M. Longfield-Jones, "The Case History of 'Sir H.M.,'" *Medical History* 32 (1988): 449.

16. Exquemelin, *The Buccaneers of America*, 82.

17. *Calendar of State Papers, Colonial: America and West Indies*, vol. 10 (London: Her Majesty's Stationery Office, 1896), 231.

18. *Calendar of State Papers, Colonial: America and West Indies*, vol. 12 (London: Her Majesty's Stationery Office, 1899), 415.

19. Stephen Leslie, ed., *Dictionary of National Biography*, vol. 5 (London: Macmillan, 1886), 124.

20. *Calendar of State Papers*, vol. 7, 298.

21. Don Carlos Seitz, Howard F. Gospel, and Stephen Wood, *Under the Black Flag: Exploits of the Most Notorious Pirates* (Mineola, NY: Courier Dover, 2002), 87.

22. Exquemelin, *The Buccaneers of America*, 199.

23. David F. Marley, *Pirates of the Americas*, vol. 2 (Santa Barbara, CA: ABC-CLIO, 2008), 838.

24. Exquemelin, *The Buccaneers of America*, 81–82.

25. Ibid., 124.

26. *Calendar of State Papers*, vol. 10, 121.

27. *Calendar of State Papers, Colonial: America and West Indies*, vol. 11 (London: Her Majesty's Stationery Office, 1898), 678.

28. Étienne Montauban, *Relation du voyage du Sieur de Montauban, capitaine des flibustiers, en Guinée en l'an 1695* (Amsterdam: J. Louis de Lorme, 1698), 367.

29. William Dampier, *A New Voyage Round the World* (New York: Dover, 1968), 21.

30. Exquemelin, *The Buccaneers of America*, 151.

31. C. Lovat Fraser, *The Lives and Adventures of Sundry Notorious Pirates* (New York: McBride, 1922), 20.

5

LAIRS

Upon entering the Darién,
commend yourself to Mary;
your entry is in her hand,
your exit lies in God's.
                    —Engraved on a Panamanian coastal keep, as noted
                                by Father Severino de Santa Teresa

No vessel or crew during the late 17th or early 18th century could possibly have remained at sea for any great length of time—at most, only for a few months—before their crudely preserved supplies of food and drink would begin to grow foul; the firewood necessary for cooking their meals to run low; and the wooden ships themselves to require repairs, especially when operating in warmer climes. Shore bases were, therefore, essential for all vessels, so they could resupply and refit on a regular basis. Naval warships and merchantmen routinely enjoyed access to major port facilities, but some privateers—and virtually every pirate—had to rely on other, more unconventional arrangements.

Usually, freebooters had to seek out a remote and defensible bay in which to rest, careen, hunt, fish, barter, and rearm—far from any official scrutiny—and to stay safe from any danger of a sudden attack during this vulnerable period while their ship lay immobile and defenseless. Uninhabited bays far from busy sea lanes were normally chosen for

these retreats, preferably with approaches screened by some nautical obstacles such as offshore reefs or shoals, to minimize any chance
detection by passing patrols or transient vessels. A fresh water source,
wood, and plenty of game in the vicinity were also desirable features
to sustain an encampment ashore.

Because of the benign climate prevailing in the tropics, Caribbean
rovers already carried aboard their ships everything necessary for setting up such a camp, beginning with their hammocks—which were
ideally suited for sleeping in the open air—plus a few large cauldrons
and pots from the galley for cooking, plus each man's personal utensils for eating. The pirate chronicler Alexandre-Olivier Exquemelin recorded how the French *flibustiers* among whom he had served during
the 1660s would sail into a concealed anchorage, where all would go
ashore to set up their individual tents on land. Since the pirate ship
would first have to be lightened, so as to be warped up close to the
beach to then be tilted over and careened,

- its guns, powder barrels, and heavy rounds would all be ferried a
  shore as an initial step and installed into defensive batteries on land;
- its sails, yardarms, blocks, and rigging would be unslung and used
  to erect large pavilions ashore, the largest being destined to serve
  as a mess hall and others to protect general stores, while shipboard
  machinery was also used to operate the wooden hoists on land;
- the highest point of land around would be chosen as a lookout spot
  and kept manned around the clock, with a means for signaling down
  to the main camp below by day or night; and
- a rough campground would be cleared, firewood and foodstuffs
  gathered, and some sort of perimeter established, although seldom
  lined with any kind of defensive pickets or palisades.

Pirates normally felt safe enough to lounge confidently in their base
camps, seldom bothering to send out patrols to sweep against any
potential attack or to erect any defenses beyond the initial batteries
installed to cover their anchored vessel.

Such self-assuredness could sometimes prove misplaced, of course,
as when the buccaneer chronicler William Dampier recorded how
the New England freebooter, Captain Thomas Paine—while serving
illegally under a French commission in the summer of 1681—had
crept his damaged 10-gun, 100-man ship into Panama's Bocas del Toro
Archipelago to effect repairs, and

> having built a tent ashore to put his goods in while he careened his
> ship, and some men lying there with their arms, in the night the Indi-

ans crept softly into the tent and cut off the heads of three or four men, and made their escape; nor was this the first time they had served the privateers so.[1]

Whenever possible, pirates would compel their prisoners or slaves to perform all of this manual labor, as well as the heaviest work in lightening, tilting, and cleaning their ship's hull. Veteran West Indian rovers, inured to mosquitoes and accustomed to the regional diet, were capable of living in such a setting for weeks, even months on end. In one noteworthy case, Jean-David Nau l'Olonnais ordered his *flibustier* flotilla to disperse prior to a planned raid in 1668, and so his followers vanished into a variety of jungle-fringed harbors scattered along the coast of Belize, subsisting quite comfortably in them for three months—until a Spanish galleon was announced as having arrived in the Bay of Amatique opposite, as had been expected—at which point the French freebooters reassembled, seemingly out of nowhere, for a surprise attack.

A few of these 17th-century pirate haunts have survived into the present day as sun-bleached shantytowns, although most have silently vanished over the centuries, their last few traces being swallowed up by the jungle.

HAVENS FROM STORMS

In addition to providing temporary sanctuary for marauders wishing to effect repairs and recuperate, these out-of-the-way anchorages also permitted pirate ships to ride out bad weather—especially during the West Indian hurricane seasons, whose patterns had become well known to experienced seamen after a century and a half of observation. Typically, rovers who found themselves far from home or otherwise impeded from putting into a major port whenever such threats portended would seek out a sheltered and uninhabited harbor to avoid experiencing the perils from such ferocious storms out on the open waves. Captain Stede Bonnet's boatswain Ignatius Pell, for instance, confessed to the South Carolina authorities in 1718 that the crew of the pirate sloop *Revenge* had chosen to linger for a month and a half in the Cape Fear River estuary, because they had wished to wait out the hurricane season before returning toward Saint Thomas in the distant Virgin Islands.

Today, just as in that era, most hurricanes started forming in June, usually over the western reaches of the Caribbean in the initial stages of any season. A lull frequently ensued in July, after which the activity and intensity of eruptions shifted into the Lesser Antilles, with the number of hurricanes peaking by October. Although the island of

Guadeloupe seems to have borne the brunt of many such storms over the centuries, these often proved less severe than elsewhere, as these hurricanes were often just gaining strength while in these latitudes. As they moved eastward and northeastward, they escalated and roared much more destructively through Hispaniola, Cuba, or the Bahamas before veering up past North America's Atlantic Seaboard, and eventually dissipating out over the ocean. About eight such monster storms would appear in the West Indies during any normal season, although sometimes as many as a dozen might erupt.

Naturally, such phenomena were feared by all seamen—whether pirates, privateers, merchant sailors, or naval professionals. In fact, many a freebooter would lose his life to such storms throughout this era, including some seasoned Antillean hands:

- One of the earliest privateers to operate out of Jamaica, the Belgian-born Adriaen van Diemen Swart, died when his frigate *Griffin* was driven deep into the Gulf of Mexico by a huge storm in August 1664, only five of his crewmen emerging alive when its dismasted hull eventually swirled helplessly onto the coast of Florida.

- Two years later, Francis, Lord Willoughby—the resident governor-general of the English Leeward Islands—was lost with almost 1,000 men when his entire 20-ship fleet, sailing to the relief of Saint Kitts during the Second Anglo-Dutch War, was engulfed by a massive hurricane on the night of August 4–5, 1666.

- The notorious Corsican-born privateer Giovanni Michele, better known among his Spanish colleagues as the corsair Juan Corso, disappeared somewhere along the Gulf Coast of the modern United States, during a storm in May 1685.

- Likewise, the next year, the cruel *flibustier* chieftain Grammont's flagship *Hardi* vanished with all hands, when it was caught by a storm off the Azores.

- The Dutch-born rover Jan Erasmus Reyning survived 30 years of combat, imprisonment, and disease in the Caribbean, only to perish in a storm while anchored peaceably off Bilbao in the Bay of Biscay.

- Black Sam Bellamy's crippled flagship *Whydah* was driven to its death on Cape Cod by a howling storm during the night of April 26–27, 1717 (O.S.), with only 2 of the 146 men aboard surviving that horrific night.

- And the luckless Charles Vane would have his sloop smashed by a powerful storm off Honduras in February 1719, being one of a handful of survivors to crawl onto an uninhabited island, from where he was eventually rescued—only to be recognized and carried prisoner into Port Royal, to be hanged.

THE PIRATE CAMP

Unable to obtain basic necessities such as foodstuffs and drink except through theft, most rover bands had to gather some kind of a stockpile of provisions from interceptions or raids before being able to retire into a lonely bay to dismantle, disarm, and careen their ship. Bonnet, for example—his sloop *Revenge* having been stripped of everything of value by Blackbeard—was reduced to rummaging through merchantmen transiting along the Virginia coast, until after a month he finally managed on July 29, 1718 (O.S.), to take "a sloop of fifty tons, bound from Philadelphia to Barbados laden with provisions . . . as also another of sixty tons from Antigua to Philadelphia having on board rum, molasses, sugar, cotton, and indigo."[2] These supplies allowed him to steer for the Cape Fear River estuary in North Carolina and set up a camp ashore to begin careening his *Revenge* in preparation for clearing toward the Antilles.

While living in such encampments ashore, pirates tended to observe the same basic regimen as they observed aboard ship. Like most people during the 17th and 18th centuries, prior to the invention of electric lighting,

- they worked from sunup to sunset, usually rising at daybreak and sleeping in only on Sundays;
- at dawn, the night watch would be relieved and any prisoners released from confinement;
- the pirates ate two meals a day, once in the morning and again in midafternoon, in gatherings around a communal kettle;
- they held their food down on wooden plates with forks and cut and passed portions into their mouth on the tip of a sharp knife;
- spoons were also employed, and each individual's set of utensils was designed to fold up or nestle into a portable kit to be carried upon their person;
- work on the ship and its equipment would quickly resume, no pirate captain ever being truly at ease until his vessel was ready to put back out to sea;
- smoking tobacco in pipes was commonplace, with even children of the era indulging in the habit;
- the daily work pace eased as the tropical heat built up in the afternoon, before a halt was finally called;
- after the main meal of the day had been consumed, pirates often broke up into groups and entertained themselves with target shooting, competitions, music, gambling, and plays;

George Lowther with his pirate ship *Happy Delivery* careened off the West African coast in 1721, so as to burn off barnacles encrusted on its hull. Note his crewmen gathered around a bowl of tobacco in the tent behind, temporarily erected using one of the ship's canvas sails. (Edward Rowe Snow, *Pirates and Buccaneers of the Atlantic Coast* [Boston: Yankee Publishing Company, 1944])

- at sundown, prisoners would once again be confined for the night and a watch set;

- in fair weather, pirates would sleep in their hammocks—slung between trees—or on the ground at spots they had already claimed, a short distance away from the main campfire, or retire into tents if heavy rain threatened; and

- most pirate captains allowed individual crewmembers to remain unsupervised around the campfire after lights-out, since desertion was unlikely in such a remote locale.

Depending on circumstances, armed boat parties might sally in pursuit of any passing vessels, especially if the pirates suspected that their anchorage had been spotted. If any stay became protracted, foraging parties might begin venturing ever farther afield to hunt, fish, or gather food, as fresh new supplies were constantly needed; and if such needs grew more pressing, larger detachments might be sent along the coast in boats or inland on foot to raid Spanish towns or rustle livestock. The entire pirate camp might be relocated if local stocks of fish, game, or fruit became too depleted.

Natives could prove hostile if pirate bands drained their resources excessively or otherwise acted abusively, but on most occasions, both groups got along well, united by their hostility against the Spaniards. A particularly warm welcome from the locals might extend the length of any pirate stay, even coming to intermingle with their women. As has been noted, Nau l'Olonnais's *flibustiers* were able to reside comfortably in Belize for three months in 1668, and such lengthy layovers were also not uncommon among the lost communities of runaway slaves along the southern Cuban coast.

In other more stark landscapes, though, such as lonely Samaná Bay on Hispaniola or many desert isles in the Bahamian archipelago, pirate stays would be much briefer. For eventually the weather would begin to clear, trade winds would begin to blow, merchant traffic would resume, and pirate ships would put back out to sea in quest of prey.

EARLY HIDEOUTS

The first generation of Caribbean buccaneers had quickly learned how to adapt to living in the New World, many having served in the ranks of early European smugglers who—unlike the commanders of major commercial convoys or royal squadrons, who had to keep to deep-water routes for greater safety—had deliberately probed into the

maze of reef-lined islands and along the stretches of dark, silent tropical coastlines in search of suitable anchorages. Both the northwestern
shores of Hispaniola and southern Cuba had provided a multitude
of such resting spots for the earliest interlopers, being far removed
from Spain's major plate fleet routes, which passed much farther to
the south.

All of these early haunts would have several features in common:

- They lay near or behind daunting maritime barriers, which scared
  away most legitimate oceangoing traffic.
- Their immediate approaches were often additionally intertwined
  with treacherous shallows, which posed an extra deterrent against
  any pursuing warship that drew too much water.
- The contours of such hideouts were difficult to discern from out
  at sea, a seemingly solid-looking coastline often dissolving into a
  string of offshore isles, with twisting inner channels and concealed
  bays swimming into view once smaller vessels had ventured closer
  inshore.
- These lairs lay far from any major ports or towns, whether inhabited by the Spaniards or any other nationality.
- They could not be easily surprised by a column of troops approaching from overland.

A few of the more infamous pirate bolt-holes are herewith described,
although many more existed, most being occupied on a more fleet-
ing and transitory basis.

Gardens of the Queen or South Cays of Cuba

Cuba is a long, narrow island, and its southern coast is lined for several hundred miles by a string of lush offshore isles, one archipelago
in particular having been dubbed the "Gardens of the Queen" by
none other than Christopher Columbus. Despite their great natural
beauty, these waters also abound with countless reefs, rocks, and
deceptive channels, all perilous hazards for old-time sailing ships.
Spanish charts from that era recorded many clusters along this expanse as *abrojos* or "eyes-open" stretches, where mariners should proceed with extreme caution. Yet for privateers and pirates, who enjoyed
firsthand knowledge of its topography, this Cuban labyrinth could
provide abundant refuges in which to rest and resupply at ease, so
that the Gardens would remain a popular destination for weary marauders throughout the age of piracy.

Its dark green shoreline often appears as unbroken terrain from out at sea, yet dissolves into many twisting passages and hidden inlets upon moving in closer. Rovers could therefore careen their ships unseen on a fine, sheltered, sandy beach while keeping uninterrupted watch out to sea. Sometimes they would camouflage the protruding masts of their ships by tying on large branches or palms, so as to blend in against the jungle backdrop. Commonly known among the English in the 17th century as the South Cays, this stretch of Cuban coastline would be visited by virtually every notorious raider from that era:

- Adriaen van Diemen Swart and Gerrit Gerritszoon or "Rok Brasiliano" are known to have spent several months living among its islands as early as 1663.
- Edward Mansfield led his outlaw flotilla into its waters two years later, anchoring offshore with easy familiarity.
- Henry Morgan convened his first rendezvous as newly anointed pirate "Admiral" in the south cays of Cuba, early in 1668, being joined there by the likes of John Morris and Edward Collier.
- Exquemelin first stepped onto the same Cuban beaches that same year as a follower of Nau l'Olonnais.

William Beeston, later destined to become Jamaica's royal governor, recorded in his diary that he had departed Port Royal on January 31, 1672 (O.S.), in command of the 40-gun frigate HMS *Assistance* "to the south cays of Cuba after [rogue] privateers and pirates, by the desire of the Governor of Santiago [de Cuba]."[3] More than seven years later, Governor Lord Carlisle would also dispatch the newly arrived, 32-gun frigate HMS *Success* under Captain Thomas Johnson into this same maze, to run down the pirate Peter Harris—but when this particular Royal Navy warship sighted and chased that renegade through the archipelago's shoal waters in late November 1679, it blundered onto a sandbank and tore out its bottom, being irrecoverably lost— while Harris laughingly made good his escape. Two and a half years afterward, the great Laurens de Graff would also choose to anchor among these Cuban keys to sell his mass of booty from the sack of Veracruz to Jamaican buyers.

For decades, *guardacostas* would steal along the shorelines of the Gardens of the Queen, making occasional captures—yet they could never succeed in discouraging its many piratical visitors, smugglers, or poachers. As late as the summer of 1722, the pirate captain Thomas Anstis would relax comfortably amid its brilliant waters for a couple of months with his ship *Morning Star* and brigantine *Good Fortune* awaiting news of a potential royal pardon.

Abraham's Cay or Bluefields, Nicaragua

Another favorite pirate haunt was this almost invisible harbor concealed along the mosquito-infested Caribbean coast of Central America. It was first claimed by a pair of Dutch brothers—Abraham and Willem Blauveldt—who originally hailed from the fishing village of Monnikendam near Amsterdam in North Holland. Veteran privateers from the Netherlandic campaigns against Spain, they had shifted their allegiance to the English Puritan colony installed on Providencia Island and in 1633 piloted a band of traders across to Cape Gracias a Dios to create an outpost among its Moskito natives.

Reconnoitering farther south from this base, the Blauveldts entered a wide, sheltered anchorage at the mouth of what the Spaniards knew as the Escondido or "Hidden" River. Dense tropical foliage made its contours almost indistinguishable from out at sea, no sea traffic passed nearby, and no Spaniards lived in its general vicinity, because the local Indians were hostile to them, although they could be befriended by other foreigners. The long spit of land enclosing this anchorage was severed from the mainland by shallow channels at both ends, so it provided a naturally defensible position.

The brothers had therefore sailed for England, Abraham appearing before a Providence Island Company committee meeting in Brooke House on June 14, 1637 (O.S.), to request help in founding a new colony there. He described his discovery as "a good harbor, a mile-and-a-half in breadth at its mouth, that he was two miles up the main and found the country overgrown with silk grass, and a river eight or ten feet deep, and 30 feet broad."[4] Yet the Company—drained of funds and with no returns yet from their Antillean investments—did not act upon this proposal.

The disappointed brothers turned to Dutch and Swedish interests to obtain new commissions, especially once the Puritan colony on Providencia Island was wiped out by a Spanish fleet in May 1641. Willem would operate out of New Amsterdam (modern New York City) for most of that ensuing decade, making annual privateering forays into the West Indies against the Spaniards, while Abraham seems to have taken up residence in the harbor they had jointly discovered. After the English conquest of Jamaica, a document entitled "An account of the private ships of war belonging to Jamaica and Tortudos in 1663"[5] listed one of the Blauveldts as still living and operating out of Cape Gracias a Dios with 50 men aboard a three-gun bark and regarded as an English ally.

The name Abraham's Cay would remain known long thereafter. For example, a Honduran native named Juan de la Cruz was captured off Amatique in the spring of 1666 by 30 French buccaneers foraging aboard three large boats. De la Cruz later escaped and testified to the Spanish authorities how his captors had carried him to the Cayo de Abraham, to be held captive aboard the anchored fleet of Nau l'Olonnais. This statement was corroborated by Jean Villebon, a deserter from this same French formation who asserted that the pirate ships lay "at a cay or island named Abraham," preparing for a raid upriver into central Nicaragua. Two decades later, Dampier also visited Abraham's Cay, although referring to it as Bluefield's River on the Main, explaining how: "It had this name from Captain Bluefield, a famous privateer living on Providence Island, long before Jamaica was taken."[6]

Despite occasional sweeps by Spanish expeditions in the 18th century, this mysterious and ramshackle foreign enclave somehow managed to survive, its population consisting of a curious blend of seafaring outcasts, runaway slaves, and native tribespeople. Today it is known as Bluefields Bay, the main seaport for eastern Nicaragua.

Bay of Campeche, Tris Island, or Laguna de Términos

Like the south cays of Cuba and Abraham's Cay, this huge shallow bay on the gulf coast of Mexico was also far removed from any inhabited areas as well as tricky to approach by sea, so that it, too, became a popular bolt-hole for pirates seeking a place to rest or hide during the 17th and early 18th centuries. Penetrating the Gulf of Mexico was a risky course for any foreign sailing ship, as no friendly seaports lay along the curve of its inescapable lee shores, while the waters closest to the Yucatán Peninsula were shallow and dotted with numerous rocks, sandbanks, and other maritime hazards.

After braving such dangers and arriving opposite the Laguna de Términos, its coastline appeared very low and scrubby, its climate hot and muggy, with only two muddy channels that allowed small vessels sufficient clearance to enter—although not large warships. Once inside, its inner shoreline was lined with dense tropical mangroves amid extensive marshes that were often flooded by overflowing rivers. Few natives lived in these torrid backwater inlets during colonial

times, and no Spaniards, who regarded this entire region as unhealth-
ful and unappealing. The Laguna de Términos was in fact considered a tropical no-man's-land between the provinces of Tabasco and
Yucatán without any recognized residents or overland communication. The Laguna was actually enclosed by a long, narrow, sandy island
long ago christened as Isla Triste or "Sad Island," which the English
misunderstood as Trist or Tris, and which has since been formally
renamed by the Mexican authorities as Isla del Carmen.

The first English interlopers had infiltrated this area perhaps as
early as 1658, shortly after the conquest of Jamaica, and five years
afterward Commodore Christopher Myngs led a major expedition
that devastated the nearby seaport of Campeche. More adventurers
began growing familiar with the Laguna, soon dubbing it the Bay of
Campeche (often misspelled as Campeachy in the correspondence of
the day). They seem to have initially been attracted to its coastline
by the wild cattle browsing aimlessly amid the scrubby savannas of
abandoned Xicalango Point, which they slaughtered in such numbers
that it became known to the English as Beef Island.

But what really attracted the ensuing wave of trespassers and permanent occupiers would be the large stands of logwood trees, whose
resin fetched handsome prices in Europe, being used there as a strong
dye for tinting cloth. Legend has it that pirates first learned of its
profitability when the veteran Jamaican privateer Captain William
James carried off a Spanish ship full of logwood and was astonished
at the price its cargo fetched once he sailed it into port to dispose of
this prize. Until then, he had supposedly "known so little of its real
value, that he had burned much of it for fuel on the voyage."[7]

When news of this rich seizure spread, hundreds of poachers began descending on the Laguna to set up logging camps hidden deep
inside its mangroves and eke out a living by felling trees for sale.
They subsisted much as their *boucanier* contemporaries on Hispaniola, except rather than hunting and butchering wild cattle to sell meat
to visiting vessels, the baymen stockpiled trees along riverbanks to
supply merchantmen that came calling. And like their French counterparts, these loggers were rugged individualists content to live beyond all government rule, supplementing their sporadic income with
raids against the local Spaniards.

Soon, merchantmen departing Jamaica began routinely circling into
the Gulf of Mexico to purchase a bulk cargo of logwood inside the
Laguna before proceeding out past Florida for their home ports in
North America or Western Europe. Sometimes they employed their
own crewmen to fell trees near the shorelines and float them out to

be hoisted aboard; other times, they purchased logs already cut by the baymen. The Spanish authorities noted this traffic and occasionally sent irregular *guardacostas* in sweeps down the coastline, which proved ineffectual and only provoked devastating counterraids. As early as 1667, Samuel Moseley of Dorchester, Massachusetts, was asked to represent his privateer friend Captain Thomas Salter of Port Royal, Jamaica, when a Spanish vessel that the latter had taken in the Bay of Campeche was illegally carried into New York City and sold off by its prize crew.

The 23-year-old future chronicler William Dampier first ventured into the Laguna in August 1675, when he shipped out of Port Royal aboard a ketch with a cargo of rum and sugar to exchange for logwood. So taken was he with the baymen's life that, after this ketch returned to Jamaica, Dampier made his way back to the bay in February 1676 and remained for more than two years, eventually departing for England in the autumn of 1678 with a goodly amount of money amassed— enough for him to marry. Of his experiences among the English loggers during their heyday, he later wrote that

> they often made sallies out in small parties amongst the nearest Indian towns, where they plundered and brought away the Indian women to serve them in their huts, and sent their husbands to be sold at Jamaica; besides they had not forgot their old drinking-bouts, and would still spend £30 or £40 at a sitting on board the ships that came hither from Jamaica, carousing and firing of guns three or four days together.[8]

Many 17th-century rovers frequented the Laguna de Términos, viewing it as an inaccessible base of operations. During the summer of 1669, for example, the rogue privateers Joseph Bradley, Gerrit Gerritszoon—better known as Rok Brasiliano—and Jelles de Lecat retired into its waterways to recuperate for a couple of months, after having intercepted a Cuban vessel laden with flour so as to furnish themselves with supplies. De Lecat even laid in a cargo of logwood before departing, and then ironically obtained a Spanish commission a couple of years later to the patrol the Laguna as a *guardacosta*. Governor Sir Thomas Lynch of Jamaica countered by sending the idled privateer John Morris in late January 1672 to take the renegade "Captain Yellowes," but Morris merely smuggled slaves and other goods into Campeche, then loaded his own ship with logwood before returning.

The mulatto Cuban corsair Diego Grillo was reputedly prowling the Laguna in 1673. Five years afterward, Captains George Spurre and Edward Neville recruited scores of heavily armed baymen from their hidden river warrens and led them in a stealthy advance that surprised Campeche at dawn on Sunday, July 10, 1678, resulting in much booty. Eight years afterward, when Jamaica's governor Hender Molesworth was angrily attempting to recall the outlaw John Coxon, he wrote complainingly to London in mid-November 1686:

> I hear that Coxon is cutting logwood in the Gulf of Campeachy, and has written to his friends that he has given up privateering and means to earn an honest living. I shall nonetheless send the proclamation declaring him a pirate to those parts by first opportunity.[9]

Molesworth followed this up by issuing a warrant on November 24, 1686 (O.S.), commissioning "Captains Richard Cubitt and Conway to apprehend John Coxon, the pirate, said to be logwood-cutting in the Bay of Campeachy."[10]

After enduring pirate raids out of the Laguna for several decades, the Spaniards finally organized an expedition that materialized off its entrance on December 11, 1716, expelled numerous trespassing vessels they caught inside, and then ferried ashore materiel to begin erecting a small fort, thereby barring future access. An attack seven months later from three buccaneer sloops failed to dislodge this Spanish garrison so that the Bay of Campeche was henceforth denied to pirates.

Bocas del Toro

The exact origin of the curious name for this maze of islands—literally the "Mouths of the Bull," which lie intermingled along the lush northwestern coastline of the modern Panamanian Republic—has been lost to history yet apparently began as a Spanish navigational warning for sailors. Much like "Mouths of the Dragon" warned of the unexpected dangers to be encountered from currents in the Gulf of Paria, the Bocas del Toro cautioned seafarers against wandering into this lonely Panamanian maze, where sailing ships might become lost among its disorienting topography until wrecked ashore—much like travelers in ancient times who had the misfortune to wander into the maze containing the Bull of Minos, becoming ever more bewildered until they met their fate.

Such a reputation naturally suited West Indian rovers, who knew that they could confidently congregate among its offshore islands, invisible from out at sea and thus safe from any chance Spanish naval patrol, or even an overland military sweep. Exquemelin mentioned the buccaneer John Davis of Jamaica as one captain who had used this archipelago as a lair since early on, recording how: "For a long time he had been lurking in the Gulf of the Boca del Toro, on the look-out for ships from Cartagena bound for Nicaragua."[11] The privateer Edward Mansfield also frequented this archipelago with his pirates, grateful to be able to anchor amid its channels with impunity. The buccaneer chronicler Dampier remembered the Bocas del Toro as "a place that the privateers use to resort to as much as any place on all the coast, because here is plenty of green tortoise, and a good careening place" (although adding the commentary that its "Indians here have no commerce with the Spaniards, but are very barbarous and will not be dealt with").[12]

After their joint sack of Portobelo in February 1680, Captains Coxon, Robert Allison, and Bartholomew Sharpe gleefully redistributed their booty and then dispersed into their favorite anchorages within the Bocas del Toro "to make clean our ships, there being the best place to careen our ships, by reason there is good store of turtle and manatee and fish."[13] For the next half century or more, the archipelago would provide refuge for many more outlaws and never be conquered by the Spaniards.

Coxon's Hole, Roatán Island

Lying roughly 25 miles off the north coast of Honduras, this long and narrow tropical isle—only 5 miles across at its widest point and 37 miles long—is noteworthy for its natural beauty. Along with smaller neighbors such as Útila, Guanaja, Barbaretta, Morat, and Pigeon Cay, this grouping would become known as the Bay Islands to the many poachers, runaways, and outlaws who would frequent them during the early 18th century. During Spain's conquest of the Americas, Roatán had been much too poor and remote to attract any claimant, after which Spanish transatlantic galleons had tended to circle wide around Cape Gracias a Dios at the northeastern tip of Honduras, because of the dangers posed by the Quita-sueño bank or Mesoamerican barrier reef lurking farther out at sea.

European smugglers had therefore found this lush island uninhabited except for native fishermen and runaway slaves, so Roatán had become a regular stopover for interloper ships. Soon, some permanent year-round residents appeared, and their number multiplied, so that four Spanish warships are known to have landed 450 Cuban militiamen on Roatán as early as July 1650 in a vain attempt to catch some of its English settlers before they melted away into its mangroves, and these troops departed empty-handed. The capture of Jamaica four years later by Oliver Cromwell's huge expedition brought an end to Spanish strategic hopes of ever clearing Roatán, and the island became a favorite haunt for generations of buccaneers.

The great Laurens de Graaf regularly visited, and a historic assembly of pirates was held on one of Roatán's beaches on April 7, 1683, to discuss a projected assault against the main Mexican seaport of Veracruz. Doubters among the throng of hundreds of freebooters who had gathered were reputedly swayed when the fierce *flibustier* chieftain Grammont bellowed at them: "I would believe it almost impossible, except for the experience and valor of those who hear my words."[14] The plan was endorsed with a roar of acclamation, so that a fleet of five pirate ships and eight lesser craft departed with 1,300 to 1,400 raiders, stealing into the Gulf of Mexico and winning this prize.

Another frequent visitor was the notorious John Coxon, who, after roving on both sides of the law throughout the 1670s and 1680s, is believed to have retired from the sea altogether to live out his remaining years on Roatán, whose principal harbor consequently became known as Coxon's or "Coxen's Hole—today Coxen Hole, the capital and most populous town on that island. Local legend avers that the old pirate was still alive there as late as 1697.

As logwood purchases out of the primitive encampments lining the nearby shores of Belize increased during the early 18th century, pirate visits to Roatán likewise continued apace. The entry of Blackbeard into Coxen's Hole was witnessed in early February 1718 by an alarmed Captain William Wade of the sloop *William and Mary*, who later reported that there "came in a ship of about 40 guns and a sloop of 10 commanded by . . . Edward Thatch, having in all about 250 men (70 or thereabouts being Negroes)," accompanied by two prizes. These threatening cutthroats forced Wade to dump his valuable cargo of logwood overboard as well as to beach his sloop so as to act as a makeshift dock for them, providing a platform for their prisoners to careen and clean their vessels' hulls. The brutish Thatch remained in Coxen's Hole for several weeks, seizing whatever additional vessels happened to enter, before finally burning his two prizes and departing in mid-March 1718. Wade was lucky that his *William and Mary* was not also torched, so he was able to refloat his sloop, salvage much of his jettisoned cargo, and eventually limp back into Jamaica to tell his tale.

LOST STRONGHOLDS

In addition to the remote bolt-holes often favored by pirates, selected because they were far removed from major sea traffic and difficult to find or penetrate, there were also major seaports—which, during the early days of the golden age of piracy, had openly welcomed such visitors, only to gradually become denied to them.

Tortuga Island, Haiti

Strategically situated six miles off the northwestern coast of Hispaniola sits the rocky low-lying island of Tortuga, measuring 22 miles long and only one mile wide. Because of their "pernicious" dealings with foreign smugglers, all Spanish residents who lived along its shoreline opposite had been relocated on orders from Madrid as of 1605 to be clustered closer to Hispaniola's capital of Santo Domingo. Compelled to leave behind their planted fields because of this abrupt removal, plus thousands of free-ranging cattle and pigs, this abandonment meant that henceforth foreign ships would find an easy means of refreshing their provisions, to say nothing of a tempting expanse for permanent occupation.

Cautiously, the first foreign trespassers erected their base camps on Tortuga because of its natural impregnability and only made forays across to the empty mainland opposite. Tortuga's northern side is so rock-bound as to still be nicknamed today as the Iron Coast, but its southern side contains a sheltered anchorage accessible via a pair of channels, with abundant stands of timber, fresh water, and "a very clear sandy bottom," according to the chronicler Exquemelin.[15] In the spring of 1630, some English Antillean colonists transferred onto Tortuga under Anthony Hilton, joining its handful of resident French and English hunters or buccaneers and installing a six-gun battery to protect its harbor. To ensure regular visits from merchantmen, Hilton and his lieutenant, Christopher Wormeley, furthermore signed an agreement with England's Puritan-owned Providence Company so that Tortuga became known for a while as Association Island.

In January 1634, a Dominican expedition guided by a young Irish turncoat took Tortuga's 300 inhabitants by surprise, butchering Hilton along with 194 others before throwing down its defenses and retiring with 39 captives. Wormeley departed for Virginia shortly thereafter, leaving behind a few-score frightened survivors to eke out a meager subsistence. Late in August 1642, the longtime French Antillean resident and engineer François Le Vasseur arrived with 40 Huguenot followers and a commission to displace Tortuga's unpopular English leader, Captain James Flood. The latter tamely quit for the Bahamas, leaving Le Vasseur to assume office and rename Tortuga as New Normandy (a name that also did not stick). A large fortress was built atop a promontory and called Fort de la Roche.

French buccaneers out of Tortuga raided Cuban towns in January and August 1652, provoking a Spanish counterexpedition that conquered their island base by February 1654. The victorious Dominicans even installed a garrison, yet this occupying force was withdrawn in August 1655, during the aftermath to the English conquest of Jamaica, so that Tortuga was contested by English and French buccaneers over the next few years. The latter eventually prevailed, although rovers of every nationality would still be drawn to Tortuga because of the liberal hand with which its governor issued licenses. The untamed colony would flourish as a *flibustier* stronghold until growing French power led to the establishment of large new towns on Saint-Domingue's mainland as of the 1670s. Tortuga would decline in importance until eventually unbridled roving would be reined in as of the late 1680s.

Port Royal, Jamaica

Immediately after the conquest of Jamaica by Cromwell's Western Design expedition in May 1655, its 7,000 English soldiers quickly dwindled to 2,500 through disease and want, while its naval squadron shrank to 10 warships. Given the precarious posture that these losses implied, its surviving officers eschewed the ex-Spanish capital of Santiago de la Vega—lying exposed on a plain six miles inland—in favor of erecting their main citadel at the tip of a long spit of sand enclosing the anchorage of Caguaya or Cagway. This easily defendable position had the further advantage of keeping sea communication open, and the Commonwealth commissioner, William Brayne, moreover decided in July 1657 that, since there was by then "the fair beginning of a town upon the point of this harbor," he intended that all State storehouses and private traders should be concentrated there as well, "which will soon make it a flourishing place."[16]

Because of continuous Spanish wartime threats, Governor Edward D'Oyley also began freely granting commissions to any and all privateers—whether English or foreign—as well as helping them to dispose of their booty, resupply, and effect repairs. D'Oyley even sold prizes on easy terms to likely campaigners, such as when Maurice Williams bought the Spanish frigate *Avispa* or *Wasp* for £120 in May 1659, renaming it *Jamaica*. The English Puritan governor furnished this captain with a patent, sold him five additional cannon from out of the State warehouses to help arm this vessel, and even circulated a

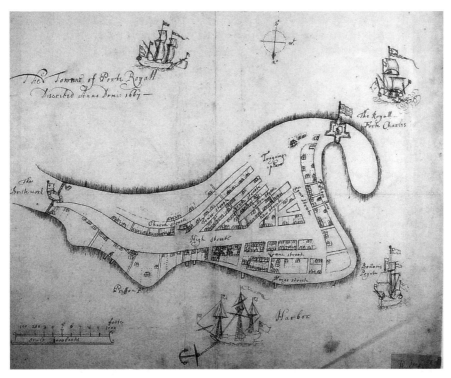

Early map of Jamaica's Port Royal, drawn in 1667, with north at bottom. An English ship is shown circling around its sandy tip, under the guns of "Royal Fort Charles," before passing Bon Amis Point and coming to anchor inside its sheltered harbor. (With the permission of the Provost, Fellows and Scholars of The Queen's College Oxford)

proclamation allowing Williams to recruit sailors out of Commodore Christopher Myngs's State flagship, with the words "that such seamen aboard the *Marston Moor* frigate that will go along with the aforesaid Captain Maurice Williams, may have liberty to go on board the said *Jamaica* frigate at their pleasure."

Not surprisingly, Jamaica became a magnet for corsairs of all nationalities and its principal seaport a welcoming haven. By the summer of 1660, the town of Cagway boasted roughly 200 houses, with a permanent population of 600 to 700 people, not including its Commonwealth garrison or hundreds of transient seafarers. When reports from London that same August 1660 indicated that the deceased Cromwell's government had collapsed and Charles II had been installed on the throne, Cagway was renamed Port Royal. D'Oyley worried because his subsequent attempts to rein in the activities of the free-spirited rovers, after a tentative peace had been concluded in 1661 with Spain back in Europe, merely vexed Port Royal's populace, who had come to "live only upon spoil and depredations."[17] Yet when Jamaica's first royal governor—Thomas, Lord Windsor—arrived to assume office in August 1662, he reintroduced a highly aggressive privateering policy against Spanish America, even during peacetime.

For the next decade or more, Port Royal welcomed visits from privateers and pirates of every stripe, many rallying under the banner of Henry Morgan, a captain in the Port Royal militia regiment. Eventually, though, the plantation owners who were starting to dominate Jamaican affairs deplored the excesses being committed by these privateers, which threatened the peaceful expansion of their sugar, cacao, and tobacco exports. Thanks to the disproportionate political power wielded by this elite—only large landowners being permitted to sit as representatives in Jamaica's assembly or on its council—they were able to gradually curtail buccaneering through legislation.

By the mid-1680s, Port Royal had become less welcoming for outright renegades, so that wilder spirits had begun shifting elsewhere. Then at 11:40 A.M. on Wednesday, June 7, 1692 (O.S.), an earthquake struck with such ferocity that much of the northern section of the town slid into the harbor, at least two rows of buildings and some 2,000 of 6,500 inhabitants being swallowed up in 30 to 40 feet of water. Another 2,000 people succumbed from the tidal wave that followed almost immediately thereafter, swamping many of the remaining dwellings and even bursting open the graveyard, adding to the subsequent spread of disease. Such a dramatic catastrophe was widely interpreted abroad as divine punishment, Port Royal's lurid past as a buccaneer roost leading some moralists to label it "the wickedest place on earth"—although not having been previously known as exceptionally licentious compared to many other seaports.

Frightened survivors nonetheless rebuilt on the mainland opposite, where a major new city called Kingston was soon created. Although Port Royal eventually reemerged, it never reclaimed its former prominence.

Madagascar

As the 17th century was drawing to a close, freebooters who for decades had prowled in the West Indies or the Americas discovered a virgin new hunting ground halfway around the world, in the Indian Ocean. Given how perishable food and drink were throughout this entire era, rovers had to make the thousands of miles of sea voyage out to the Red Sea in stages, one of their crucial stopovers after round-

ing the Cape of Good Hope being Madagascar: a huge, thinly populated island about 250 miles off the southeast coast of Africa.

Madagascar measures about 1,000 miles from north to south and is
nearly 360 miles wide at its center, making it the fourth largest island
in the world. Its straight eastern coastline gives way to a narrow band
of plains, quickly rising to a mountainous spine whose forests are
often shrouded in mists because of the humid trade winds that are
constantly wafting in from the Indian Ocean. Innumerable coves and
inlets dot its northwestern and southwestern sides, with beaches ideal
for pirates to covertly careen their weather-beaten ships, plus ample
access to fresh water and many food sources, including a rich variety
of citrus plants. Hundreds of miles long and far removed from any
European supervision, Madagascar was to briefly become a notorious pirate base. Lairs developed in Ranter Bay, St. Augustine's Bay,
on Reunion Island, Mauritius, Johanna Island, Fort Dauphin, and especially Saint Mary's Island.

On November 28, 1697 (O.S.), Captain Thomas Warren of HMS
Windsor wrote the following description of this island to the East India
Company:

> The master of ship from Madagascar, whom I met, gave me the follow-
> ing account: There is a small island called Santa Maria at the northeast
> part of Madagascar, where the pirates have a very commodious har-
> bor to which they resort and clean their ships. Here they have built a
> regular fortification of forty or fifty guns. They have about 1,500 men,
> with seventeen sail of vessels, sloops and ships, some of which carry
> forty guns. They are furnished from New York, New England, and the
> West Indies with stores and other necessaries. I was informed that if they
> could obtain pardons, they would leave that villainous way of living.[18]

A mariner from New York City named Adam Baldridge had set up a
trading outpost on Saint Mary's Island as early as January 1691 and
made a fortune selling supplies from reputable New York merchants
to a stream of booty-laden cutthroat crews.

When Queen Anne's War erupted early in the 18th century, many
rovers found renewed employment elsewhere as privateers, so Madagascar declined as a pirate haven. By 1711, fewer than 100 remained on
Saint Mary's Island, reputedly living in squalor and with little money.

Nassau, Bahamas

The last major stronghold, which was to flourish ever so briefly during the very closing stages of the golden age of piracy, was the forlorn

capital of the Bahamas—a private outpost that had been long neglected by its owners back in London. Indeed, the beautiful yet remote
Bahamian archipelago had not even been occupied until late during
the colonization period, when some settlers transferred onto New
Providence Island in 1666, so named in memory of another earlier
Calvinist outpost that had been eradicated by the Spaniards on Providencia or Santa Catalina Island. Despite only measuring 58 square
miles, being rather flat, and covered with brushwood and lagoons,
New Providence Island was surrounded by crystalline waters and
enjoyed one of the most delightful climates in the entire archipelago—
neither too rainy, as occurred farther northwest, nor too hot and arid
as to its southeast.

Its main anchorage also proved to be exceptionally good, approach-
able via a pair of deep-water passages (one of which was dubbed the
Tongue of the Ocean), as well as sheltered from gales and hurricanes
by an 80-foot ridge rising just 400 yards south of its beach. This harbor
offered respite from sea currents because of a five-mile-long offshore
cay, eventually christened Hog Island. Vessels of more than 500 tons
could not easily traverse its 14-foot-deep, reef-lined bar, yet its inner
roads stretched out for three and a half miles long by one-third of a
mile wide.

A small seaside settlement named Charles Town soon materialized,
while back in London a group of six high-born friends of the king—
known collectively as the Lords Proprietors of Carolina—rewrote the
Bahamian company charter in November 1670 to displace its original Puritan shareholders. Otherwise, they left its colonists to shift for
themselves, supplementing their meager fishing and agricultural activities by scavenging for wrecks or ambergris as well as trading with
any vessel that chanced to call. This eagerness to please visitors meant
that West Indian privateers soon found Charles Town a most obliging
bolt-hole to dispose of their booty.

To avenge descents made upon Florida and Cuba, the Spaniards
devastated New Providence Island with a pair of raids in 1684, so that
a couple hundred frightened Bahamian survivors departed for Jamaica, while another 50 resettled at Casco (Maine). The archipelago
remained devoid of any recognizable English presence until December 1686, when a small contingent returned from Jamaica under the
preacher Thomas Bridges. The tiny colony revived, although its remote
locale and commercial insignificance meant that it remained largely
ignored by its absentee rulers. When the ruffianly Colonel Cadwal-
lader Jones acted as self-proclaimed governor from 1690 to 1693, he
even refused to acknowledge the authority of England's new mon-

archs William and Mary, until he was succeeded in August 1694 by the more loyal and ambitious Nicholas Trott.

The Bahamian capital began a modest reformation under Trott, with construction of a 28-gun wooden fort. It was officially renamed Nassau the following year in honor of the queen's Dutch-born consort William, prince of Orange-Nassau. Yet its old contacts with pirates continued: in late April 1696, the notorious Captain Henry Every dropped anchor at Royal Island, sending a boat with four spokesmen into Nassau to offer Trott a £1,000 bribe to permit their stolen flagship *Fancy* into port and its renegade crew to disperse. Every had mutinied a year and a half previously at La Coruña, Spain, venturing to the Far East and eventually robbing the Mogul trader *Ganj-i-Sawai* of £200,000 off Bombay.

Now seeking to escape back into civilian life along with his 200 cutthroats, Every was allowed to sail into Nassau masquerading as Henry Bridgeman, his *Fancy* being falsely recorded as an "interloper" or unlicensed slaver from the Guinea Coast with an unregistered cargo of ivory and slaves. The corrupt Trott agreed to have this incriminating ship made over into his care, after which it was stripped of everything of value—including its 46 guns, 100 barrels of gunpowder, small arms, 50 tons of ivory, sails, blocks, and so forth—and allowed to drift ashore, to be pounded to pieces by the surf. With this telltale piece of evidence destroyed, Every and his men disappeared from the Bahamas aboard passing ships. When news of this fraud reached London, Trott was relieved of his post and a vice-admiralty court was appointed for Nassau in February 1697.

But the lawless outpost proved difficult to govern, the entire Bahamian archipelago becoming so depopulated by Cuban raids and disruptions to its commercial traffic during Queen Anne's War that only 27 families remained on New Providence Island by the time these hostilities ceased in April 1713. There was no private governor in residence amid the burned remnants of Nassau; nor was there any assistance forthcoming from the lord proprietors in England. Unemployed West Indian rovers therefore began drifting into these unpatrolled waters, especially after a Spanish plate fleet was wrecked on the nearby Florida coast in late July 1715, sparking an onrush of fortune seekers and other desperadoes into these waters.

The open roadstead at Nassau consequently became busier and, in the absence of any authorities, ruled by such renegade captains as Benjamin Hornigold. Over the next couple of years, pirates such as a young Edward Thatch would bring in prizes to pillage them with impunity, chase away honest settlers through their drunken excesses, and even install guns in the decrepit old fort to control its anchorage. Finally, the Crown in London ordered the Council of Trade and Plantations to enact measures "to dislodge those profligate fellows or pirates that may have possessed themselves of the island of Providence, and may, if not driven from thence in time, commit depredations on His Majesty's subjects or those of his allies trading in those parts of the world."[19]

Pardons were offered to any outlaws willing to submit, before an expedition arrived outside Nassau's bar on the afternoon of July 26, 1718 (O.S.), bearing a new governor designate, Woodes Rogers— himself a battle-scarred ex-privateer who had circled the globe and captured a Manila galleon and had been selected for his toughness. He was accompanied by 250 new colonists and five warships. Most of the more defiant pirates had already left the Bahamas for other hunting grounds, so that Rogers stepped ashore next morning, greeted by an honor guard of 300 boozy pirates under Hornigold and several lesser captains, who all swore fealty to the Crown.

Yet none of these chieftains was employed in organizing militia companies, repairing the fortress, erecting a new barracks and battery, or any other improvement. Disappointed, they soon began to drift away, and Rogers informed his superiors in London later that same summer of 1718: "We have scarce half of those who have been pirates left, for they soon became weary of living under restraint, and are either gone to several parts of North America, or engaged themselves on services at sea, which I was willing to promote, for they are not the people I ought to think will make any land improvements, and I wish they may be faithful at sea."[20]

NOTES

1. William Dampier, *A New Voyage Round the World* (New York: Dover, 1968).

2. C. Lovat Fraser, *The Lives and Adventures of Sundry Notorious Pirates* (New York: McBride, 1922), 107.

3. *Interesting Tracts Relating to the Island of Jamaica, Consisting of Curious State Papers, Councils of War, Letters, Petitions, Narratives, etc., Which Throw Great Light on the History of That Island from Its Conquest down to the Year 1702* (St. Jago de la Vega, Jamaica: Lewis, Lunan and Jones, 1800), 289.

4. *Calendar of State Papers, Colonial: America and West Indies*, vol. 1 (London: Her Majesty's Stationery Office, 1860), 253.

5. *Calendar of State Papers, Colonial: America and West Indies*, vol. 5 (London: Her Majesty's Stationery Office, 1880), 177.

6. David F. Marley, "La désertion du boucanier breton Jean Villebon au Costa Rica, 1669," *Généalogie et Histoire de la Caraïbe* (France) 215 (June 2008): 5585–5587.

7. E.A. Cruikshank, *The Life of Sir Henry Morgan* (Toronto: Macmillan, 1935), 274.

8. Dampier, *A New Voyage.*

9. *Calendar of State Papers, Colonial: America and West Indies*, vol. 12 (London: Her Majesty's Stationery Office, 1899), 275.

10. Ibid., 288.

11. Alexandre-Olivier Exquemelin, *The Buccaneers of America*, trans. Alexis Brown, introd. Jack Beeching (London: Penguin, 1969), 83.

12. Dampier, *A New Voyage*, 38.

13. John Franklin Jameson, *Privateering and Piracy in the Colonial Period: Illustrative Documents* (New York: Macmillan, 1923), 90.

14. David F. Marley, *Sack of Veracruz: The Great Pirate Raid of 1683* (Windsor, Ontario: Netherlandic Press, 1993), 13.

15. Exquemelin, *The Buccaneers of America,* 29.

16. Thomas Birch, ed., *A Collection of the State Papers of John Thurloe*, vol. 6 (London: Printed for the executor of the late Mr. Fletcher Gyles, 1742), 391.

17. *Calendar of State Papers*, vol. 5, 21.

18. *Calendar of State Papers, Colonial: America and West Indies*, vol. 16 (London: Her Majesty's Stationery Office, 1905), 71.

19. *Calendar of State Papers, Colonial: America and West Indies*, vol. 29 (London: Her Majesty's Stationery Office, 1930), 210.

20. *Calendar of State Papers, Colonial: America and West Indies*, vol. 30 (London: Her Majesty's Stationery Office, 1930), 375.

6

PLUNDER

Some replied that they were but few for such an undertaking, upon which Morgan said if they were few in number, each man's portion would be so much the greater.

—Alexandre-Olivier Exquemelin,
The Buccaneers of America

Not surprisingly, pirates were notorious for being callously heavy handed in stripping their victims of everything they owned, whether valuable or not. When the Spanish lawyer Andrés Caballero had the misfortune to be intercepted by a pack of such ruffians off Santo Domingo in the summer of 1673, it was later recorded that he "was made prisoner by the English, who took from him his clothes, money, silverware, and a slave that accompanied him"[1] before marooning this middle-aged gentleman on a lonely stretch of the Venezuelan coast, where he perished from ill usage. And a decade later, pillagers from another pirate ship off the West African coast—having tortured the officers of the Royal African Company ship *Eaglet* with thumbscrews to reveal their riches—warned its injured captain as they departed his gutted vessel to shift anchorage or else risk being sighted by Jean Hamlin's prowling *Trompeuse* as well, who would doubtless "take all he had."

And what freebooters did not steal they frequently destroyed out of sheer malice. Selected randomly from an unending list of examples, we might mention the following:

- After the New York privateer John Markham had surprised the impoverished Mexican fishing village of Tampico in April 1684, its traumatized survivors would recount how his thugs had stolen "wheat, fish, sugar, the church's ornaments and its silver, as well as clothing,"[2] and one buccaneer in particular—John Tudor—had even bragged to them that he had been with Laurens de Graaf at the sack of Veracruz that previous year, at which he thereupon "burned down a house and with his companions drank a barrel of spirits."

- Master Robert Lurting would lament that, after his fully loaded merchantman *Nicholson* had been captured in Lynnhaven Bay, Virginia, by Captain Louis Guittard's *La Paix* in April 1700, these vandals had proceeded to drop anchor and amuse themselves during a drunken binge by wantonly tossing overboard "about 100 hogsheads of tobacco, besides bulk tobacco, clothing, and several materials of the ship."

- In April 1717, after pillaging a Boston-owned sloop, Captain Black Sam Bellamy wished to restore this vessel to its master, yet his cutthroats voted otherwise, so that he swore at his victim: "Damn my blood, I'm sorry they won't let you have your sloop again, for I scorn to do anyone a mischief, when it is not for my advantage," and then they watched together as it slid smoldering beneath the waves.

But the very mercenary nature of the pirates' cruel calling meant that what they mostly craved was riches, particularly in the form of ready money or jewelry.

CURRENCY

Coinage was a rare and scarce commodity during the mid-17th century, paper money not yet having been introduced and not nearly enough precious metals being then in circulation. To compensate, the remote and neglected private outposts in the Antilles—still in the earliest stages of their economic development—substituted produce to serve as local currency, such as when Governor-General Francis, Lord Willoughby, reported to London in February 1664 that he was collecting taxes in the form of sugar on Barbados, as it constituted "the ready money of the island."[3]

One of the principal reasons that the first generations of West Indian rovers would be made so welcome by its colonists, and eventually even be lured as far north as New England or Canada, was that these marauders typically arrived flush with money taken from their Spanish victims, whose coinage was so abundant as to be universally acceptable. The metal currency of Spain came in three basic denominations during this era, two being gold coins and one silver:

doubloons, the largest gold coins minted by Spain, their real name of *doblón* signifying a piece of money worth double its face value of 16 reals

ducats, a smaller gold coin originally called a *ducado,* worth 11 reals

pieces of eight, the English translation for the silver coins known in Spanish as *pesos de ocho reales,* or pesos worth eight reals

The latter were being minted in such vast amounts out of Mexican and Peruvian mines that they would eventually come to circulate all around the world, being accepted as far away as China and India.

Pieces of eight were already the most common form of currency in England's Antillean colonies, their value having been pegged at four and a half shillings or four shillings sixpence apiece. The coins were often further chopped up into eight segments to provide lesser variants toward making change (from which ancient practice has come down the modern expression of two bits being equivalent to a quarter). On November 19, 1691, Sir William Phips—in his newly appointed capacity as governor of Massachusetts—would write to his friend Increase Mather: "There is practically only Spanish money in New England, and many of the people have been cheated by bad money."[4]

Colonial officials went to great pains to prevent coinage from being extracted from their jurisdictions, to the extent of stamping distinctive holes through the centers of foreign coins to discourage their circulation elsewhere. Such mutilated coinage, for instance, featured uniquely heart-shaped holes on the island of Dominica, while a visitor to Boston noted in late April 1675 that: "Their money is of pretty good silver; in the middle of it is a pine tree (with which the country abounds)."[5] The silver pieces punched out by a press from the center of such coins were known as dumps, which were also melted down to further supplement the local currency. Less than four years later, Jamaica's governor, Lord Carlisle, would candidly report to London in January 1679:

Some of the French in Hispaniola are very desirous to trade with Jamaica, and bring us cacao and moneys for the manufactures here of England. Without this trade, privately or publicly carried on, it will be hard to manage an inland trade in this island, for all ships from Ireland, Bermudas, New England, and New York, laden with provisions, carry off ready money for them; and ready money is so scarce that unless we be relieved by private trade with the Spaniards, our want thereof will be very great.[6]

As a result, fresh infusions of silver coinage were desirable on account of the stimulating effect they could have on the economy—not only of a single seaport but an entire island or colony—so that officials were always watchful for pirate vessels looking to spend their booty, because they represented one of the few potentially large-scale sources of new currency. For example, when Jean-David Nau l'Olonnais came away from his sweep through the neutral Laguna de Maracaibo in the summer of 1666, the plunder he had garnered and shared out among his 400 followers was calculated at "260,000 pieces of eight in ready money, wrought silver, and jewels," plus another "100 pieces of eight for every man in linen and silk goods, as well as other trifles."[7] Jamaican officials therefore eagerly greeted home the English participants in this raid and sought to entice their French colleagues into port as well.

In contrast, when Captain John Coxon and other freebooters began returning to Jamaica in late July 1677, after having helped sack the small Colombian port of Santa Marta, Governor Sir Thomas Lynch could scarcely conceal his disappointment when he tersely wrote to his superiors in London: "The plunder of the town was not great, money and broken plate [i.e., silver] about £20 a man."[8] Yet seven years afterward, excited New England officials would resort to extraordinary measures in order to attract two nefarious yet richly laden pirate ships—Michiel Andrieszoon's *Mutine* and Jan Willems's *Dauphine*—as they sailed up the Atlantic seaboard after having relieved two Dutch West Indiamen of a fortune in Spanish money off Cuba. A disapproving Governor Edward Cranfield of neighboring New Hampshire would write to London by the end of August 1684:

> A French privateer of 35 guns [*Mutine*] has arrived at Boston. I am credibly informed that they share £700 a man. The Bostoners no sooner heard of her off the coast than they dispatched a messenger and pilot to convoy her into port, in defiance of the King's proclamation [of March 1684, prohibiting aid and abetment to rovers]. The pirates are likely to leave the greatest part of their plate behind them, having bought up most of the choice goods in Boston. The ship is now fitting for another expedition.[9]

Eventually, royal decrees restricting access into port by pirates would curtail visits by such blatant lawbreakers, although sufficient cash—in the right hands—could still buy complicity from pliant authorities for any outlaws on the run with blood-stained booty. Among a few examples are:

- In April 1694, Rhode Islander Thomas Tew returned into Newport with stolen Mogul treasure worth more than £100,000, paying off his 40-odd hands with shares ranging from £1,200 to an eye-popping £3,000 apiece—this in an age when skilled merchant sailors might earn £15 in a year. When this Red Sea marauder subsequently approached honest John Easton, Quaker governor of that private colony, for a new privateering license, Easton asked where he intended to use it. "Where perhaps the commission might never be seen or heard of," Tew replied darkly, offering to buy it for £500. The good Quaker refused, so Tew instead sailed to New York, purchasing one for £300 from its more accommodating royal governor, Benjamin Fletcher.

- Two years later, the mutineer Henry Every—object of a worldwide manhunt for having risen and run away with his ship and then criminally looting £200,000 from another Mogul trader off of Bombay—had ample funds available with which to offer a bribe of £1,000 to the corrupt private governor of the Bahamas, Nicholas Trott, to allow this renegade ship into Nassau's harbor to be scuttled, after which Every and his 80-odd men discreetly disappeared with their booty aboard passenger ships, blending back into civilian life.

- And even Blackbeard could use his ill-gotten money to purchase a pardon in the summer of 1718 from North Carolina's obliging governor, Charles Eden—furthermore buying a home, marrying (for the 14th time), and settling down briefly in that young, struggling colony, before Thatch's old criminal ways reasserted themselves and he ventured back out to sea, only to be killed before the year was out.

Ready money could give peace of mind to even the most illiterate rank-and-file pirate; a sense of accomplishment, satisfaction, and future security. The master of the intercepted pink *Baltimore* recorded that his captors appealed to his sailors to join their ranks off Carolina in April 1700, pointing out how: "You sail in merchantmen for 25 shillings a month, and here you may have seven or eight pounds a month, if you can take it."[10]

And in one particularly telling scene observed after Sam Bellamy's capture of the rich slaver *Whydah* in the Windward Passage in late February 1717, which was loaded with African elephant tusks, gold dust, West Indian sugar, and indigo—as well as £9,000 in hard currency—his 180 cutthroats assembled ceremoniously in his captain's cabin to witness the counting out of 50 pounds apiece in coins as each man's share, which were then put into bags and stowed "in chests between decks, without any guard,"[11] in true brotherhood fashion.

GOLD

Unlike silver pieces of eight, golden coins were rarely seen in circulation. The purity of Spanish doubloons and ducats moreover declined notably during the 17th century, because that government's financial woes hit rock bottom following repeated bankruptcies. In addition to their low grade of manufacture, Spain's gold coins—referred to in general as pistoles among the English—were all too often clipped around their edges as well, further reducing their weight and monetary value. Such clipped coinage was known as light money and naturally was viewed with dim skepticism. A group of 30 Royal Navy sailors, discharged in England at the conclusion of King William's War in October 1697, complained to Parliament about their "payment in Spanish gold." One described the fraudulent practices employed by the agent at Falmouth:

> That at that time, he received twenty pistoles of Mr. [Daniel] Gwyn for Richard James, all of them wanting weight, among which were doubloons that wanted two shillings and two shillings, sixpence of weight; the whole loss, by exchanging the gold, came to twelve shillings.[12]

Although Spanish gold coins might be held in low esteem, other coins, such as the Portuguese *moeda d'ouro* or *moidore* were more highly regarded, while the precious metal itself remained as highly coveted as ever, often in its rawest form.

Gold nuggets and gold dust were frequently employed as currency by traders and seamen, the following being but a few references to this practice among piratical rovers:

- In late February 1680, Captains John Coxon and Robert Allison intercepted an eight-gun Spanish ship as it arrived off Portobelo from Cartagena bearing 30 slaves, timber, salt, and corn—plus 500 pieces of gold hidden at the bottom of a jar of red wine (which Coxon "wronged the party of by keeping it to himself,"[13] according to a disgruntled follower).

- After scouring the West African coast for prizes, the French corsair Hamlin landed near Cape St. John's in June 1683 to divide up his spoils, his 190 minions reputedly receiving shares worth "30 pound weight of gold a man," before gleefully redistributing themselves aboard two ships and parting company.

- Around this same time, a prize crew from George Bond's pirate ship carried the English merchant vessel *Gideon* into Danish Saint Thomas, storing its plunder ashore and being "given an ounce of gold dust a man," presumably as a down payment against the sale of this booty.

- In early May 1684, Laurens de Graaf stole in darkness upon an unwary 14-gun Spanish privateer, which was sailing in the night with a prize, capturing both and discovering next morning that the corsair contained "quinine and 47 pounds of gold."

- The next month, the Jamaican privateer Peter Harris "the Younger" surprised the stockaded Panamanian mining camp of Santa María el Real with 100 buccaneers and 300 Darien native allies, massacring its defenders and sharing out about 24 ounces of gold dust per man among his followers, while leaving "the other gross plunder to the Indians."

Because no system of public banking existed during the late 17th and early 18th centuries, all seafarers risked losing their savings in the event of a shipwreck or other catastrophic event at sea. Therefore, golden items such as earrings or rings were favored as a portable means of carrying wealth on one's person, gold chains being especially prized because they could be sold off link by link in times of difficulty ashore. Few merchant sailors could ever afford such ostentatious adornments, especially in peacetime, so gold chains naturally aroused suspicion—such as when Master Nicholas Jones tellingly observed, after John James's pirate crew had ransacked his sloop *Roanoke Merchant* off the Virginia coast on July 27, 1699 (O.S.)—that he had noted how "ye company and Captain himself to have gold chains about their necks,"[14] valuable items that could only have been acquired through plundering previous victims.

Six years earlier, when the privateer captain Thomas Tew had informed his assembled hands at sea that he proposed to violate his commission by venturing into the Indian Ocean to illegally hunt for neutral shipping, they supposedly signaled their willingness to join in this criminal enterprise by chanting: "A gold chain, or a wooden leg, we'll stand by you!"[15] However, displaying such extravagant wealth could also compromise any freebooter's return into civilian life. An edition of the newspaper *American Weekly Mercury* reported how four of Bartholomew Roberts's followers had slipped ashore in Chesapeake Bay early in 1720, traveling inland until they found a tavern "where they might ease themselves of their Golden Luggage." But they spent their money so lavishly—one even purchasing the freedom of several indentured women servants for the princely sum of £30—that this extravagance brought them to the attention of the local authorities, who promptly jailed them on suspicion of piracy. At their hanging, it was revealed that they had "brought on shore with them, in Spanish gold and gold dust, upward of 1,500 pounds sterling."

Roberts himself, when he appeared on deck to fight his last battle in February 1722, would be described by surviving crewmen as having been splendidly dressed in a crimson waistcoat and breeches, with a hat with a big red feather in it—plus numerous gold chains dangling about his neck. Yet lesser gold items could prove equally useful. After the avaricious Elias Haskett had arrested and supplanted the mulatto privateer captain Read Elding from office as the private governor of the Bahamas during the summer of 1701, the usurper had subsequently demanded that his prisoner's fellow corsairs provide an extortionate bribe of 50 pistoles toward his release, and then

> was not contented with that sum, but told deponent that Elding must also send him a rich ring, and a piece of plate of value, which ring and a silver tankard was carried by deponent to Haskett for a bribe, and also some pieces of dry goods, and a set of gold buttons, and three gold drops.[16]

Some gold was obtained out of Spanish American captures, but most was acquired out of vessels that had called at the slave stations of mod-

An assortment of gold and silver Spanish coins, as well as a ring, raised by modern salvors from the wreckage of Black Sam Bellamy's flagship *Whydah*, lost near Cape Cod in late April 1717. (Richard T. Nowitz/Corbis)

ern Ghana, where this precious metal was locally mined. Marauders plying off these waters were aware of this output, many having previously served aboard slavers. Hamlin must have been doubly pleased when he anchored his pirate flagship *Trompeuse*—disguised as a Royal Navy warship—near one such unsuspecting victim in May 1683, suddenly opening fire and sending across an armed gang, who discovered their prize to be a 20-gun Dutch vessel out of Flushing loaded "with 70 pounds of gold on board and abundance of liquor."[17] Nine years later, the French slaver *Bonaventure* would be captured and found to have "on board two chests about three foot in length, 16 inches in breadth, and 16 inches depth, with gold and silver."

In late November 1717, the brutish Blackbeard would be equally delighted to find—upon intercepting the 300-ton French slaver *Concorde* near Martinique, which he retained as his new flagship under the name of *Queen Anne's Revenge*—that it too contained a hidden cache of 20 pounds of gold dust. And only one month before he was slain off the African coast, Roberts had brashly stood into the anchorage at the port of Ouidah, his *Royal Fortune* brushing aside its feeble defenses so that his boat parties could board 11 slavers lying in its roads—for which he demanded a ransom of eight pounds of gold dust apiece. All but one master ashore agreed to pay, whose vessel was thereupon set ablaze and sunk, with 80 slaves still fettered alive in its hold.

JEWELRY

As has been noted, the wearing of earrings and other pieces of jewelry had been quite commonplace among seafarers ever since ancient times, being a simple yet effective means of carrying personal wealth aboard ship. During the 17th and 18th centuries, passengers and sailors alike often converted their wealth into such ready valuables before a voyage. For example, when the English-born Dominican priest Thomas Gage was preparing to depart Guatemala in January 1637, he found that during his dozen years of residence he had accumulated almost 9,000 pesos or pieces of eight, which he

> thought would be too cumbersome for a long journey; whereupon I turned about 4,000 of them into pearls and some precious stones, which might make my carriage the lighter; the rest I laid up, some in bags, some I sewed into my quilt, intending in the way [i.e., during his forthcoming trip] to turn them into Spanish pistoles.[18]

However, the Spanish frigate that carried him out to sea was promptly intercepted off the Central American coast by the Dutch mulatto privateer Diego Lucifer, whose greedy corsairs quickly ransacked Gage's baggage and relieved him of his carefully concealed wealth.

Pirates were, of course, always eager to seize such valuables. Officials in Veracruz estimated that the booty carried away by Laurens de Graaf's and the Sieur de Grammont's rapacious raiders in May 1683 totaled 800,000 pesos in coins, 400,000 worth of wrought silver, and 200,000 in "gold chains, charms, jewels, and pearls."[19] Like too much currency, such flashy treasure could also create complications whenever rovers attempted to blend back into civilian life. When Bartholomew Sharpe and 10 of his weather-beaten companions disembarked from the passenger ship *White Fox* at Plymouth on March 25, 1682 (O.S.), taking rooms at the Anchor Inn on Salpeter Bank, it was not long before people noticed that the luggage of these lowly seafarers contained the princely sum of "several thousands of pounds and several portmanteaux of jewels and of gold and silver, coined and uncoined."[20] Less than two months later, they were arrested in London on suspicion of piracy and brought before the high court of admiralty at Southwark to stand trial—although all charges were quickly thrown out for lack of any material witnesses to their crimes, perpetrated halfway around the world in the Pacific Ocean.

The same would occur six years later, when Edward Davis and two companions reached Virginia in June 1688, only to be almost immediately arrested by Captain Simon Rowe of HMS *Dumbarton* because of the £1,500 worth of battered Peruvian silver they had brought with them. Davis and his men at first denied ever being privateers, then recanted, but insisted that this booty had been procured in the South Sea merely to help them "spend the remainder of their days honestly and quietly."[21] Arrested, they were shipped to England to stand trial, and, although eventually cleared after a lengthy proceeding, this trio was obliged to cede £300 of their loot in March 1693 toward the building of a new college in Virginia, which became William and Mary.

An even worst fate allegedly befell the pirate Joseph Morris, one of Henry Every's cutthroats, who, after their hunted ship had managed to be successfully slipped into Nassau and scuttled, freeing the outlaw crew to disappear into civilian life with their ill-gotten gains, Morris was supposedly left behind in the Bahamas when he went mad after "losing all his jewels upon a wager."

SLAVES

Among the many iniquities steeped into their very character, pirates dabbled in slavery, albeit on the illegal periphery of this heartless trade.

In preindustrial times, manual laborers were in great demand for virtually every agricultural or commercial enterprise, so slaves commanded
high prices—which fired the rovers' mercenary instincts, regardless of
the fact that many blacks and mulattos had risen high among the ranks
of the buccaneer brotherhood itself. Indifferent to the suffering of others, though, pirates routinely forced hapless natives such as Indian
fishermen to toil for months, even years on end, in their service. In one
of many instances, a New York merchantman arrived at Port Royal,
Jamaica, in late September 1682, to report that Bahamian marauders
had recently "taken a *piragua*, a *barco luengo*, diverse Indians from Florida and seventeen from Cuba, whom they have sold for slaves."[22]
Upon hearing this news, Governor Sir Thomas Lynch exclaimed that
the Bahamians might well regret "the consequences of this folly and
rapine."

Individual black captives would be compelled to perform the heaviest
work aboard pirate ships, while larger numbers were sold off as booty.
For example, the Scottish-born Jamaican privateer James Browne—
operating lawlessly with an outdated French commission early in 1677—
attacked the Dutch slaver *Goude Zon* or "Golden Sun" while it was
standing into Cartagena with a consignment of 200 slaves. Browne reappeared in a remote Jamaican bay by that same May 1677, to disembark
and begin clandestinely selling off 150 of them to eager local planters.
When the royal governor, Lord Vaughan, learned of these contraband
dealings, he had Browne arrested and convicted of piracy. However,
a sympathetic House of Assembly petitioned Vaughan for a reprieve,
twice, before finally dispatching the provost marshal with a signed
order from the speaker to stay this execution—who arrived a half hour
too late.

Slaves would continue to be regarded as prizes of war throughout
the age of piracy. When Joseph Bradley's bloodied assault columns at
last prevailed against the Spanish defenders of Chagres Castle in January 1671, it was recorded that they fought their way inside "the castle
and put all to the sword, saving none but slaves and such as hid themselves."[23] Nor were freebooters the only ones who behaved thus: when
the Royal Navy ketch *Quaker* of Captain Christopher Billop pursued
and fired on a strange sail off Nevis in June 1682, he discovered it to be
the *Providence* of London, whose master had no license to trade in the
New World and so had come out from Africa as an interloper with
215 slaves to sell surreptitiously.

This interception had taken place within plain view of everybody
in Nevis's capital of Charlestown, who then saw the ketch stand away
with its prize for the French half of Saint Kitts rather than return into

port. When Billop did eventually reappear five days later, only 96 slaves were left aboard *Providence*—a dozen suffering from smallpox, the rest having been illicitly sold off. Charged with fraud and embezzlement, Billop refused to come ashore to face the authorities, instead sailing *Quaker* for England without orders. No wonder that Nevis's island council would describe him to the Council of Trade and Plantations in London as "one of the worse men we ever saw in the King's service, and the most unfit to continue in it."[24] (Dismissed from the Royal Navy, Billop resettled in New York and would be authorized in 1686 to establish "a ferry upon the southwest side of Staten Island" as well as becoming that island's surveyor.)

In a similar vein, as the pirate expedition of Laurens de Graaf and the Sieur de Grammont had prepared to evacuate Sacrificios Island—engorged with immense booty following their sack of Veracruz in May 1683—in one final act of cruelty, armed parties swept through the throngs of terrified Spanish captives and pitilessly culled almost 1,500 blacks and mulattos to carry off as slaves, ignoring the pleas of those who were freeborn. Three months afterward, warships of the Armada de Barlovento ran down some of these same pirate vessels near the Cayman Islands and succeeded in recuperating the prize ship *Nuestra Señora de Regla*—which, in a desperate bid to escape, had been set ablaze by its freebooter crew despite 90 slaves still aboard, who managed to extinguish these flames.

As Antillean plantations began to grow during the early 18th century, slave-stealing raids and counter-raids became a routine feature of regional warfare, eagerly embraced by privateers on both sides. And even after peace had been restored after a dozen years of hostilities in 1713, pirates would still continue to find slaves to be profitable plunder. When Captain James Martel intercepted the slaver *Greyhound* in the autumn of 1716, while it was bound from Guinea toward Jamaica, he relieved it of gold dust, elephants' tusks, and its 40 healthiest captives—a sufficiently large band of laborers to tempt him into steering for Saint Croix in the Virgin Islands to careen, where his flagship was destroyed by a Royal Navy warship.

Another instance of pirates acting as human traffickers occurred in late August 1718, when the renegade Charles Vane blockaded Charleston, South Carolina, and snapped up the 80-ton brigantine *Dorothy* as it brought in 90 slaves from Guinea, retaining this vessel as his new flagship. The slaves were transferred out and crammed aboard the sloop of his unwilling subordinate, Charles Yeats, who, one evening while lying at anchor, managed to slip his cable and outrun the furious Vane up into the safety of the North Edisto River. From there, Yeats sent a message overland to South Carolina's governor, requesting permission to surrender under the terms of the royal amnesty for piracy in exchange for bringing in this valuable consignment of slaves. The offer was accepted, and Yeats and his mercenaries were welcomed, and even "had their certificates sign'd" by that grateful official.

MISCELLANEOUS PILLAGED GOODS

Not surprisingly, pirate gangs that were not able to wrest enough money or jewelry from their hapless victims, might resort—whenever practicable—to wholesale theft of commercial cargoes or bulk produce, with the intention of selling it off at cut-rate prices to unscrupulous buyers. In a few instances, rovers might not even recognize the true value of their plunder: the Jamaican privateer Captain William James, for example, allegedly made off with a Spanish prize during the early 1660s that was full of lumber, only to be astonished upon reaching port to learn that it was actually logwood—which commanded princely prices because it was used in the production of a highly coveted, indelible dye. Until then, James had supposedly "known so little of its real value, that he had burned much of it for fuel on the voyage,"[25] thus depriving himself of a small fortune.

Indigo was another expensive commercial commodity. On September 26, 1679, Captain John Coxon and a mixed pack of his piratical colleagues captured a Spanish merchantman in the Bay of Honduras while it was busily loading with a shipment of this valuable export. Leaving a large amount of indigo behind simply to rot on the beach, the freebooters then sailed to Jamaica to dispose of their bulky loot. It was reported at Port Royal that

> There has been lately taken from the Spaniards by Coxon, Bartholomew Sharpe, Bothing, and Hawkins [Richard Sawkins?] with their crew, 500 chests of indigo, a great quantity of cacao, cochineal, tortoise shell, money, and plate. Much is brought into this country already, and the rest expected. Those that pay custom for their goods, land it at noonday and share it.[26]

The governor vainly tried to prevent the introduction of these ill-gotten gains, but the rovers threatened that, in retaliation, "they would leave their interest in Jamaica and sail to Rhode Island or to the Dutch, where they would be well entertained."[27] And despite naval patrols, these goods were smuggled ashore and sold, to the noticeable benefit of both the island's economy and treasury.

Less than four years later, Laurens de Graaf and his engorged squadron staggered away from their sack of Veracruz, steering their groaning vessels into the maze of islands off Cuba's southern coast to clandestinely sell off this mountain of goods to smugglers who came stealing across to meet them from Jamaica. Such covert sales of stolen items would continue throughout the entire age of piracy, right through to Jean Lafitte's days at Barataria near New Orleans.

As late as the autumn of 1716, Captain James Martel—having intercepted the 20-gun *John and Martha* off Cuba and learning that it was loaded with logwood and sugar—laughingly commanded its unfortunate master to tell his owners that the pirate captain "would take care it should be carried to a good market."[28] And even the oafish Blackbeard recognized the potential value of such commodities when he returned in September 1718 into his backwater home port of Bath, North Carolina— accompanied by a heavy-laden French merchantman, which he had allegedly spotted adrift and abandoned near Bermuda.

In reality, Thatch had intercepted two such French vessels at sea, each bearing a rich cargo of sugar and cocoa. He had compelled both French crews to concentrate all their goods aboard one ship, then to sail away aboard the empty one, thus leaving him to make for North Carolina with his one bulging prize. A court of inquiry quickly convened by its compliant local authorities obliged Blackbeard by ruling that he could keep the ship along with its valuable cargo, then furthermore— at Blackbeard's suggestion—agreed that the prize itself was leaking dangerously and should be scuttled—eliminating all evidence of his crime. In payment for these fraudulent rulings, the thuggish rover gave 60 hogsheads of sugar to Governor Eden and 20 to the provincial secretary, Tobias Knight.

CAPTAIN KIDD'S LOST TREASURE

Pirates enjoyed an exaggerated reputation, both during their contemporary era as well as today, of amassing much greater hoards than they ever actually possessed. This reputation may have sprung in part from the boastful nature of many freebooters, plus the lurid tales that were repeatedly circulated among the public about their misdeeds, during an era when news sources were otherwise relatively primitive and underdeveloped. In one of many instances, local legend on the Dutch island of Curaçao still maintains today that the notorious caper Jan Erasmus Reyning left treasures hidden in various caves along its coastline, although none has ever been found.

Romanticized depiction by Howard Pyle of Captain Kidd burying part of his booty. Although Kidd did indeed smuggle some caches ashore, most were soon seized by the Crown authorities —yet rumors would persist for centuries thereafter of unrecovered portions still waiting to be found. (Merle Johnson, comp., *Howard Pyle's Book of Pirates* [New York: Harper & Brothers, ca. 1921])

In another proven case of exaggeration, Master Richard Burgess of the ship *Maryland Merchant* out of Bristol solemnly averred before the Crown authorities in Virginia that the pirates who had ransacked his vessel in Lynnhaven Bay on July 26, 1699 (O.S.), already carried "£3,000,000 sterling in gold and silver" in their hold and were commanded by none other than the most wanted outlaw of that day, Captain William Kidd—although both of these facts proved patently untrue. Kidd had actually been captured three weeks previously in New York City, while the pirate who pillaged the *Maryland* in Lynnhaven Bay was Captain John James, who had been so hard pressed at the time that he and his men almost immediately thereafter eagerly fell upon "the cargo of corn and pork from a North Carolina sloop."[29]

However, historical records do confirm at least one tale of piratical treasure. While Kidd had been desperately steering up the Atlantic seaboard that same spring of 1699, knowing himself to be an outlaw wanted on a worldwide warrant, he did pause on more than one occasion to clandestinely deposit portions of his booty ashore among trusted friends, such as the 67-year-old retired Captain Thomas Paine of Conanicut Island, Rhode Island. After Kidd proceeded into Boston and was arrested on July 6, 1699 (O.S.), a massive search was instituted by the Crown authorities to find his scattered caches of treasure.

Most were quickly unearthed, yet the holding left with Paine was overlooked until a few weeks later, after Kidd's wife Sarah—who had also been imprisoned—covertly wrote the following letter, pleading to receive some of the funds entrusted to Paine:

> Captain Payen [*sic*],
>
> After my humble service to yourself and all our good friends, this cometh by a trusty friend of mine who can declare to you of my great grief and misery here in prison, by who I would desire you to send me 24 ounces of gold, and as for all ye rest you have in your custody, shall desire you for to keep in your custody, for it is all we have to support us in time of want, but I pray you to deliver to the bearer hereof the above-mentioned sum, whose name is Andrew Knott.[30]

Months later, during Knott's own interrogation by the authorities, he would recall that

> he went to Captain Payne's house on Cononicutt [*sic*] Island and received from Captain Payne 7 bars of gold weighing 1¾ lb., being weighed by a pair of steelyards. Payne fetched the gold from out of an inner room and took Knott's receipt. Knott saw no more gold than what Payne brought out, and upon the road on his way homeward, the weight of the gold broke his pocket, and he lost one of the bars. The other six he brought to Boston and Capn Kidd's servant maiden, Rebecca, came to Kidd's house and fetched the gold to Kidd, who later gave Knott 20 pieces of eight for his journey and trouble. The journey took five days.[31]

When confronted with these charges, Paine at first denied everything, arguing that he had refused to help Kidd, because he knew that "my house would be searched."[32] Later, Paine surrendered 18 ounces of gold dust to the Crown, saying that it had merely been a small gift that he had forgotten accepting from the fugitive Kidd. Yet despite the deep suspicions held by royal officers, no charges were ever laid against the Rhode Islander and no more treasure discovered—until more than a century and a half later, when a stray gold ingot fell out of Paine's chimney as his historic home was undergoing some renovations.

NOTES

1. David F. Marley, *Pirates of the Americas*, vol. 1 (Santa Barbara, CA: ABC-CLIO, 2010), 68.

2. Ibid., 236.

3. *Calendar of State Papers, Colonial: America and West Indies*, vol. 5 (London: Her Majesty's Stationery Office, 1880), 189.

4. *Calendar of State Papers, Colonial: America and West Indies*, vol. 13 (London: Her Majesty's Stationery Office, 1901), 569.

5. *Calendar of State Papers, Colonial: America and West Indies*, vol. 9 (London: Her Majesty's Stationery Office, 1893), 221.

6. *Calendar of State Papers, Colonial: America and West Indies*, vol. 10 (London: Her Majesty's Stationery Office, 1896), 319.

7. Alexandre-Olivier Exquemelin, *The Buccaneers of America*, trans. Alexis Brown, introd. Jack Beeching (London: Penguin, 1969), 104.

8. *Calendar of State Papers*, vol. 10, 19.

9. *Calendar of State Papers, Colonial: America and West Indies*, vol. 11 (London: Her Majesty's Stationery Office, 1898), 678.

10. Philip Alexander Bruce, *Institutional History of Virginia in the Seventeenth Century*, vol. 2 (New York: G. P. Putnam's Sons, 1910), 213.

11. George Francis Dow and John Henry Edmonds, *The Pirates of the New England Coast, 1630–1730* (Salem, MA: Marine Research Society, 1923), 119.

12. *Journal of the House of Commons*, vol. 12, *1697–1699* (London, 1803), 680.

13. Marley, *Pirates of the Americas*, vol. 1, 91.

14. Ibid., 659.

15. Dow and Edmonds, *Pirates of the New England Coast*, 85.

16. *Calendar of State Papers, Colonial Series: America and West Indies*, vol. 20 (London, 1912), 364.

17. Marley, *Pirates of the Americas*, vol. 1, 171.

18. Thomas Gage, *English-American* (London: Routledge, 1928, reedition of 1648 original), 332.

19. David F. Marley, *Sack of Veracruz: The Great Pirate Raid of 1683* (Windsor, Ontario: Netherlandic Press, 1993), 62.

20. Derek Howse and Norman J. Thrower, eds. *A Buccaneer's Atlas: Basil Ringrose's South Sea Waggoner* (Berkeley: University of California Press, 1992), 27.

21. *Calendar of State Papers, Colonial: America and West Indies*, vol. 13 (London: Her Majesty's Stationery Office, 1901), 20.

22. Marley, *Pirates of the Americas*, vol. 1, 77.

23. *Calendar of State Papers, Colonial: America and West Indies*, vol. 7 (London: Her Majesty's Stationery Office, 1889), 91.

24. *Calendar of State Papers,* vol. 11, 262.

25. E.A. Cruikshank, *The Life of Sir Henry Morgan* (Toronto: Macmillan, 1935), 274.

26. *Calendar of State Papers,* vol. 10, 430.

27. Ibid., 444.

28. Johnson, *General History,* 38.

29. *Calendar of State Papers, Colonial: America and West Indies,* vol. 17 (London: Her Majesty's Stationery Office, 1908), 390.

30. John Franklin Jameson, *Privateering and Piracy in the Colonial Period: Illustrative Documents* (New York: Macmillan, 1923), 223–224.

31. Ibid.

32. Howard M. Chapin, "Captain Paine of Cajacet," *Rhode Island Historical Society Collections* 23, no. 1 (January 1930): 30.

7

WEAPONS, SHIPS, AND TACTICS

Each man shall keep his piece, cutlass, and pistols at all times clean
and ready for action.
> —From the written articles of Captain
> Bartholomew Roberts's pirate charter

Pirates rose to power during the late 17th and early 18th centuries
because of their firepower, hit-and-run tactics, and seamanship. No
matter how few in number, most bands thought that they could carry
any town or rich merchantman through mobility, surprise, and superior musketry, while their thirst for booty would eventually lead them
on epic transoceanic voyages—even global circumnavigations—in
quest of prey.

WEAPONRY

The earliest buccaneers had quickly come to appreciate the tactical
advantage that firearms gave them over their more numerous, brave,
yet underequipped Spanish foes. There were no armament factories
and few powder mills in the Americas during this era, so virtually all
weapons and most ammunition had to be imported into the Antilles
from Holland, France, or England. Commonwealth officials on newly
conquered Jamaica, therefore, would take the step of supplying guns
out of their own warehouses to English and foreign privateers alike

to bolster their strikes against the Spaniards during the initial phases of that island's occupation. In contrast, access to imported muskets, pistols, and blunderbusses was to remain so severely restricted in the viceroyalties on the American mainland because of Spain's closed-door trade policies that firearms would remain an expensive and rare luxury among the Spanish American defenders.

Naturally, West Indian freebooters proved eager customers for any and all manner of weaponry brought into their unregulated harbors by European traders, and they soon came to amass considerable arsenals through purchase or barter with visiting vessels. The chronicler Alexandre-Olivier Exquemelin, upon personally joining the ranks of the *flibustiers* himself during the late 1660s, later remarked of lawless Tortuga Island off Haiti: "Here they sold their plunder to merchant ships at anchor in the roadstead, and with the money bought necessaries such as powder, bullets, and other useful arms."[1]

The disparity in firepower between the buccaneers and their victims had quickly become so evident that when a Spanish coast guard patrol recaptured the ship *Nuestra Señora del Honhón* in Mexico's Laguna de Términos during the summer of 1680—after having been in piratical hands for 11 months—the Spaniards could not refrain from commenting on how well supplied they found it, "with arms, powder, cannon balls, grenades, and other explosives."[2] Seven years later, another Spanish coast guard vessel was captured by English pirates in the Philippines, and its humiliated commander would later recall how they openly "jeered and laughed" at his tiny clutch of arms and ammunition.

Confidence in their superior firepower would often lead rovers into rash and reckless attacks, even when knowing themselves to be heavily outnumbered—such as when the Sieur de Grammont slipped ashore into the port of La Guaira with only 47 followers before dawn on June 26, 1680, to seize its sleeping garrison commander and 150 soldiers in their beds. After quickly looting several buildings, Grammont began fighting his way back toward his anchored ship, through hundreds of aroused Venezuelan militiamen, who only succeeded in slashing him across the neck with a machete, slaying nine of his buccaneers, and wounding several more before he sailed away.

In the unusual event of two equally well-armed West Indian contingents meeting in battle, the effects of mutual gun volleys could prove devastating. In late April 1666, after news had reached the shared island of Saint Kitts of an outbreak of Anglo-French hostilities back in Europe, 1,400 English militiamen had marched against a concentration of 350 Frenchmen at Pointe de Sable. This English host was spearheaded by

260 Jamaican buccaneers under Lieutenant-Colonel Thomas Morgan, who drove directly toward the French center—only to be ambushed by a company of musketeers hiding behind a hedge under Bernard Lafond de l'Espérance. Despite suffering horrific casualties, the buccaneers fought their way through and succeeded in fatally wounding the French commander; yet the Jamaican survivors thereupon received a heavy artillery blast that felled Morgan and destroyed the last of his men's courage, as only 17 of their original 260 members had emerged unhurt from this ferocious firefight.

Not surprisingly, when such dense fusillades were unleashed against ill-armed Spanish American formations, the results would prove cruelly lopsided. Henry Morgan's 1,200 freebooters had advanced up Mata Asnillos Rise toward Panama City on the morning of January 28, 1671, ascending to find 1,200 inexperienced militiamen and 400 riders drawn up in a battle line at its top to oppose them, possessing few firearms and no artillery. As the 300-man buccaneer vanguard circled out to deploy against the defenders' right, the undisciplined Panamanians on that flank suddenly rushed across the field at their foes. This wild charge was smashed by a rippling reply of well-aimed gunfire, more than 100 Panamanians being slain with the buccaneers' opening volley. Such murderous fire, to which the defenders could scarcely make reply, sowed panic throughout the remainder of their battle line, so that within less than 10 minutes they broke and fled—leaving behind 400 casualties, compared to a mere 15 injured freebooters.

Conversely, when deprived of their fire power, pirates could be rendered just as helpless. On April 30, 1686, the *flibustier* chieftain Nicolas Brigaut stood in toward Matanzas, Florida, aboard a captured galliot flying false Spanish colors, hoping to gather intelligence for a projected raid against nearby Saint Augustine. Watchful Spanish soldiers appeared along the Matanzas shoreline, and worsening weather then caused the galliot to run aground on its bar. Unfazed, Brigaut's men—"carrying their arms in their mouths"[3]—waded ashore on the morning of May 2 and "dug holes in the beach, from which they poured a heavy fire into the Spanish troops." Although outnumbered, they were able to drive away the Spaniards, killing four and wounding seven—although their galliot remained stuck fast.

Brigaut therefore opted to abandon it, stealing ashore under cover of night and a heavy downpour with his 40 marauders and some captives, to trudge southward in hopes of being rescued by his waiting commander, Grammont. The rains erased the spoor of the Frenchmen's footsteps from the sand, so that they had seemingly vanished. After covering almost 25 miles, the buccaneers met a band of about

50 or 60 Indians, who beckoned them in a friendly fashion to a meal, before abruptly shooting arrows and wounding six *flibustiers* and then vanishing.

Shaken, Brigaut and his men took refuge on an offshore sandbank to await their rescuers, but a prisoner escaped from there by swimming ashore and carried word of their location into Saint Augustine. A column of 50 Spanish soldiers consequently exited in pursuit, chancing upon the stranded pirates at their most vulnerable moment: as 19 of the *flibustiers* had "left the bar to swim ashore, carrying their muskets and powder in waterproof bags"[4] to forage along the desolate shoreline. The waiting Spaniards sprang out of concealment and massacred them before they could prime their weapons, then proceeded out onto the sandbank to dispatch the rest—in their blood fury, even mistakenly murdering the pirate's Spanish captives—before dragging Brigaut and a black pirate named Diego back into Saint Augustine to be interrogated and hanged shortly thereafter.

Muskets

By far and away the most favored firearm among 17th- and 18th-century pirates was the musket, not their ship's artillery. The French chronicler-priest Jean-Pierre Labat even recorded how Antillean *flibustiers* regarded a dozen well-aimed muskets to be the equivalent of a heavy gun. Innovations and design improvements that had made 17th-century muskets lighter and more portable, as well as more reliable through the introduction of flintlock firing mechanisms, facilitated their use by raiders at sea and on land. Pirates preferred surprising and blazing away at their startled foes, shocking them into submission or retreating if they should offer any serious resistance. This ability to inflict casualties from a safe distance while minimizing their own losses fit in well with their self-serving mercenary instincts as well as their tactical predilection for instilling fear into intended victims.

For example, when Henry Morgan and 400 freebooters burst upon the sleeping city of Portobelo at daybreak on July 11, 1666, a shaken Spanish survivor would later relate how they had swarmed down its quiet streets deliberately firing "off their guns at everything alive, whites, blacks, even dogs, in order to spread terror."[5] And Exquemelin would subsequently recount how the president of the Audiencia in distant Panama City—astonished to hear that Morgan had carried this heavily fortified harbor with such a slender force—sent a messenger

asking that he might be allowed to see the weapon which had given him such power. Morgan received the President's envoy with great civility, and gave him a French musket with a barrel four-and-a-half feet long, firing a one-ounce bullet; he also sent a cartouche which he'd had expressly made in France, containing thirty cartridges full of powder. He charged the messenger to tell his master that Morgan presented him with this musket, and that within a year or two he would come to Panama, to fetch it back.[6]

Although probably fictitious, this story nonetheless underscored the buccaneers' awareness and belief in the importance of firepower.

Even their antagonists would acknowledge this fact. In the wake of the piratical assault against Mexico's main seaport of Veracruz in May 1683, Spanish interrogators would record how Laurens de Graaf and the Sieur de Grammont had explicitly instructed their minions while assembling at their Honduran rendezvous to bring along as many firearms as possible for this venture—a detail ruefully corroborated by surviving Spanish eyewitnesses, such as

- Ensign Félix Gabriel de Arteaga, who testified that his company had been peppered in the darkened streets of Veracruz by freebooters equipped "with four or five weapons" apiece, as his frightened troops had huddled near the Santo Domingo Convent;
- Ensign Diego Medina Barba, badly wounded as twin columns of *flibustiers* had converged upon the governor's palace behind an unrelenting fusillade, "as each one of them carried three or four firearms";
- while numerous traumatized civilians would describe how bands of pirates had moved unconcernedly through the throngs of captives being held on Sacrificios Island, as each one was armed "with three firearms and a short sword or cutlass."

Similar reports of pirates being festooned with a profusion of sidearms would be recorded for decades. As late as September 1720, the master of a tiny Bermudan sloop victimized in the Grenadines by Bartholomew Roberts would tellingly note about these 130 marauders: "Every man double armed, and mostly Englishmen."[7]

Pirates would rely upon their musketry not only on land but in ship-to-ship encounters as well. Labat stated that *flibustiers* were particularly inclined to pepper merchantmen with volley fire alone, then board, as their prizes would not suffer as much damage as from the round shot of heavy artillery. Impoverished Cuban corsairs—who could not afford to purchase heavy cannon or cannonballs—also resorted to this same tactic, as when the Jamaican sloop *Hereford* was riding out a storm off Cuba's coastline in August 1683, only to be beset by "a *piragua* of 50 men, who at once opened fire of small arms and dangerously wounded one man."[8] Two and a half years later, Captain

Edward Goffe of the pink *Swallow* would endure an almost-identical experience, when two Cuban *guardacosta* galleys "came up to my ship's side and without hailing, poured in a volley which killed two men and wounded five or six, and then making fast to my ship's side, tried to board her."

Goffe, though, at least managed to defeat these corsairs after a bloody half hour of gunfire, and the tables would be turned by musketry on other occasions as well: perhaps most ironically in March 1718, when the tiny sloop *Dolphin*—whose crew had mutinied and turned pirate—trailed after a group of vessels they had spotted straggling away from Utila Island, believing them to be traders departing the nearby Honduran coast with purchased cargoes of logwood. Closing on their intended victim as evening fell, the pursuers menacingly challenged this rearmost vessel, only to receive a hail of musket balls by way of reply and were forced to surrender, discovering that the ships were actually part of a pirate flotilla under none other than Blackbeard himself.

Pistols

Seventeenth-century muskets could be fired fairly accurately at medium range but were slow and cumbersome to reload, so buccaneers often carried several pistols as well, so they could continue firing as the distance narrowed against their foes. A clear example was offered during the piratical surprise attack against Veracruz at dawn on May 18, 1683, when a long column of French *flibustiers* had snaked into its main plaza out of the gloom and unleashed a volley of musket fire at the astonished Spanish sentries guarding the governor's palace. Rather than pause to reload, these rovers had pressed in with pistols drawn to storm the building's gates. A young Spanish ensign, Medina Barba—who had fallen to the ground wounded from this initial fusillade—later recounted how he was also shot in the pit of his stomach with a pistol as this line of French pirates had swept over him.

Fighting men acknowledged the murderous effects of such close-range gunfire by dubbing anyone or anything they regarded as outstanding or invincible, as being pistol-proof. The articles of Ned Low's band of cutthroats in 1723 would even specify that: "He that sees a sail first, shall have the best pistol, or small arm aboard of her." Pirates usually sported at least two pistols in addition to their musket, cutlass, or dirk, referring to themselves as being "harnessed" when fully armed. The usual usage of this array of weaponry was to be described after Elias Haskett had deposed the mulatto privateer Read Elding as acting governor of the private colony of the Bahamas, only to in turn be removed himself when Elding and his fellow rovers launched a countercoup by seizing its principal fort and magazine in October 1701, and then

> with swords, pistols, and other arms went to the Governor's House in Nassau, where [Haskett] then was, and fired into it, at him; but the shot missing him, one of the confederates was wounded, by which means they left off firing and betook themselves to their swords, with which they seized the Governor, wounded him in several places and immediately carried him away to the Fort, and there loaded with irons and confined him a close prisoner.[9]

The typical armament of well-accoutered pirates was also noted when Captain Sam Bellamy intercepted a small pink off Cape Cod on the morning of April 26, 1717 (O.S.)—the 53rd and final vessel taken during his 11-month reign of terror—and sent across a prize crew of seven pirates from his damaged flagship *Whydah,* whom an eyewitness later recalled as clambering over the pink's side "armed with their musquets, pistols, and cutlashes." And when the famed Bartholomew Roberts emerged from his cabin aboard *Royal Fortune* to fight his last battle off West Africa's Cape Lopez on the morning of February 10, 1722 (O.S.), surviving crewmen would afterward recount how he had been wearing a crimson waistcoat and breeches, a hat with a big red feather, numerous gold chains, and a silk sling with two pairs of pistols thrust into it.

Blunderbusses

This powerful, short-range firearm apparently originated in The Netherlands, its curious name believed to have been an English garbling of its original Dutch name *donderbuis,* which combined *donder,* meaning thunder, and *buis,* signifying a pipe or tube. Throughout the 17th and early 18th centuries, a blunderbuss was recognized as a distinct type of muzzle-loading musket, characterized by a very short barrel with a large bore and a flared muzzle—which supposedly could spray a cluster of small shot in a wider pattern, yet was actually intended for ease in reloading. Blunderbuss barrels were usually made of steel or brass, less than two feet in length (compared to at least three feet, and often more, for contemporary muskets), resulting in a compact yet murderous firearm at close quarters—similar to a modern sawed-off shotgun.

Although limited in range, the gaping muzzle of blunderbusses meant that they could be more easily reloaded with powder and

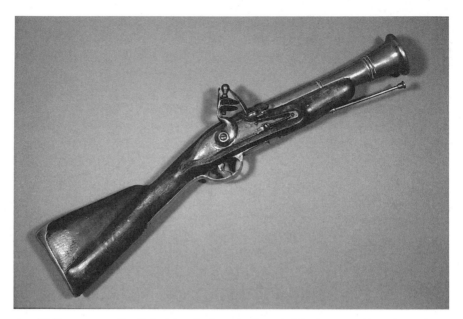

An 18th-century English blunderbuss, identifiable by its short large-bore barrel, flared at its end for ease in reloading; a powerful and fearful weapon favored by pirate boarders. (Private Collection/Peter Newark Historical Pictures/The Bridgeman Art Library)

shot under difficult circumstances—such as in a heaving boat or at night—making them popular weapons for boarding parties comprised of pirates or privateers, as well as for military assault columns. The discharge of a blunderbuss was moreover notoriously loud, adding to their shock effect in battle, and this blast would reverberate especially heavily in close confines—such as aboard a crowded sailing ship. (Indeed, because of its notoriously loud report, *blunderbuss* became a common nickname during that era for any noisy or argumentative person; for example, the following wry observation was recorded in London in January 1672, on the eve of the Third Anglo-Dutch War: "The master of yesterday's packet-boat, a very blunderbuss, says it was reported our Ambassador had demanded free trade in all their [Dutch] plantations in the Indies."[10])

The sound of a blunderbuss could be so penetrating that after Laurens de Graaf had led 800 freebooters silently into the darkened streets of Veracruz and positioned them for a simultaneous citywide attack at dawn on May 18, 1683, the agreed signal to launch this attack was to be the firing of three blunderbusses. These reports echoed the length of Veracruz and were so unmistakably distinct that the Spanish ensign Medina Barba—awake early that fatal morning, enjoying a cigar on his home's balcony—immediately recognized them as weapons foreign to Veracruz and called out a vain warning to the sentries standing guard outside the nearby governor's palace before the pirate assault columns closed in.

Grenades

Hand grenades were another weapon often favored by buccaneers who wished to move swiftly and break up concentrations of enemy resistance in battle without being encumbered by heavy ordnance. In fact, iron shells packed with gunpowder and ignited by a burning fuse were becoming an important piece of military hardware during the 17th century. In the closing stages of the Second Anglo-Dutch War, for example, the Committee of Plantations in London directed in January 1667 that Governor-General Lord Willoughby should have his military stores on Barbados augmented by "20 iron guns and 800 hand grenades."[11]

Because of their volatility, such charges were usually entrusted to veteran soldiers known as grenadiers, with steady nerves under fire. Untrained militiamen could not be allowed to handle grenades without hazard to themselves and others. Governor Thomas Dongan of New York commented in September 1687—during an upsurge of peacetime border infringements by the French out of Canada—that he had "grenade shells enough, but nobody understands how to use them."[12]

Many buccaneers, having sprung from military backgrounds, knew how to employ hand grenades to devastating effect. When Laurens de Graaf and the Sieur de Grammont stole over the walls into the sleeping city of Veracruz on the night of May 17, 1683, most of their 800 freebooters melted into its darkened streets, but two assault columns silently formed up to storm the Spaniards' principal pair of defensive bastions at first light. A survivor in the Caleta Bastion later related how, at a signal, "a group of some forty enemy with a white [French] flag"[13] came sprinting through the twilight, tossing grenades and shooting inside this redoubt, before swarming up a sand dune onto the bastion's roof and compelling its five frightened soldiers to surrender. The blasts of these grenade detonations were plainly heard three-quarters of a mile away, on San Juan de Ulúa Island.

Likewise, when Captain François Grogniet came gliding out of the darkness to land on the outskirts of Guayaquil and storm that city by surprise at dawn on April 20, 1686, his *flibustiers* waded into the dense brush around the small anchorage of Casones (near modern Aguirre and Elizalde Streets), only to be challenged by a Spanish sentry and have

French print depicting a soldier igniting a hand grenade, 1688. In armies of that era, only veterans would be entrusted with such lethal charges in the heat of battle. Privateers and pirates also employed them at sea to subdue resistance with a few frightening blasts. (Author's Collection)

a gun exchange erupt, whose noise aroused the sleeping inhabitants. Rain also started to fall, but, even so, the French paused in a large house after disembarking for their grenadiers to light their tinders before advancing at daybreak with "flags flying and drums beating" to overwhelm the Ecuadorian defenders.

Pirates often extemporized grenades out of whatever containers were available to them, such as glass bottles. For example, the French priest Labat recorded how when, early in 1694, the *flibustiers* of Capitaine Pinel swarmed over the bows of an 18-gun English ship off Barbados, its crew barricaded themselves inside their forecastle. Pinel's boarders countered by finding a small hatch

> through which they flung a glass jar filled with gunpowder and surrounded by four or five lit fuses, which ignited the powder when the

jar burst and burnt seven or eight Englishmen so horribly, they called for quarter.

Cutlasses

Seventeenth- and early 18th-century naval seamen, privateers, and pirates alike favored a particular type of short, heavy saber or slashing sword known as a cutlass—a name that had first been recorded in English usage as early as the 16th century, probably derived from the French version *coutelas* of the original Italian *coltellaccio*, meaning a large, heavy knife with a broad cutting edge. Used as sabers by mounted cavalrymen, cutlasses were thicker and not as long as other contemporary swords, featuring a straight or slightly curved blade sharpened along its cutting edge plus a solid cupped or basket-shaped hilt to protect the sword hand.

It made for a fearsome weapon in close-quarter combat and, because of its reduced length, could be more comfortably carried by parties crowded into boats or wielded with greater ease among such impediments as rigging lines and low deck beams aboard ship. Unlike the aristocratic rapier, it did not require prolonged training to master its use, while its blade was sturdy enough to even prove useful in shipboard emergencies that might require hacking through heavy cordage, canvas, or wood. Pirates additionally employed them as tools ashore, such as to chop firewood or to clear brush.

Cutlasses were commonplace to all seamen in the West Indies. For example, when Juan de Alarcón's Cuban corsairs slipped silently ashore in January 1684, a half mile east of Charlestown (modern Nassau) in the Bahamas, it was later recorded how a certain Captain Clarke, "being out of doors near the waterside, some men in ambush shot him through the thigh and cut his arms with a cutlass, and then they marched away with all haste to the town, firing into some houses as they went."[14] And when, five years later, the English garrison commander emerged from beleaguered Fort Pemaquid in Maine to negotiate with its native besiegers,

> he found the Indians all well armed with new French fuzees, waist-belts, and cutlasses, and most of them with bayonet and pistol, grey and black hats on their heads, and some of them with colored wigs.[15]

On the outbreak of Queen Anne's War early in 1702, the private colonists living in South Carolina would specifically request from London two dozen artillery pieces, plus "10 small patereras [*sic: pedreros* or swivel guns], 20 blunderbusses, 200 fusees, 12 doz. of hand granadees, 200 cutlasses, 3 cwt. [hundredweight] of match powder, great shot and fusee bullets proportionable, without which it will be morally impossible for us to make our defense."[16]

Yet by the early 18th century, the cutlass was becoming increasingly identified only with piracy because of the propensity of such outlaws to wield them while delivering flat-bladed beatings or punitive cuts, in incidents that were becoming ever more widely reported. Just one of many such accounts occurred when Captain Charles Vane and his vicious followers aboard the pirate flagship *Ranger*—who bore a particular grudge against all Bermudans—captured the sloop *Diamond* of Master John Tibby off Rum Key in the Bahamas during the spring of 1718. A sailor named Nathaniel Catling later testified that

> after beating them all, the pirates of the *Ranger* hanged up deponent by the neck until they thought he was dead. Perceiving he began to revive, one of them cut him with a cutlass over the collar-bone, till one of their own gang contradicted it.[17]

Swivels

Smaller pirate bands often prowled or hid along jungle-lined shorelines aboard single-decked vessels equipped with multiple oars—low, nimble craft that were difficult to spot against this dark backdrop and could move upwind, traverse shallows, or charge swiftly in quick bursts of rowing after their prey. Not big enough to mount proper artillery, these small craft relied on a few swivel guns strategically placed in bow and stern that could be easily traversed in almost any direction to unleash a deadly blast of grapeshot. (Master James Wilkins of Philadelphia described being shot at by one such swivel aboard a Cuban *guardacosta* while standing some distance away on the shoreline, which missed "but fell among some sugar canes that grew near, in which it cut down a wide lane."[18])

Ironically, because of their meager resources and limited access to imported armaments, the Spanish American corsairs who hunted pirates often featured less expensive swivels—known as *pedreros* among the Spaniards—aboard their simple, yet heavily manned patrol boats, making them formidable opponents in an engagement. During the summer of 1681 off the steamy Central American coast, it would take a full hour for Captain George Wright's *barco luengo* armed with four guns and 40 hard-bitten pirates to subdue a Spanish tartan out of Cartagena armed with only four swivels and 30 corsairs.

And although they packed a potent wallop, swivels were also light enough to be manhandled into position atop gun stands by only a pair of sailors, making them a useful armament for hit-and-run operations. When the brigantine of Gerrit Gerritszoon (also known as Rok Brasiliano) was wrecked on the Yucatan coast in late December 1669, a Spanish cavalry patrol chanced upon this pirate chieftain and his men as they were hastily burying two rescued bronze swivel guns and some 60 iron balls on the sandy beach—evidently hoping to steal a local boat from nearby and then return to unearth and arm it with these concealed weapons. Likewise, the tiny 35-ton sloop *Prophète Daniel* of Antoine Bernard of Martinique only had "a crew of seventeen men, two guns, [and] two swivel-guns" when it joined the pirate fleet of Laurens de Graaf and the Sieur de Grammont in the sack of Veracruz in May 1683.

For larger freebooter groups operating on the high seas, a favorite combination was to use a major vessel armed with heavy cannon as a flagship accompanied by a smaller, swifter consort armed with multiple light weapons (including swivels and grenades) for running down and overawing merchantmen. For example, two famous Dutch-born freebooters who dropped anchor off northwestern Jamaica in the autumn of 1687 were sailing in such a tandem, described by the English authorities as: "Yankey [Jan Willems] has a large Dutch-built ship with 44 guns and 100 men; Jacob [Evertsen] has a fine bark with ten guns, 16 patararoes [*sic*], and about 50 men."[19]

Pirate vessels would continue well into the 18th century to feature numerous swivels. Captain Benjamin Hornigold reportedly put out to sea from the lawless lair of Nassau in January 1716 with his sloop *Mary,* "having on board 140 men, six guns, and eight patararas [*sic*]."[20] Six years later, Captain George Lowther would be encountered with his 100-ton Rhode Island sloop *Happy Delivery,* mounting 8 cannon and 10 swivels.

Slavers were often fitted with extra swivels as well, many pointed inward to be instantly discharged to quell any sudden mass insurrection but which also made them doubly welcome as prizes for pirates. The additional armament allowed them to transfer some of these swivels aboard other prizes to augment the strength and reach of their flotilla. Edward Davis, for example, was delighted to intercept a Dutch slaver off West Africa's Cape Three Points in June 1719 that was bristling with 32 cannon and 27 swivels and that he renamed the *Royal Rover*—soon becoming Bartholomew Roberts's first flagship. Edward England's *Royal James,* Sam Bellamy's *Whydah,* Blackbeard's *Queen*

Anne's Revenge, and John Fenn's *Morning Star* also all began their piratical service as captured slavers.

SHIPS

Generally speaking, pirates preferred sailing aboard small, swift vessels that could easily overhaul merchantmen, outrun or outmaneuver naval pursuers, work into shallow waters, and be careened by relatively few hands. Major strikes organized by the earliest buccaneers required the assembly of a host of such minor vessels to gain strength through numbers. For instance, the fleet that Henry Morgan gathered in December 1670 to assault Panama was made up of 28 English and 10 French vessels, the largest being his own 22-gun, 120-ton flagship *Satisfaction* and François Trébutor's 14-gun, 100-ton frigate *Sainte-Catherine.* All the rest were smaller, some of the tiniest ones displacing as little as 12 tons, while five craft did not even have any guns

Bermuda sloop at anchor off the Boston Lighthouse, 1729. Note the tilt or "rake" of its single mast and elongated bowsprit, which made such vessels very fast and agile, greatly sought after by pirates. Armed gangs would crowd aboard for quick chases of merchantmen, outrunning any naval pursuers before retiring into lonely coves, to enjoy their spoils. (Fotosearch/Getty Images)

mounted—yet such an unimpressive flotilla transported a combined total of 1,850 freebooters across the sea and landed them at Chagres, from where they fought their way over the isthmus and into the streets of Panama City.

At the peak of piracy's power, successful commanders would come to lead their own individual squadrons, directing operations of satellite vessels and storing all the booty garnered aboard one main flagship. When such leaders combined forces, their strength could be imposing: the fleet that Captain David Mitchell of the 48-gun frigate HMS *Ruby*—the most powerful Royal Navy warship then stationed in the West Indies—chanced upon off Cuba's Isla de Pinos in April 1685 included the great ships and accompanying squadrons of the Sieur de Grammont, Laurens de Graaf, Michiel Andrieszoon, Jan Willems, and Jacob Evertsen, such a daunting group that this naval officer dared not try to carry out his orders by demanding the surrender of the English renegade Joseph Bannister's 36-gun *Golden Fleece*, which was plainly visible at anchor within their midst.

Yet such agglomerations of major and minor vessels also required crewmen numbering into the hundreds, who were difficult to keep supplied on a regular basis, to say nothing of satiated with enough booty when it had to be divided up among so many unpaid freebooters. And as royal decrees began undermining the wartime role of privateers and denying more ports to renegade rovers, the advantages of operating a small craft with a limited number of hands began to reassert themselves. An example of such calculated self-interest was provided by the Rhode Islander Thomas Tew, who departed lonely Bermuda in January 1693 with 46 hard-bitten veterans aboard his eight-gun, 70-ton sloop *Amity*—armed with a commission purportedly authorizing an attack against the powerful French slaving stronghold of Gorée in West Africa, although Tew actually intended to sail his tiny vessel around the Cape of Good Hope to attack rich, lightly armed, neutral shipping in the Indian Ocean and Red Sea. After an epic 15-month, 22,000-mile voyage, he stole back into his home port of Providence with an immense fortune in ill-gotten gains, far from any threat of prosecution and able to pay off his twoscore seamen with astonishing sums.

Obviously, a pirate captain did not need a large and heavily armed ship in order to be successful, especially since most roved merely to satisfy base selfish motives rather than to battle their nation's enemies during time of war. Small and swift vessels such as sloops were therefore preferred, those designed and built on Bermuda being especially coveted because of their superior speed and handling. When Captain

Christopher Goffe was sent out of Boston aboard the privateer *Swan* in August 1691 to chase away a pair of marauding Bermudan sloops under Captains Thomas Griffin and George Dew that had been making a nuisance of themselves through a string of offshore interceptions of supposed New England smugglers, Goffe soon returned into Nantasket to glumly report to the authorities that "they could sail two feet to his one."[21] And when Captain Benjamin Candler of HMS *Winchelsea* made a sweep through the Virgin Islands hunting for Sam Bellamy in May 1717, he reported that he found only a few pirate collaborators living ashore:

> When we came, they hid themselves in the rocks; one Ham, a notorious villain living on Beef Island, was on board of Bellame [*sic*] the Pirate when he was here, and as soon as they fired a gun at Virgin Gorda, he betook himself to a Bermuda boat he has and his negroes, and lurked about the creeks and islands until we were gone.[22]

The most infamous captains of piracy's last hurrah during the early 18th century all began their careers in command of small, fast, nimble, and heavily manned sloops:

- Sam Bellamy started as captain of the 10-gun *Mary Anne* in June 1716, crammed with 90 hardened freebooters.

- Gentlemanly Stede Bonnet cleared Barbados in April 1717 with his own custom-built, six-gun, 60-ton *Revenge,* allegedly with 125 hired crewmen stuffed aboard.

- After a losing encounter against a Spanish warship, Bonnet limped into Nassau that same August 1717, where his *Revenge* was upgraded with six extra guns and put back out to sea with 100 hands under its new commander, Blackbeard.

- Howell Davis and Thomas Anstis shipped out of Nassau in 1718 as crewmembers aboard the merchant sloop *Buck,* only to mutiny and take it over "with [four] other rascals" so as to go "a-pyrating."

Although Bellamy, Blackbeard, Davis, and many other rovers would all wind up in command of much larger flagships, they still retained sloops as part of their formations for the day-to-day work of running down prizes on the high seas. And in the end, Blackbeard even abandoned his 36-gun, 300-ton flagship *Queen Anne's Revenge* in North Carolina's Beaufort Inlet in June 1718, betraying and marooning hundreds of his followers, to escape upriver with only 20 loyal hands left aboard his favorite sloop, *Adventure*—the vessel on which he would be shot, hacked, and stabbed to death only a few months later.

Types

Sailing ships were built in many different shapes and sizes during the late 17th and early 18th centuries, certain designations being variously applied to different configurations according to a particular region, seaport, or opinion. Generally speaking, though, the following were the main categories of vessels operating at sea during the golden age of piracy:

ships, the largest class of vessels afloat, typically displacing from 300 tons and upward, characterized by having three square-rigged masts, plus a couple of full-length decks

frigates, smaller ships that displaced from 120 tons upward and also featured three square-rigged masts, yet only a single complete gundeck

barks or barques, usually displaced less than 100 tons and sported two square-rigged masts plus a fore and aft mizzenmast

brigs or brigantines, smaller vessels characterized by a square-rigged foremast and mainmast alone, without any third mast

ketches, whose distinctive silhouette consisted of a tall mainmast amidships plus a smaller mizzenmast astern

sloops, recognizable because their low hulls, usually sported a single mainmast and an unusually extended bowsprit

snows were a type of brig featuring a small additional trysail directly behind the mainmast

The term *galley* also appears repeatedly in historical records for this period, but rather than referring exclusively to vessels of that ancient design—such as Roman biremes or triremes that were rowed by multiple banks of oarsmen—it actually meant an added feature on some 17th- and 18th-century ships that had been pierced with strategically placed holes so they could be propelled with long sweeps, in addition to their sails. When Captain Kidd, for example, secured a commission and was preparing to depart London in December 1695 to hunt pirates in the Far East, he and his investors bought the brand-new, 287-ton frigate-galley *Adventure* at Deptford, which was armed with 34 guns and pierced for 46 sweeps, a significant advantage for moving through shallow inshore waters and up rivers. Kidd was to even avail himself of this feature a year later, while approaching the Cape of Good Hope in company with the Royal Navy squadron of Commodore Thomas Warren; fearful that his best seamen might be impressed by this understrength naval formation, Kidd took advantage of the opportunity when all the ships became becalmed to row out of sight. Slavers were often fitted out as galleys to allow them to work in and out of remote anchorages, although this mobility also made them a favorite prize among pirates. After Captain James Martel had seized the 20-gun *John and Martha* off Cuba in the autumn of 1716, he cut it down by a deck and retained it as his new flagship.

Yet curiously, very tiny boats such as piraguas—a crude type of Antillean coastal craft or riverboat made from a simple hollowed-out log—often contained the most dangerous bands of pirates, small desperate groups hunting to find larger vessels. The young Breton adventurer Jean Villebon worked his way up the Central American coastline in one such gang during the summer of 1668, being one of 26 *boucaniers* piled aboard two piraguas, questing for prey. Even when overturned by the waves, these tough and unsinkable craft merely drifted ashore, where the pirates could retrieve them—their weapons and tools still safely lashed to the gunwales and their powder dry inside gourds sealed with wax.

Acquisition and Replacement

Needless to say, pirates stole their vessels, and often upgraded from undersized, older, or otherwise unsatisfactory ships through ever larger captures. Captains Kidd and Stede Bonnet were among the rarest of commanders in that they originally went to sea aboard custom-built, purchased vessels. Most renegades began as members of a pirate splinter faction or mutineers aboard merchantmen, running away with the ship on which they were serving. Perhaps the most infamous example of this latter practice was provided by Henry Every, who, in May 1694, was first mate aboard the heavily armed private frigate *Charles II*, long delayed in the Spanish port of La Coruña on a projected salvage expedition to the West Indies. Every led 85 disgruntled, unpaid crewmen in a mutiny, slipping out to sea past the batteries one night to set the captain and 16 loyal hands adrift in a boat next morning, saying to them as they parted company: "I am a man of fortune, and must seek my fortune."[23]

True to his word, Every sailed this stolen frigate—now renamed the *Fancy*—to the Far East, where after a year and a half of adventures, he succeeded in boarding the enormous Mogul trader *Ganj-i-sawai* off Bombay in September 1695, pillaging it of the immense sum of £200,000. Returning to the West Indies, he and his pirates were faced with the problem of quietly disposing of *Fancy*, so as to disperse back into civilian life with their loot. Dropping anchor in the sparsely populated Bahamas, they bribed the corrupt private governor at Nassau to enter harbor and make this vessel over to him, supposedly "to take care of her for use of the owners." But once this crooked deal was struck, *Fancy* was stripped of everything of value—46 guns, many smaller arms, 100 barrels of gunpowder, 50 tons of ivory, sails, and blocks—and deliberately untied two days later to drift ashore and be destroyed by the surf. With this telltale piece of evidence against them obliterated, Every and his men could vanish from the Bahamas aboard various visiting ships, never to be seen again.

Although pirates came to have favorite vessels, most nonetheless abandoned them whenever it suited their purposes or their usefulness was at an end, seemingly without any qualms. Criminally wrested from victims in most cases, and in any event impossible to sail into Crown-controlled seaports where they might be recognized, they were viewed as expendable liabilities. Countless examples abound of marauders disposing of their vessels:

- Captain Kidd beached and burned his *Adventure* on Madagascar late in 1698 to sail for the West Indies aboard his 400-ton Indian prize *Quedah Merchant,* which he in turn abandoned there after buying the sloop *San Antonio,* so as to steer stealthily for home aboard this non-descript vessel by June 1699, hoping to avoid detection.
- In late February 1717, a mere two months after capturing and rearming his prize *Sultana* as his new flagship, Captain Sam Bellamy gave it away to the dispossessed master of the two-year-old, 300-ton slaver *Whyduh,* which he preferred to retain as an even better vessel.
- Intending to disband his flotilla in June 1718 and sneak ashore into civilian life, Blackbeard apparently ran his large *Queen Anne's Revenge* aground on purpose in North Carolina's lonely Beaufort Inlet to strip it of everything of value before marooning hundreds of his followers and disappearing upriver with 20 loyal hands and the bulk of his booty aboard the sloop *Adventure.*
- Even the great Bartholomew Roberts, regarded as a fine seaman, would exchange flagships with astonishing frequency during his 20-month career—often giving his new ones the same or similar names, either out of personal preference or possibly to confuse any future legal proceedings. He abandoned his original *Royal Rover* in favor of *Royal Roger,* then christened at least four of his captures as successive *Royal Fortunes.*

Such callous disregard for the property of others meant that pirates could wreak a heavy toll on peacetime shipping. Two weeks after seizing the six-gun brigantine *Rebecca* in the Cayman Islands, Ned Low abandoned it in June 1722 off Nova Scotia in favor of the brand-new,

80-ton schooner *Mary,* which he in turn forsook shortly thereafter in the Azores for the French pink *Rose,* only to then accidentally overturn it while attempting to careen at Surinam. Limping to the French-held island of Grenada crammed aboard a prize schooner named *Squirrel,* Low and his men captured a sloop there, which they named the *Ranger*—all of this destruction transpiring during the span of only six months, before the year 1722 was even ended.

TACTICS

Although the earliest buccaneers preyed upon Spanish shipping, their greatest successes came through assembling at an agreed-upon rendezvous in numbers, then sailing to a quiet anchorage and using light craft to steal undetected upon Spanish towns to ransack and extort their wealth before dispersing with whatever booty they could garner. These West Indian rovers became remarkably adept at penetrating far up muddy rivers or silently forging through steamy jungles to emerge by surprise deep inland, eventually making forays across the Isthmus of Panama in such numbers as to raid uncontested in the Pacific Ocean for years. At the peak of their powers, pirate fleets even seized major seaports such as Panama City, Veracruz, and Campeche and held them with impunity.

Yet the escalating size of such land assaults meant that inevitably freebooters would exhaust all targets within easy reach of the Caribbean that were capable of paying out significant dividends, when spoils had to be shared out among so many. Commanders consequently became more calculating in their designs, realizing that proceeds from a single, yet rich, capture could prove much more rewarding if split up among only a small number of participants. As a result, during King William's War—with French merchant prizes swept clean from the seas—American mercenaries uncovered the value of sailing halfway around the world to prey upon neutral argosies plying through the peaceful Red Sea. Such slow, lightly armed ships could scarcely defend themselves against the nimble sloops crowded with gun-toting desperadoes, and their exotic cargoes fetched fantastic profits once sailed home to New England, thousands of miles from the scene of such crimes.

Some pirate commanders such as Laurens de Graaf and Bartholomew Roberts might indeed have been great seamen, capable of brilliant tactical maneuvers—yet most captains would concentrate single-mindedly on hunting down merchantmen and avoiding naval warships. Pirate vessels rarely engaged in ship-to-ship artillery duels, as commercial vessels invariably tried to outrun or evade their pursuers, then obligingly surrendered once the marauders drew close. There was relatively little profit—and considerable danger—in directly challenging a warship, so most pirates only fought against navy vessels when they became cornered.

On Land

As noted, the early buccaneer companies made their mark by gathering into flotillas, then sailing to raid Spanish American towns by surprise. Many of their leaders came from a military background—such as Henry Morgan and the Sieur de Grammont—so they directed their expeditions like amphibious forces, like marines. Their followers' familiarity with West Indian conditions meant that first they had to be allowed to steal sufficient supplies, then sail together to a quiet anchorage, and use light craft and guides to creep undetected along the coastline or up rivers, drawing close to their target in nocturnal stages, until finally bursting upon their unsuspecting victims at dawn.

Yet the battle discipline of these polyglot bands was also quite good, as veteran members realized that concentrated volleys were needed in order to retain their advantage over more numerous foes. Seventeenth-century buccaneer armies routinely marched into action behind fluttering flags and beating drums, much like contemporary regiments. Such conduct was quite familiar to rank-and-file members, many Caribbean freebooters being discharged soldiers. When Captain Edward Collier disgorged his landing force from six pirate ships outside Riohacha (Colombia) at daybreak on October 24, 1670, they marched upon its four gun keep with such disciplined purpose that the Spanish garrison was convinced they were regular royal troops recently arrived from England—until they drew closer, and the pirates' true identity became apparent.

Yet buccaneers actually maneuvered into battle in somewhat looser firing lines and discharged their weaponry more independently than European regiments of that day. Governor Juan Álvarez de Avilés of Guayaquil, who personally confronted the piratical assault columns that loomed out of the darkness and carried his city by storm in April 1687, would later write to his superiors describing how "the enemy advanced on all sides, but not in closed ranks, rather without order, which has always been their way of waging war, separated from each other by two or three paces, jumping and crouching and shooting, rushing into our trench at different points simultaneously."[24]

These tactics remained constant throughout most of the 17th century, and, although West Indian formations were eventually considered inferior to the professional royal regiments sent from Europe to supplant them, freebooters remained an effective auxiliary strike force—especially where booty was involved. During the French invasion of Jamaica in King William's War, for example, Laurens de Graaf led 1,500 *flibustiers* ashore at Carlisle Bay on the night of July 28, 1694, advancing the next morning against the 250 English militiamen guarding its town with a dozen artillery pieces. By approaching cautiously in a loose formation at an oblique angle and holding their fire until they came within point-blank range, the French were able to loose a murderous volley of musket fire that drove the defenders out of their trenches and across the river, leaving the *flibustiers* free to pillage the town's buildings.

What eventually brought an end to such land actions was the lack of returns from these assaults. As royal strongholds multiplied, the pirates' disembarkations early during the 18th century ended in abject failures, so that their focus returned to the sea.

At Sea

Pirate vessels usually preferred to bear down on targeted merchantmen at an oblique angle, peppering their intended victims with musket fire before rushing in to carry the ships through boarding. Marauders furthermore counted upon fear unnerving any thoughts of resistance, facilitating their captures through displays of menacing devices such as blood-red flags (threatening no quarter) and often unleashing a ferocious initial volley. A classic example of such intrepid action was recounted by Exquemelin, of when Captain Pierre François of Dunkirk—aboard a small bark manned by only 26 rovers—stole upon a Colombian pearling fleet in calm weather off Las Rancherías, near Ríohacha. These *flibustiers* had come rowing along its shoreline and even glided past a Spanish warship anchored a mile and a half away, in deeper water, by masquerading their bark as a coaster peacefully approaching out of Maracaibo.

Closing upon the pearling fleet's flagship, a two-masted vessel bearing eight guns and 60 armed men, Captain François suddenly called upon it to surrender and avoided the ragged broadside the Spaniards fired in reply. During the lull while they were struggling to reload, the French closed the range and felled several Spanish with accurate musket fire before swarming aboard. Then, to deceive the distant warship that all was still well, the Spanish ensign was left flying and the vacated French bark was scuttled, giving the impression that the defenders had successfully repelled this assault. It was only

Seventeenth-century buccaneers aboard a tiny coastal craft, stealing upon an unwary Spanish galleon at sundown, as imagined by Howard Pyle. (Merle Johnson, comp., *Howard Pyle's Book of Pirates* [New York: Harper & Brothers, ca. 1921])

when François weighed some time later and stood out to sea that the man-of-war realized what had transpired and cut its cable to pursue. The bold Frenchmen were only undone at the last minute, when their prize's mainmast collapsed during the ensuing chase, or else they would have escaped scot-free.

Similar tactics of bearing in quickly from an oblique angle and relying solely upon musketry would be observed in countless other piratical encounters over the ensuing decades, both at anchor and upon the open sea. In just one of many instances, Sir Henry Morgan—temporarily acting as Jamaica's governor in January 1681, after the death of the official titleholder—dispatched a flotilla to arrest the outlaw privateer Jacob Evertsen in Bull Bay and recorded how this delegated force bore in indirectly on this pirate brigantine and its prize and, upon boarding,

> received three musket shot, slightly wounding one man, and returned a volley killing some and wounding others of the privateers. Everson and several others jumped overboard, and were shot in the sea near shore.[25]

And in November 1685, Lieutenant-Governor Hender Molesworth of Jamaica wrote a description for his superiors in London of similar tactics being employed by the hard-bitten mercenaries serving aboard Cuba's coast guard vessels:

> These galleys and periagos [sic: piraguas] are mostly manned by Greeks, but they are of all nations, rogues culled out for the villanies that they commit. They never hail a ship; and so they can but master her, she is certain prize. They lurk in the bushes by the shore, so that they see every passing vessel without being seen. When our sloops are at anchor, they set them by their compasses in the daytime, and steal on them by night with so little noise that they are aboard before they are discovered.[26]

This preferred tactic of attacking another vessel through gaining an advantageous angle and raking its decks with musket fire—not heavy artillery rounds—was even to be observed in clashes between rival privateers. In late September 1689, Captain Samuel Pease's Massachusetts colonial sloop *Mary* emerged from Boston and sighted the renegade vessel of Thomas Pound near Tarpaulin Cove, overhauling it in a stiff south-southeasterly wind. Pease hoisted the king's jack and fired a shot from his main gun across the renegades' forefoot (the only artillery round discharged this day), to which they responded by affixing "the red flag of piracy at the mainmast top."[27] Pease thereupon fired a single musket shot, followed by a full volley, directly into the renegades' hull and, as the distance narrowed, called on them "to strike to the King of England." Pound could be clearly seen on his quarterdeck brandishing a sword and shouting back above the wind: "Come aboard, you dogs, and I will strike you presently!"

A heated exchange of musketry ensued, but no more heavy rounds. Pease's sloop, being more nimble, ran down to leeward of the renegades—normally a tactical disadvantage, but not on such a blustery day. The heeling caused by the strong wind raised *Mary*'s weather side as a bulwark to protect his marksmen, while allowing his loyal crewmen to fire downward upon the more exposed renegades. After a murderous gunfight, *Mary* finally surged alongside the renegade craft, and boarders subdued them in a fierce hand-to-hand struggle, during which muskets were swung about as clubs, leaving four pirates dead and a dozen wounded, only two remaining unharmed to surrender.

Almost 30 years later, virtually the same tactics would be used when two South Carolina sloops closed in on Stede Bonnet's pirate sloop *Royal James* at first light on September 27, 1718 (O.S.), as it lay at anchor in the Cape Fear River estuary. Pouring in musket fire from both sides, Bonnet weighed and steered close to the western shoreline to escape these privateers but ran aground. The Carolinian sloops moved in on the stranded *Royal James*, yet also grounded, one "within pistol-shot of the pirate, on his bow; the other right ahead of [Bonnet], almost out of gun-shot."[28] Over the next five hours, the immobilized vessels exchanged musketry, the pirates having the advantage in that their deck was tilted away from their opponents, so that 10 South Carolinians were killed and 14 wounded, compared to a dozen casualties aboard Bonnet's vessel.

Yet this battle was ultimately decided when the rising tide lifted the Carolina sloops free, while leaving *Royal James* still hard aground. Bonnet and his outnumbered men could only watch helplessly as their foes quickly repaired their rigging and then closed in on their own paralyzed vessel from oblique angles, unleashing simultaneous musket volleys to cover their final, devastating assault with boarding parties. In a despairing gesture, Bonnet called upon his gunner to blow up *Royal James*'s powder magazine, but his pirate crew chose to surrender. All were carried prisoners into Charleston, "to the no small joy of the people of Carolina,"[29] according to a contemporary report.

Avoiding Ship Duels

As the 17th century gave way to the 18th, pirate vessels would engage in artillery exchanges ever more rarely. Even the great Laurens de Graaf was reluctant to offer battle after his *Neptune* had been caught off Mexico's Alacrán Reef in September 1685 by the Armada de

Barlovento flagship *Santo Cristo de Burgos* and vice-flagship *Nuestra Señora de la Concepción*. He survived by outmaneuvering these two antagonists all day (the Spaniards noting how he often supplemented his cannon salvoes with musket volleys), then—as darkness fell—took the desperate expedient of jettisoning *Neptune*'s main artillery altogether to gain the wind and claw away overnight, escaping via the Yucatan Channel.

Most pirate crews held a dim view of captains who chose to engage warships. Less than five years later, William Kidd—while still employed as an honest privateer during the opening stages of King William's War in the Antilles—helped battle five French warships off the island of Saint Martin in late January 1690. Despite emerging from this hard-fought encounter, his 80 to 90 mercenary crewmen felt aggrieved about Kidd's "ill behavior," resenting their involvement in a line-of-battle engagement with scant booty to be won. Consequently, when Kidd went ashore at Nevis, a group of mutineers unilaterally made off with his 20-gun *Blessed William* and £2,000 worth of loot, leaving him to vainly pursue them to New York.

More than 30 years later, a like fate befell the tough Edward England after he led his 34-gun flagship *Fancy* and 36-gun consort *Victory* in a direct frontal attack against a trio of East Indiamen anchored off Johanna Island near Madagascar on the morning of August 17, 1720 (O.S.). Two of these large merchantmen weighed and escaped out of the bay, but Captain James Macrae's *Cassandra* fought back defiantly until its hull was riddled with heavy rounds, so that it had to be beached to allow its survivors to escape onto land. The pirates angrily took possession of their hard-won prize, discovering £75,000 worth of European trade goods aboard—not the high-priced Oriental treasures they had expected. Furious at the heavy casualties they had endured in capturing an outward-bound Indiaman, England's minions voted him out as captain, banishing him from their company altogether with a few loyal adherents aboard a small boat. It was said that he barely reached Saint Augustine's Bay on Madagascar and died there shortly thereafter in abject poverty.

And if a large Indiaman should prove such a formidable adversary for pirates by this second decade of the 18th century, they were even more powerless against naval warships. Such a lesson would be driven home on the morning of February 5, 1722 (O.S.), while the brilliant Bartholomew Roberts was lying at anchor off Cape Lopez with his flagship *Royal Fortune*, plus the smaller consorts *Great Ranger* and *Little Ranger*. When a tall sail appeared offshore, Roberts—assuming it to be a rich merchantman—ordered his subordinate James Skyrme to pursue with *Great Ranger,* watching through his glass as this prey slowly wheeled and clumsily began running away before the wind, as if afraid. The pirate sloop exited and gradually overhauled, Skyrme opening fire with his bow chasers at 10:30 A.M., by which time Cape Lopez had fallen well below the horizon. As the gap continued to narrow, *Great Ranger's* decks became lined with exultant, cutlass-brandishing pirates, while above them fluttered a bewildering array of flags, including a black Jolly Roger.

But suddenly at 11:00 A.M., this large ship swiftly bore up to starboard, ran out two tiers of heavy guns, and let fly with a crushing broadside. The pursuers were appalled to learn that they had been lured directly beneath the muzzles of Captain Chaloner Ogle's 50-gun warship HMS *Swallow,* which pounded them into submission in a one-sided exchange that saw 10 pirates killed and another 20 wounded (including Skyrme, whose leg was blown off), out of a crew of 100 cutthroats—without suffering so much as a single casualty aboard the Royal Navy vessel. Ogle subsequently returned into Cape Lopez five days later and annihilated Roberts's formation, in the process slaying this last great pirate chieftain.

NOTES

1. Alexandre-Olivier Exquemelin, *The Buccaneers of America,* trans. Alexis Brown, introd. Jack Beeching (London: Penguin, 1969), 69.

2. David F. Marley, *Pirates of the Americas,* vol. 1 (Santa Barbara, CA: ABC-CLIO, 2010), 74.

3. Ibid., 540.

4. Ibid., 541.

5. Peter Earle, *The Sack of Panamá: Sir Henry Morgan's Adventures on the Spanish Main* (New York: Viking, 1981), 58.

6. Exquemelin, *The Buccaneers of America,* 139.

7. *Calendar of State Papers, Colonial: America and West Indies,* vol. 32 (London: Her Majesty's Stationery Office, 1933), 167.

8. *Calendar of State Papers, Colonial: America and West Indies,* vol. 11 (London: Her Majesty's Stationery Office, 1898), 725.

9. *Calendar of State Papers, Colonial: America and West Indies,* vol. 19 (London: Her Majesty's Stationery Office, 1910), 699.

10. *Calendar of State Papers, Domestic: Charles II, January 1672* (London: Her Majesty's Stationery Office, 1897), 70.

11. *Calendar of State Papers, Colonial: America and West Indies,* vol. 5 (London: Her Majesty's Stationery Office, 1880), 443.

12. *Calendar of State Papers, Colonial: America and West Indies,* vol. 12 (London: Her Majesty's Stationery Office, 1899), 434.

13. David F. Marley, *Sack of Veracruz: The Great Pirate Raid of 1683* (Windsor, Ontario: Netherlandic Press, 1993), 29.

14. *Calendar of State Papers, Colonial: America and West Indies,* vol. 11 (London: Her Majesty's Stationery Office, 1898), 578.

15. *Calendar of State Papers, Colonial: America and West Indies,* vol. 13 (London: Her Majesty's Stationery Office, 1901), 114.

16. *Calendar of State Papers, Colonial: America and West Indies,* vol. 20 (London: Her Majesty's Stationery Office, 1912), 97.

17. *Calendar of State Papers, Colonial: America and West Indies,* vol. 30 (London: Her Majesty's Stationery Office, 1930), 264.

18. *Calendar of State Papers, Colonial: America and West Indies,* vol. 37 (London: Her Majesty's Stationery Office, 1937), 158.

19. Marley, *Pirates of the Americas,* vol. 1, 588.

20. *Calendar of State Papers, Colonial: America and West Indies,* vol. 29 (London: Her Majesty's Stationery Office, 1930), 139.

21. Marley, *Pirates of the Americas,* 570.

22. *Calendar of State Papers,* vol. 29, 369.

23. *A Complete Collection of State Trials and Proceedings for High-Treason,* vol. 5 (London, 1730), 7.

24. Marley, *Pirates of the Americas,* vol. 1, 347.

25. *Calendar of State Papers,* vol. 11, 7.

26. Ibid., 721.

27. Marley, *Pirates of the Americas,* vol. 1, 741.

28. C. Lovat Fraser, *The Lives and Adventures of Sundry Notorious Pirates* (New York: McBride, 1922), 109.

29. Ibid., 110.

8

TORTURE

In cold blood, they did a thousand cursed things.
—Lament of a Spanish survivor of the four-week
pirate occupation of Ríohacha, Colombia, 1670

While some individual pirates might have been capable of admirable feats of bravery, inspirational leadership, and skillful seamanship—as well as acts of generosity and a rare spirit of equality for that unenlightened age—their calling nonetheless remained a very cruel one. Whenever in large numbers, pirates routinely stole whatever they wanted from others by force, compelled the weak to serve them through threats or outright enslavement, and savaged their hapless victims to extract as much wealth from them as possible—or simply for their own gratification. As early as January 1670, a well-educated young gentleman had written from Port Royal to his collegial friend, Lord Arlington, the secretary of state at Whitehall, describing many of the vices prevalent among the rough-hewn frontier society that was just then emerging on Jamaica, including some unsavory details:

It is a common thing amongst the privateers, besides burning with matches and such like slight torments, to cut a man in pieces: first some flesh, then a hand, an arm, a leg, sometimes tying a cord about his head, and with a stick twisting it till the eyes start out, which is called "woolding." Before taking Porto Bello [in July 1668], thus some were

used, because they refused to discover a way into the town, which was
not [i.e., did not exist]; and many in the town, because they would not
discover wealth they knew not of. A woman there was by some set bare
upon a baking stone and roasted, because she did not confess of money
which she had only in their conceit; this he heard some declare boasting,
and one that was sick, confess with sorrow.[1]

Such wanton cruelty sprang from many sources, not least the very
callousness of the age. Already, irregular warfare had been sustained
for many decades in Europe and its overseas colonies through heartless acts of pillage, as only a few royal forces ever received regular
pay or supplies. Looting had therefore become an accepted norm for
all fighting men while on campaign and would prove especially so in
the unregulated waters of the Antilles, to say nothing of vast, lonely
stretches of open ocean.

Society moreover remained rigidly segregated throughout this
period, its benefits being enjoyed almost exclusively by the privileged
elites, with corporal punishment being freely meted out among the
lower orders. Sailors aboard peacetime merchantmen were commonly
struck with canes or the lash, only grudgingly fed or paid, and all too
often subjected to the whims of their master or ship owner without
any legal recourse or hope of betterment. Indeed, any hint of defiance
might result in a charge of mutiny, punishable by flogging or hanging. And, as has been noted, many rovers had suffered personally as
menial members of these downtrodden lower classes throughout their
early lives, before striking out vengefully as freebooters.

PRODUCTS OF A BRUTAL AGE

Life was cheap during the 17th century, heartless blood sports such
as dog fighting, bear baiting, and ratting being frequently staged for
popular amusement, all featuring confrontations specifically designed
to end in mutilation, suffering, or death. Boxing consisted of brutish and primitive maulings, while duels to the death were commonplace as well. Even legally sanctioned punishments meted out by the
authorities were unimaginably barbarous by today's standards. When
the Quaker preacher James Nayler was convicted of blasphemy in
London in December 1656, he was condemned—after heated debate
among Oliver Cromwell's deeply offended Puritan leadership as to
the most painful remedies available—to be exposed to vicious public
abuse in the pillory for a couple of hours, then to be whipped through
the streets, branded on the forehead with the letter B, and to have a

hole burned through his tongue with a hot iron before being flung back into prison.

And after the Dutch commodore Cornelis "Kees the Devil" Evertsen had reclaimed the West Indian island of Saint Eustatius from English forces in June 1673, he learned that three sailors had murdered its governor during this occupation. Determined to make an example of these Dutch culprits, he ordered them to draw lots, as only one was to be given a quick death through hanging—the other two being condemned to keelhauling, flogging, and marooning on a desert isle.

On execution day, all three were paraded to the gallows and had nooses placed around their necks, yet only one was actually turned off to die. The remaining two were then rowed out to the anchored flagship *Swaenenburgh*, where each was hoisted out to dangle from his wrists at the tip of its main yard. A weighted line was tied to their feet, and the other end was passed underneath the hull and run up to the opposite tip of the yardarm. An oil-soaked rag was tied over their mouths and noses to prevent outright drowning, after which each was dropped into the sea and the line hauled in, so as to tug them beneath the ship in suffocating agony over its sharp barnacles, emerging—barely conscious, battered, bleeding, soaked in salt water, and dangling upside down—on the far side of the vessel. This terrible ordeal was repeated three times for each prisoner, after which the broken men were cast onto separate uninhabited cays, to die lingeringly and alone of hunger, want, and exposure.

Similarly, when the Corsican-born mercenary Biagio Michele or "Blas Miguel" violated a Spanish truce with the French *flibustiers* of Hispaniola by launching an ill-fated strike against Petit-Goâve with only 65 Cuban corsairs at dawn on August 10, 1687, the infuriated French authorities angrily condemned him and his two principal lieutenants to be "broken alive" on the wheel—a dreadful death in which each prisoner was tied naked and spread-eagled onto a large wheel, to receive a series of bone-shattering blows over the course of several hours, writhing helplessly in excruciating pain under the hot sun before eventually expiring or being mercifully dispatched by a final coup de grâce. The 42 surviving Cuban corsairs were furthermore sentenced to be hanged all around Miguel, only two—a young boy and a black man—being spared because they had been forced to join the raiders.

These terrible sentences were carried out two days later, Miguel being slowly battered to death atop a stage specially erected in Petit-Goâve's execution ground, while the whites, mulattos, Indians, and

A contemporary woodcut of the execution of Stede Bonnet for piracy. (Charles
Johnson, *A General History of the Robberies
and Murders of the Most Notorious Pyrates*
[London: Rivington, 1724])

blacks who had accompanied him were strung up one by one, to thrash
and eventually fall silent all around his prone, dying figure.

FEARSOME JURISPRUDENCE

The vast majority of horrid punishments were administered publicly during the 17th century, supposedly to serve as a deterrent
to the general populace as well as to shame the condemned. When
the 32-gun frigate HMS *Success,* newly arrived from England, was
wrecked—through a Jamaican pilot's negligence—while pursuing the
pirate Peter Harris off the South Cays of Cuba in early December 1679,
a naval court of inquiry condemned this unfortunate subordinate "to
receive seven lashes aboard every commissioned ship, thrice, one
day after another,"[2] as an example to the rest.

In another instance of judicial vindictiveness recorded six years
later, an English laborer chanced to blurt out a few angry insults about
Charles Osborne, justice of the peace for the county of Middlesex, so

the judge avenged this slight by sentencing the malefactor—the week before Christmas 1685—"to be stript of his middle upwards on the next Thursday, and to be whipt on his back till his body should be bloody, at the hinder part of a cart from the west end of Rosemary Lane to the place called the Armitage."[3]

Following the restoration of the monarchy to England's throne in 1660, the number of crimes punishable by death had soon begun to soar from 50 to well over 100, such statutes eventually coming to encompass even such seemingly trivial offences as stealing any item valued at more than five shillings or writing a threatening letter. Executions and floggings had long been regarded as entertainments by the general public, with seats and refreshments freely sold to spectators who flocked to callously witness the demeanor of the condemned man during his last few dreadful minutes. Dennis McCarthy, an ex-prizefighter hanged for piracy at Nassau in 1718, would be long remembered for having stood gamely on the gallows—bedecked in colored ribbons, as was then customary among boxers—and telling his admiring audience that his friends had often joked that he would die in his shoes, "and so to prove them liars, he kicked off his shoes amongst the crowd, and so died without them."[4]

Given such pitiless examples of officially sanctioned barbarity, pirates would have little trouble devising fiendish torments of their own with which to terrify or abuse their victims. And rather than serving as a deterrent, the severity applied by 17th-century legal systems merely meant that the rovers themselves—like other contemporary criminals—grew hardened, behaving wantonly whenever enjoying the upper hand, while fatalistically vowing never to be taken alive so as not to be subjected to such dire fates. The French chronicler Ravenau de Lussan personally observed how even the great pirate chieftain Laurens de Graaf, fearful that he had blundered into a Spanish *armadilla* off the Venezuelan coast in January 1685, ordered two powder kegs brought up on deck and stove in so he would be able to blow up his ship with his own hand—for instant death was preferable "to falling into the hands of men who gave no quarter and would inflict on us hideous tortures, beginning with the captain."[5]

- Likewise, the desperate pirate crew of Louis Guittard's *La Paix* would retreat below decks under the withering fire of HMS *Shoreham* in Virginia's Lynnhaven Bay on April 29, 1700 (O.S.), and threaten to ignite the 30 barrels of gunpowder stored in its hold and die in the blast—along with 50 or so incarcerated English captives—unless they were granted quarter.

- As boarding parties swarmed aboard Stede Bonnet's grounded pirate sloop *Royal James* at the mouth of North Carolina's Cape Fear River on September 27, 1718 (O.S.), he, too—in a despairing gesture—ordered his gunner George Ross to detonate its powder magazine, only to have his surviving crewmen overrule this command and hoist a white flag.
- And while Captain James Skyrme's *Great Ranger* was being riddled by heavy rounds from the powerful warship HMS *Swallow* off the West African coast on February 5, 1722 (O.S.), a half dozen desperadoes fled below into its magazine and stuck a pistol into a barrel of gunpowder, pulling the trigger to blow everyone aboard into oblivion—without noticing in the gloom that this particular barrel was only partially full, so that, although these would-be suicides were horribly burned, their ship did not explode or sink.

And at the subsequent hearing held at the English slave factory at Cape Coast Castle, 52 of Skyrme's pirates were duly condemned to hang, 20 to serve as manual laborers in the Royal African Company's gold mines (a fate that none of them survived), plus 17 more to be transported in chains to Marshalsea Prison in London—only 4 reaching that destination alive.

TORTURE FOR PROFIT

The principal motivations behind the brutal torments inflicted by pirates on their captives sprang from avarice, cruelty, and a misdirected thirst for revenge. The wartime practice of extorting goods and wealth from hapless victims had originated long before the earliest buccaneers. During such recently concluded European conflicts as the Thirty Years War and English Civil War, ill-disciplined bands of unpaid soldiers and sailors had frequently resorted to such harsh measures—sometimes by heartlessly preying upon their own long-suffering civilian populace simply to meet their most basic necessities such as food, drink, or shelter. And ever since medieval times, fighting men had also been offered large bribes to spare the lives of high-ranking noblemen or officers taken upon the battlefield, often retaining such prize captives for weeks or months on end, until every last penny could be squeezed out of their family or friends at home. Such ransoms had furthermore been routinely demanded for Christians taken and held as slaves by the Barbary pirates of North Africa, the Salé or Sallee rovers being among the most ruthless of these practitioners.

West Indian privateers had quickly adopted such tactics as their own, finding them admirably suited to their own narrow self-interests. Starting with their first Spanish American strikes, freebooters would deliberately target as many prominent citizens as possible. Money was rare and banks nonexistent during the 17th century, so currency was commonly concealed in private homes or aboard merchantmen and only revealed to captors under great duress. Unsalaried and unscrupulous young marauders, serving for a share in whatever booty might be obtained, quickly realized the value of extracting details on such hidden treasures, after which they also extorted payments of additional ransoms against the release of their prey from worried family members or friends.

The Ordeal at Veracruz, May 1683

An infamous case that typified these hard-hearted piratical practices was recorded in vivid detail by the eyewitnesses interviewed by the Mexican authorities after the abrupt seizure and four-day pillage of the port city of Veracruz in May 1683 by 800 rovers under Laurens de Graaf and the Sieur de Grammont. Already familiar with this city's approaches and layout, the marauders had stolen silently over its low walls at night, taken up positions outside major buildings and homes in the darkness, and caught its sleeping garrison and citizenry utterly by surprise when explosive fusillades erupted at dawn. Captain Jorge de Algara, a militia officer who happened to be patrolling the streets that night, was cornered and beaten into submission, later reporting that one of his buccaneer captors had gleefully informed him in broken Spanish: *Tú eres capitán y tienes muchos dineros* ("You are a captain, and have much money.")

A couple of thousand terrified captives were then herded into La Merced Church as dawn broke, from where leading citizens would be led out one at a time that same morning, to be tormented. A wealthy Irish-born merchant named John Murphy declared that he was dragged out at 8:00 A.M. into a jeering mob of corsairs awaiting him in the Plaza Mayor and "received by Lorencillo himself [de Graaf]."[6] The Irishman's hands were tied behind his back, and he was hoisted up to swing on the city scaffold, painfully suspended from his inverted arms—a brutal 17th-century military punishment known as the *strappado*. As he dangled there,

> with terrible pain and hurt, they told him to confess where he had his money and silver, to which he responded that those who had entered his house had taken everything.[7]

This could not be, his tormentors insisted, but Murphy gasped out that he had been left penniless. Even his silver service, which had been cast

The strappado, a painful public punishment, as depicted in *The Miseries and Misfortunes of War* by Jacques Callot, 1633. (Grosjean Collection, Paris, France / The Bridgeman Art Library)

down the well before the looters had penetrated into his home, had been retrieved. At this,

> Lorencillo slashed him in the head with his cutlass, opening up a serious wound, then clubbed him many times on the body, almost killing him, before having him cut down and taken upstairs into the Governor's palace, where a pirate surgeon attended him.[8]

Nor was Murphy's ordeal entirely over, for after being patched up and thrust into a small cell where the Spanish governor already lay covered in his own wounds, Grammont entered and, pointing a carbine directly in the Irishman's face, ordered him to confess what monies he and his neighbors had. Again Murphy replied that he had lost everything and did not know his neighbors' wealth, at which the *flibustier* chief stormed out angrily.

Outside, the cruel business continued, as other prominent citizens and clerics were brought forth to undergo similar brutalities. Father Bernabé de Soto, the frail rector of the Jesuit college—who seemed much older than his 54 years because of his long service among the northern missions—was forced to kneel before the pirates. He was told that the governor had offered 70,000 pesos for his ransom; how much could the Jesuit raise?

The rector paused and said that he might obtain 500 pesos. "No sooner had he uttered these words" than a *flibustier* lashed him across the back with a leather strap, sending the elderly Jesuit sprawling into the dirt, where a couple more blows followed. A knife was placed at the Father's throat, then one of the Frenchmen growled that "his life would be spared, but he must irremissibly give 50,000 *pesos.*"[9]

As the Jesuit was being hustled into the Casas Reales, the Franciscan *guardián* had a noose placed around his neck and was repeatedly hoisted into the air to dangle there, before learning that his own ransom had been set at 200,000 pesos. The same figure was arbitrarily assigned for the Dominican prior, after which the pirates resorted to more wholesale methods. Barrels of gunpowder were wheeled into La Merced, and the horrified throng was told that these were about to be detonated. "This produced a great screaming and tumult," one later recounted, as men and women fought to back away from the lethal charge. Soon this shouting subsided, as de Graaf bellowed in Spanish above the din

> that if they surrendered their money, they would be spared; and when it seemed to the pirates that some hesitated, they called again for the fuses to be lit, at which the clamor returned.[10]

Eventually, a sum of 80,000 additional pesos was affixed, and the hiding places of numerous smaller caches were revealed.

The pirates then spent the next two days pillaging and vandalizing every warehouse and residence in Veracruz before providing their principal hostages with paper and pens to write pleas to their loved ones in Mexico's interior, beseeching that together they raise a combined total of 150,000 pesos as the agreed-upon ransom to secure their release and spare the city from being torched upon its evacuation. These pleas were passed to nearby viceregal officials to be forwarded inland, after which the pirates suddenly drove most of their prisoners into a long column, loaded each with a bundle of bulk booty such as sacks of flour, grains, gunpowder, and bolts of cloth and forced them to carry these riches for a mile southeastward—to be transferred offshore, as the pirate fleet had swung around to drop anchor at Sacrificios Island. Any laggards were beaten or shot if they did not keep pace in this unhappy column, so that dozens of bodies soon littered this trail. One week later, chests containing the stipulated ransom were finally delivered to the pirates, and, after culling more than 1,000 blacks and mulattos from among their throng of parched and starving captives on Sacrificios Island, the engorged freebooter fleet stood away in triumph.

Repeat Pattern of Abuse

The atrocities inflicted at Veracruz would come to be repeated many more times over the ensuing decades by other bloody-minded pirates likewise bent upon extracting as much wealth as possible from their defenseless victims. Some of the more large-scale cases would occur after major captures:

- In July 1685, de Graaf and Grammont seized another Mexican seaport—Campeche—only to be disappointed by the meager booty left behind in this forewarned city. Therefore, after six weeks of fruitless occupation, Grammont's *flibustiers* celebrated Louis XIV's feast day with fireworks and festivities on August 25, 1685, then the next morning sent a threatening message inland to the governor of Yucatán, demanding 80,000 pesos and 400 head of cattle to leave its buildings intact upon withdrawing. Refused, they torched its houses next dawn, after which Grammont paraded all his captives in Campeche's Plaza Mayor on August 28 and hanged six before the survivors begged de Graaf—"whom they knew to be more humane than the Frenchman"—to intercede so that this brutality might cease, and the cruel occupiers at last sailed away.
- Next July 1686, a roving band of buccaneers under Captain Francis Townley surprised a Spanish mule train on the outskirts of Panama

City, taking 300 captives—two of their heads being sent to the *Audiencia* president to compel him to begin supplying these pirates with cattle, sheep, and flour on a regular basis. After a month of this extortion, a sudden sortie by three Spanish vessels surprised the anchored freebooter flotilla but failed to drive it off—and an infuriated Townley sent in another 20 heads as punishment.

- Guayaquil was surprised by a stealthy pirate river force in April 1687, its terrified citizenry also being herded into its main church and the wealthiest then singled out for special attention. The wounded garrison commander, for example, was beaten on his back with sword blades in front of his weeping family while fearsome pirates roared demands at the other cowering prisoners for ransoms to be raised. To ruthlessly drive home this point, seven or eight rich Spaniards were dragged down to the riverbank as well, along with all the clerics, to witness while one was selected at random and murdered by a pistol shot before the remainder were clapped up again within the overcrowded church.

- As much as 10 years afterward, in one of the last actions of King William's War, the 900 to 1,000 *flibustiers* who had participated as auxiliaries in the siege of the Colombian port of Cartagena, reacted with like cruelty upon being cheated out of their share of booty by the French commanding general. Having angrily debated this matter for several days among themselves, the surly rank-and-file buccaneers eventually violated the capitulation terms by swarming back into the devastated city—ignoring the protests of their leaders—to round up every Spaniard they could lay their hands on and inflict savage tortures until an additional 1,000 crowns per *flibustier* was raised.

And just as famous, large-scale conquests were to be marred by these types of excesses, the unpaid rovers' insatiable thirst for plunder meant that even minor captures could often be characterized by some very dark deeds as well. The brigand crew of the lawless French renegade Jean Hamlin was notorious for being specially equipped to inflict such torments. Early in 1683, they intercepted the Royal African Company slaver *Thomas and William* while it was making from Barbados toward Jamaica. Its captain, Richard North, later recounted how these corsairs manned his vessel, transferred their prisoners aboard Hamlin's flagship *Trompeuse*, and steered into a quiet bay on the nearby coast to torture their principal captives at leisure by "squeezing their thumbs and privy members in vices, hanging them up in the brails by their hands tied behind them; and so found out what riches they carried."[11] A few months later off Cape Lopus in West Africa, some English pirates in the company of Hamlin boarded the Royal African Company ship *Eaglet* one evening and "stretched [its captain John]

Waffe and his officers, and put screws on their thumbs to make them confess what gold they had."

Unfortunately, any listing of such cruel extortions would be very long and extend right up to the end of the age of piracy. For instance, Master Robert Leonard of the snow *Eagle* out of New York had the misfortune to be manhandled by Captain Edward England's hard-hearted ruffians out in the open Atlantic in February 1718, relating how he had been

> taken and his ship plundered by a pirate ship. The commander beat him with his cutlass for not bringing to at first shot, and the pirates threatened to sink his vessel and throw him overboard with a double-headed shot about his neck, if he concealed where his money was.[12]

In another account published in the June 6–13, 1723 (O.S.), edition of the *American Weekly Mercury* newspaper, four homeward-bound New

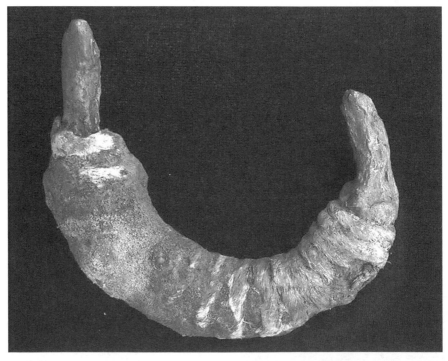

Fragment of a leg iron recovered from Blackbeard's lost flagship *Queen Anne's Revenge*, formerly a slaver; such restraints were also commonly employed on unruly crewmembers and pirate captives. This particular artifact was originally wrapped in cord so as to minimize chafing on a prisoner's leg. (Wendy Welsh/North Carolina Department of Cultural Resources)

England trading sloops had been intercepted off the western tip of Cuba that spring by a different pack of pirates under the villainous Captain Ned Low, who viciously "cut and whipped some, and others they burnt with matches between their fingers to the bone, to make them confess where their money was."

Penniless Spanish *guardacostas* were often accused of similar mistreatment for profit as well. In March 1725, Master James Wilkins of the sloop *Sarah and Mary* out of Philadelphia was intercepted off Hispaniola by a gang of Cuban corsairs while bearing a cargo of cocoa and salt homeward from Curaçao during peacetime. Even as he was clambering aboard this intercepting vessel, Wilkins "received a great blow on his head with a cutlass, and then was stripped of his coat, hat, and silver shoe-buckles."[13] The mulatto commander of this cutthroat crew refused to identify himself, and when the injured master demanded

> by what authority they took him, the Spanish Captain directed the point of his sword to affirmant's breast and answered that was commission enough for him, adding: "Goddamn you, hold your tongue or I'll run you through!"[14]

Dropping anchor off Saona Island to pillage their prize at leisure, two of these corsair crewmen thereupon

> beat him [Wilkins], and throwing a rope about his neck, threatened to hang him if he would not discover what he had on board. Among many other violences, the Spaniards inflicted a very deep wound, quite to his thigh-bone, and thereupon he shew'd 700 pieces-of-eight silver and four pistoles gold, all which they took. Then they cut and much bruised this affirmant with cutlasses by the Spanish Captain's order, because he had not discovered the money sooner.[15]

After being detained aboard for almost a month, Wilkins and two of his merchant sailors were callously dropped into the water off Saint Thomas in the Virgin Islands to swim ashore as best they could, staggering onto its beach exhausted and utterly destitute.

TORTURE FOR SPITE

During the early 18th century, the long-practiced brutalization of prisoners by pirates seemingly worsened, coming to include many spiteful acts out of sheer mean-spirited maliciousness as rovers grew ever more alienated and desperate. Sometimes an insignificant matter might provoke a vicious outburst, such as when the pirate flotilla of

Louis Guittard intercepted the brigantine *Barbados Merchant* of Liver-pool on the morning of April 23, 1700 (O.S.), about 30 leagues from the Virginia Capes. These high-strung rovers had flown into a rage after its peacetime merchant sailors had refused their offer of joining the pirates' ranks. In a sudden outburst, Master William Fletcher was stripped and almost beaten to death, after which the marauders pro-ceeded to avenge this perceived slight by cutting away all of *Barba-dos Merchant's* masts, bowsprit, sails, and rigging, disabling its helm, smashing compasses, even stealing every candle aboard to leave them helplessly adrift. Then, as Guittard's four vessels had paraded past their crippled victim to continue northeast as evening fell, the pirates called tauntingly to the traumatized crew left stranded aboard: "Why have you cut away your masts?"

Many freebooter captains and their followers nursed particular grudges, such as Charles Vane's thuggish crew aboard his flagship *Ranger,* who hated all Bermudans. As a result, after capturing the sloop *William and Martha* of Master Edward North in the Bahamian archi-pelago in April 1718, this horrified commander would later report this treatment of one of his crewmembers:

> they bound hands and feet and ty'd (upon his back) down to the bow-sprit, with matches to his eyes burning and a pistol loaded with the muzzle into his mouth, thereby to oblige him to confess what money was on board.[16]

Captain Ned Low, once a lowly rigger in a Boston shipyard, was also infamous for his savage outbursts. It was widely reported how, upon capturing the rich Portuguese ship *Nossa Senhora da Vitoria* in the Lesser Antilles in January 1723, he had allegedly butchered most of its crew in a fit of rage after its captain had deliberately dropped a bag containing 11,000 gold *moidores* into the sea rather than surrender them to the pirates. And later that same summer, Low's ruffians had openly bragged to some other appalled listeners about having burned "the *King George* and a snow belonging to New York, and sunk one of the New England ships, and cut off one the master's ears and slit his nose."[17]

Masters who had the misfortune of falling into the hands of sail-ors whom they had previously mistreated received no pity. Off Sierra Leone, the small snow *Cadogan* of Bristol was intercepted during the autumn of 1718 by Edward England's flotilla, and its master, Peter Skinner, was ordered aboard the pirate flagship *Pearl.* Immediately upon reaching its deck, Skinner was recognized by his former boat-swain, whom he had gotten rid of along with a few other troublesome hands during a previous voyage by deliberately having them pressed into the Royal Navy. Skinner had even refused to pay their overdue wages as they were being dragged off his ship, so that now the vengeful boatswain and his piratical comrades vowed to repay "all in your own coin."[18] Skinner was lashed to the windlass and pelted with broken bottles, then untied to stagger bloodily about the deck while being whipped, until he finally collapsed. Since he had been such a good master, the boatswain sneeringly told his prostrate form he would be given an easy death—and thereupon shot him through the head.

In a remarkable display of savagery in the spring of 1721, the ship *Irwin* out of Cork in Ireland was brutally sacked off the coast of Martinique by a pirate vessel—possibly Captain Thomas Antis's brigantine *Good Fortune*—and during a particularly ugly and violent frenzy, 21 of these outlaws raped and tossed a woman passenger into the sea while she was still alive, and then viciously beat another passenger in front of his family because he had attempted to intervene. By the closing stages of the age of piracy, such actions had turned most of the world against the last few rovers.

MISTREATMENT BETWEEN PIRATES

Not surprisingly, outlaw sea rovers could also heap abuse upon each other, especially whenever they moved to cast out unwanted members. For example, after capturing the galley *Providence* in late April 1699 (O.S.), the mixed pirate crew of Captain Hind fell out among themselves over command of this 22-gun prize. Hind had been defeated after a violent confrontation and marooned along with 15 other beaten colleagues on the remote, uninhabited Berry Islands on the outer fringes of the Bahamian archipelago—abandoned there with only "three small arms and a bottle of gunpowder"[19] to keep themselves alive. And as piracy turned ever more blatantly criminal and desperate during the second and third decades of the 18th century, such acts of internal violence only got worse.

Like modern street gangs, pirates would usually turn upon any individual who expressed a desire to quit their criminal group. Governor Peter Heywood of Jamaica would report to London about one such instance, when the ruffianly crew of a passing pirate sloop had burdened a tiny turtling vessel in late December 1716 with three men and a boy that they were expelling from their ship—yet not without "first whipping them inhumanely, and burning matches between their fingers, ears, and toes." In particular, the governor noted how the young lad—"who I take to be about twelve or thirteen years of age"—had been punished for having dared to say that he wanted to quit their company, at which the enraged pirates had vowed that they would not let him go "without a daudorus, as they called it—a good whipping."[20]

Individuals who stole from shipmates could also be dealt with very harshly by pirate crews, according to their own rules. Among the articles governing the conduct of followers of Bartholomew Roberts, uncovered after the sudden death of that captain—generally esteemed during his career to have been a humane commander—was one rule specifying that any member caught withholding items from any general accumulation of booty would be marooned, while any cutthroat caught stealing from another "shall have his nose and ears slit, and be put ashore where he shall be sure to encounter hardships."

During the last dark days of piracy, marauders took to pressing skilled hands and other specialists out of the merchant vessels they intercepted, obliging them to serve aboard their pirate ships—yet without necessarily inviting them to join in as full-fledged members of the brotherhood. The existence of such unfortunates, nominal shipmates yet wholly at the mercy of the most malicious elements within any crew of cutthroats, could be quite precarious, dependent on the whim of bored and often inebriated thugs. Philip Ashton, a Massachusetts sailor who had the misfortune to be forced out of a Marblehead schooner in June 1722 to serve for several months among the criminal ranks manning the flagship *Fancy* of Captain Edward Low, renowned for his cruelty, later recounted how he "could never be assured of safety from them, for danger lurked in their very smiles."[21]

NOTES

1. *Calendar of State Papers, Colonial: America and West Indies,* vol. 7 (London: Her Majesty's Stationery Office, 1889), 50.

2. Michael Pawson and David Buisseret, *Port Royal, Jamaica* (Kingston: University of West Indies Press, 1974), 67.

3. John Cordy Jeaffreson, ed., *Middlesex County Records,* vol. 4 (London, 1892), 300.

4. Dr. Philip Henry George Gosse, *The Pirates' Who's Who* (New York: Dulau, 1924), 24.

5. Ravenau de Lussan, *Journal of a Voyage into the South Seas* (Cleveland: Arthur H. Clark, 1930), 44.

6. David F. Marley, *Sack of Veracruz: The Great Pirate Raid of 1683* (Windsor, Ontario: Netherlandic Press, 1993), 47.

7. Ibid.

8. Ibid.

9. Ibid., 48.

10. Ibid.

11. *Calendar of State Papers, Colonial: America and West Indies*, vol. 11 (London: Her Majesty's Stationery Office, 1898), 519.

12. *Calendar of State Papers, Colonial: America and West Indies*, vol. 30 (London: Her Majesty's Stationery Office, 1930), 413.

13. *Calendar of State Papers, Colonial: America and West Indies*, vol. 37 (London: Her Majesty's Stationery Office, 1937), 156.

14. Ibid.

15. Ibid.

16. *Calendar of State Papers*, vol. 30, 263.

17. David F. Marley, *Pirates of the Americas*, vol. 2 (Santa Barbara, CA: ABC-CLIO, 2010), 692.

18. John, *General History*, 86.

19. *Calendar of State Papers, Colonial: America and West Indies*, vol. 17 (London: Her Majesty's Stationery Office, 1908), 445.

20. *Calendar of State Papers, Colonial: America and West Indies*, vol. 29 (London: Her Majesty's Stationery Office, 1930), 212.

21. Edward E. Leslie, *Desperate Journeys, Abandoned Souls* (New York: Houghton Mifflin, 1988), 87.

9

RELIGION

I am here deprived of converse, both with scholars and Christians, few here even of the better sort, caring to see a minister out of the pulpit.

—Rev. Francis Crow from Port
Royal, Jamaica, March 1687

Not surprisingly, the far-ranging and intermingled bands of pirates roaming across the tropical seas came from many different religious backgrounds, none being particularly distinguished for their piety. As early as 1630, Puritan zealots had established private Caribbean communes on Tortuga and Providencia Islands, from where some preyed upon passing Spanish vessels. Seven years later, an English-born Catholic priest who was traveling through these same waters aboard a Spanish merchantman, would record:

The greatest fear that I perceived possessed the Spaniards in this voyage, was about the island of Providence, called by them Santa Catarina, from whence they feared lest some English ships should come out against them with great strength. They cursed the English in it, and called the island the den of thieves and pirates.[1]

Some of these early Puritan seafarers would prove to be as rough and uncouth as any marauders who have ever sailed: men such as the transplanted Bostonian Captain John Aylett, who, while in command of a State warship at Jamaica in February 1660, had allegedly "again given himself over to debauchery and drunkenness, and he stands indicted of burglary for stealing £8 out of a chest."[2] Nine years afterward, discharged from the navy and now in command of a privateer, Aylett would be killed while dining aboard Henry Morgan's flagship *Oxford* in an accidental explosion while riding at anchor off Ile-à-Vache at the southwestern tip of Haiti, preparing for a raid against Cartagena.

Another early West Indian rover from a Puritan background would be Captain Charles Hadsell, who served with some notoriety under both Edward Mansfield and Morgan and ended his days smuggling logwood out of the Bay of Campeche in Mexico—being last recorded as having reached Port Royal in August 1675 with a small ketch, aboard which the future buccaneer-chronicler William Dampier would soon ship out as a hand. Robert Searle, Sir Thomas Whetstone, and Thomas Paine were also early West Indian freebooters who came from Puritan families.

ANTIPATHY AGAINST THE CATHOLIC CHURCH

Many of the earliest freebooters who prowled the Caribbean during the mid-17th century had been raised in various Protestant denominations—such as Dutch Calvinists and French Huguenots—and, although the young marauders themselves might not have been very observant, especially while on campaign, the historical antagonism between their faith and the Catholic Church would still color many of their actions against the Spaniards. Only a few decades earlier, Protestant prisoners had been very harshly treated by the Inquisition, and while the Holy Office might have since lost much of its power, resentments lingered.

Clerics were therefore sometimes singled out to be brutalized as prisoners in ways that would be shocking to us today. When Morgan surprised the Panamanian town of Portobelo at daybreak on July 11, 1668, his buccaneers quickly rounded up a group of prominent captives—including two friars, several women, and nuns—to act as a human shield for an assault column that was to storm its main Santiago de la Gloria citadel with torches and axes. The defenders reluctantly opened fire, wounding both friars and killing an Englishman, but were unable to prevent their fortress from being carried in a bloodbath.

Two years later, having sacked the Nicaraguan city of Granada in September 1670, the Dutch-born leader of a raiding party of Jamaican buccaneers, Laurens Prins or Lawrence Prince, drove home his

Contemporary woodcut of Henry Morgan's raiders fighting their way into the Cuban town of Puerto Principe—modern Camaguey—in March 1668. Note its church spire in the background, one of many buildings that were ruthlessly pillaged over the next three days. (Alexandre Olivier Exquemelin, *The Buccaneers of America: A True Account of the Most Remarkable Assaults* [London: Swan Sonnenschein & Co., 1893])

demand for 70,000 pesos in ransom for the release of his hostages by sending the Spanish authorities the head of a priest in a basket, and saying that he would deal with the rest of the prisoners in the same way. Clergymen were in fact considered high-value captives, commanding high ransoms, and so were often specially targeted: the French *flibustier* Captain Pierre La Garde and his English subordinate John Coxon surprised Santa Marta on the Spanish Main in June 1677, then casually carried away its bishop, Lucas Fernández y Piedrahita, when they withdrew, dropping this prelate off a month afterward at Port Royal, Jamaica. Despite his fright and discomfiture, this cleric had fared much better than his unfortunate colleagues would six years later at Veracruz; they endured fearsome mistreatment at the hands of their captors as described in chapter 8.

It was standard practice whenever buccaneers pillaged a Spanish American town to herd all their prisoners into the town's principal church, which was usually the largest building available. For example, it was recorded that, when John Morris and David Martien had surprised Granada in late June 1665, they had "secured in the great church 300 of the best men prisoners, abundance of which were churchmen, plundered for sixteen hours, discharged all the prisoners, sunk all the boats, and so came away."[3] And after the pirate horde under Laurens de Graaf and the Sieur de Grammont had withdrawn from their occupation of Veracruz in May 1683, Spaniards openly wept at the shambles left behind in its Merced Church, including the bodies of infants and elderly who had died in its heat and press. Naturally, they would seek to retaliate in kind whenever possible, such as when a Franco-Cuban raiding force surprised Nassau in September 1703 and burnt the town and church to ashes before departing.

Fully cognizant of the irreligious nature of their piratical foes, the Spanish Americans would even devise a system of passwords known as *santo y seña* or "saint and countersign," based on the Church calendar. If a vessel or fortress were approached by strangers after nightfall, they would be challenged by a sentry shouting out a saint's name at random, which was to be answered by correctly identifying the corresponding place associated with that particular saint—to a cry of "Santa Rosa," for instance, the proper reply would be "Lima;" to "San Francisco Javier," the answer was "Navarra;" and so on. This system had been introduced with heretical English or Dutch pirates in mind, as they would never have such pious answers ready on their lips. Moreover, such a flexible system permitted Spanish vessels to depart on protracted voyages without worrying about a specific password having been altered during their absence.

SUPERSTITION AND RITUAL

Catholics serving among the earliest pirates' ranks were more conflicted, in that their hostility against the Spaniards did not extend into religious antagonism. Although not exceptionally reverent, and indeed capable of wanton acts of desecration (such as the destruction of Margarita Island's church bells by the Marquis de Maintenon's French occupiers in February 1677), they were generally less hostile toward the Catholic Church than their Protestant colleagues. When

Mansfield had reclaimed Providencia Island from the Spaniards in May 1666, leading a small force comprised of 200 buccaneers—100 of them being Englishmen, 80 *flibustiers* from Tortuga, plus a few Dutch and Portuguese—his French followers had interceded to prevent the English from ransacking its church.

Maintenon returned to Margarita Island on a peaceful visit in January 1682, informing its Spanish authorities that he was under orders from his king to patrol the Caribbean against pirates and restore stolen goods. A few jewels, money, and garments were handed over, expropriated from some *flibustiers* on Martinique who had pillaged them from a Spanish piragua bearing servants of the Venezuelan bishop, Marcos de Sobremonte, as it was sailing from Cumaná toward La Guaira. On the other hand, though, this gesture was offset by the brutality with which Grammont's *flibustiers* would abuse the monastic leaders of Veracruz during their sack of that city in May 1683, this fearsome chieftain even riding his horse directly inside La Merced Church to herd its terrified clerics out into the streets, to be loaded down to act as porters for the departing pirate horde.

Naturally, religious observance was a commonplace feature of everyday life throughout the 17th and 18th centuries, regardless of one's faith or piety. Sunday was universally recognized as a day of rest, even among pirates—as late as 1722, the written covenant governing the conduct of Captain Bartholomew Roberts's crew would conclude with this final article: "The musicians shall have rest on the Sabbath Day only, by right; on all other days, by favor only." Realizing how many people slept in on Sundays, rovers would sometimes deliberately take advantage of this practice for their own nefarious ends by timing strikes to coincide with those particular mornings. For example:

- An hour before daybreak on July 10, 1678—a Sunday—a large group appeared out of the predawn darkness at one of the small landward gates of the Mexican port of Campeche, answered the sentinel's perfunctory challenge, and quietly shuffled into the streets; although rather than native worshipers come early for morning church services, as the sleepy sentry had assumed in the gloom, they were actually 160 buccaneers under Captains George Spurre and Edward Neville come to plunder the city.

- Before sunrise on another Sunday, April 23, 1684, the freebooter Captain John Markham of New York City silently disembarked a force from three frigates and eight sloops near the Mexican port of Tampico, and traumatized survivors would later relate how he then "led his men in an encircling maneuver and firing musketry at the Spaniards,"[4] until other buccaneers could overrun the startled town.

- At 4:00 A.M. on yet another Sunday, April 20, 1687, the joint pirate formation of Captains François Grogniet, Pierre Le Picard, and George Dew came gliding across the inky, muddy waters of the Guayas River, deep inside Ecuador, to surprise the sleeping city of Guayaquil.

Sometimes, raiders chose Church festival days for their descents. Late in March 1660, an expedition of 400 vengeful *boucaniers* from Tortuga Island off Haiti burst out of the jungle to surprise the Dominican border town of Santiago de los Caballeros on Easter weekend. The French priest, Jean-Baptiste Du Tertre, who subsequently recorded an account of this attack, could not refrain from adding his own commentary—that these raiders did not live to prosper from their booty, in particular the church ornaments they had impiously pillaged on that Easter Sunday, as many of them later "perished unfortunately." And when the mercenary Biagio Michele or "Blas Miguel" led a strike by Cuban corsairs against Saint-Domingue's *flibustier* capital of Petit-Goâve with the express intent of killing or capturing their great leader Laurens de Graaf, he chose to attack at dawn on a particular Sunday—August 10, 1687, which coincided with the Church feast day honoring Saint Lawrence, when de Graaf was sure to be relaxing in his home port, in anticipation of celebrating his saint day.

Yet beyond such tactical considerations, pirates—like virtually all other seamen of that age—could be quite superstitious, and thus prone to channel their trust into ritualized beliefs. Another French chronicler-priest, Jean-Baptiste Labat, noted the following ceremony in his *Memoirs* as having occurred on March 6, 1694, shortly after his arrival on the Antillean island of Martinique during King William's War:

> We were busy all this morning confessing a crew of *flibustiers* who had arrived at Les Mouillages with two prizes that they had captured from the English. The Mass of the Virgin was celebrated with all solemnity, and I blessed three large loaves which were presented by the captain and his officers, who arrived at the church accompanied by the drums and trumpets of their corvette. At the beginning of Mass, the corvette fired a salute with all her cannons. At the elevation of the Holy Sacrament she fired another salvo, at the benediction a third, and finally a fourth when we sang the *Te Deum* after Mass.
>
> All the *flibustiers* contributed 30 *sols* to the sacristy, and did so with much piety and modesty. This may surprise people in Europe, where *flibustiers* are not credited with possessing much piety, but as a matter of fact they generally give a portion of their good fortunes to the churches. If church ornaments or church linen happen to be in the prizes they capture, the *flibustiers* always present them to their parish church.[5]

Ruins of Panama's 17th-century cathedral, abandoned when the entire city was relocated into a more defensible position five miles away, a couple of years after Henry Morgan's devastating sack of the original settlement in 1671. (Steven Miric)

A much more remarkable incident had occurred a decade earlier in Veracruz's main square, when 14 pirates had been publicly executed on the morning of June 14, 1684. A witness described how the cord had burst while one of these convicted men was being garroted

> and having been retied by the executioner, broke again; at which said prisoner fell to the ground and Lic. Don Froilán del Páramo Montenegro, curate who as attending the condemned, shouted out that this man had offered himself up to the Virgin, and God did not wish him to die.[6]

Some clerics had thereupon pushed forward from the crowd, lifted the lucky pirate, and carried him to sanctuary in the Jesuit college, despite the guards' attempts to prevent their intercession.

RELIGIOUS OUTCASTS

France's Huguenots

During the 1680s, whatever lingering religious allegiances might have been held by various Antillean freebooters would undergo a defining transformation. In France, the Sun King, Louis XIV, moved to assert his absolute power over that entire nation, its overseas colonies, and peoples by subordinating all its organized religions. An assembly of Catholic clergymen had agreed in November 1681 to curtail all papal prerogatives, so that henceforth bishops could not leave France or any of its territories, legates could not arrive, royal officials could not be excommunicated, nor any ecclesiastical laws made without the king's consent. And to achieve unanimity in all religious fields, Louis also moved against his 800,000 to 900,000 Huguenot subjects by ordering royal dragoons quartered in Protestant homes as of that same year, with orders to mistreat their residents until they too converted to his new official version of Catholicism.

Amid this wave of intolerance, hundreds of thousands of Huguenots would begin to flee into Protestant realms, including many seamen in the West Indies—such as Captain Pierre LePain, who arrived at Port Royal, Jamaica, early in 1682 to request English citizenship, followed some time later by the well-known *flibustier* Captain Jean Tristan, as well as Jean Leroux, who emigrated to New York City to obtain naturalization there in the spring of 1692. Such refugees would be viewed as traitors by their former compatriots, and thus stigmatized as pirates for whatever actions they might subsequently take at sea, while being regarded as subjects of suspect English loyalty during any wars involving France.

England's Irish Catholics

A similar realignment based upon religious beliefs would occur among English freebooters as well, after the unpopular James II—a staunch Catholic—was deposed in December 1688 amid fears that he intended to impose his faith upon that Protestant kingdom. At first, some privateers who retained commissions issued by the exiled James were denounced as pirates (to which they vehemently countered that their licenses were in fact the only legitimate ones, unlike those issued in name of the Protestant usurpers, William and Mary), but most freebooters quickly conformed to the authority of these two new joint rulers.

Nevertheless, a few English Catholic rovers who had switched allegiance prior to this upheaval—such as the frustrated Captain John Philip Beare—would be joined over ensuing years by a few more professing loyalty to the exiled Stuart monarchy. One such noteworthy turncoat would be the Jamaican renegade Nathaniel Grubing or Grubbing, who—having been born on that island—proved to be exceptionally adept at leading raids after he took up service with the French of Saint-Domingue during King William's War in the early 1690s. His detailed knowledge of Jamaica allowed Grubing to steal along its familiar coastlines and lead landing parties ashore "in the night upon lone settlements near the sea, and robbing them of all they had, and away again before any notice could be given for any strength to come against him."[7] The English authorities angrily resented his defection and treachery, offering hefty bounties against his capture, as they regarded Grubing as little more than an outright criminal.

The unshakeable Catholic faith held by many Irish subjects would make them suspect in the eyes of all English authorities. The activities of Captain John Hoar or Hore, for example, were viewed with particular suspicion after he brought a wealthy French prize into Rhode Island for adjudication with his frigate *Dublin* early in 1694, despite bearing a perfectly legitimate commission from Governor Sir William Beeston of Jamaica. Thomas Burke, a peacetime pirate, would be vehemently denounced for sowing destruction among the fishing fleets off Newfoundland in the summer of 1699, before steering far south and dying near Barbados, much to the delight of Crown officers. Two decades later, reports of the widespread depredations being committed by the notorious Edward Seegar or Edward England would almost unfailingly include a mention of his Irish birth.

Even worse, the Catholic upbringing of many Irishmen would allow them to more easily switch allegiance to such foreign powers as France or Spain and be welcomed into the ranks of these traditional enemies of England. The renegade Richard Noland, after operating as an outright pirate out of lawless Nassau during the autumn of 1717, was able to transfer to neighboring Cuba and readily secure a license to patrol as a *guardacosta* for the next five years, much resented by his English victims. And during the ensuing War of the Quadruple Alliance, a Royal Navy snow would be specifically dispatched under a flag of truce from Jamaica in February 1720 to present a formal complaint to the Spanish authorities on Cuba about the privateering activities of Christopher Winter and Nicholas Brown—two Catholic rovers who were a great nuisance, preying upon English interests as licensed commanders under Spanish colors. Not surprisingly, this complaint was simply ignored.

ANTISOCIAL ANGER AND HOSTILITY

The final generation of rovers who blatantly operated as lawless criminals during the decade after Queen Anne's War had concluded in 1713 were seemingly untroubled by religious scruples, or indeed most other kinds of societal restraint. Mercenaries whose services were no longer valued or wanted, they conducted themselves as men warring against the world, desperadoes with little to lose.

Their attitude toward all religions seemed embittered by disappointments, hardened by the cruelties of everyday life. When Captain "Black Sam" Bellamy captured a Bostonian sloop in April 1717, he allegedly harangued its master, arguing that it was better to sail freely as a pirate than submit to lesser men, simply because they were rich. The master replied that he dared not break the laws of God and man, to which Bellamy derisively snorted that there was "no arguing with such sniveling puppies, who allow superiors to kick them about deck at pleasure, and pin their faith upon a pimp of a parson—a squab, who neither practices nor believes what he puts upon the chuckle-headed fools he preaches to!"[8]

As ever, the Sabbath was viewed merely as a day of rest among pirates, and sometimes as a tactical advantage for their own nefarious ends. On Friday, June 15, 1722 (O.S.), Captain Ned Low deliberately lay in wait with his brigantine *Rebecca* inside Port Roseway at the southwestern tip of Nova Scotia, knowing from past experience what to expect: in accordance with long-established custom ashore, many religious-minded New England skippers would depart the nearby Grand Banks fisheries prior to any weekend to drop anchor in a quiet harbor and spend the Lord's Day in restful contemplation without any labors beyond routine shipboard duties. Therefore, on that fateful Friday, 13 such "Sunday Keeper" fishing schooners from Marblehead began filing into Port Roseway to find the pirates already waiting for them inside; the pirates pillaged them of everything they owned.

NOTES

1. Thomas Gage, *The English-American* (London: privately printed, 1648), 270.

2. *Calendar of State Papers, Colonial: America and West Indies*, vol. 9 (London: Her Majesty's Stationery Office, 1893), 134.

3. *Calendar of State Papers, Colonial: America and West Indies*, vol. 5 (London: Her Majesty's Stationery Office, 1880), 360.

4. David F. Marley, *Pirates of the Americas*, vol. 1 (Santa Barbara, CA: ABC-CLIO, 2008), 236.

5. Jean-Baptiste Labat, *Memoirs, 1693–1705* (London: Routledge, 1970), 36.

6. David F. Marley, *Sack of Veracruz: The Great Pirate Raid of 1683* (Windsor, Ontario: Netherlandic Press, 1993), 67.

7. *Calendar of State Papers, Colonial: America and West Indies*, vol. 14 (London: Her Majesty's Stationery Office, 1903), 327.

8. Capt. Charles Johnson, *General History of the Robberies and Murders of the Most Notorious Pirates* (London: Dent, 1972), 587.

10

FLAGS

[Ned Low] made a black flag, and declared war against all the
world.

—Charles Johnson, *A General and True History*

Adventurers who joined rover bands throughout the great age of
piracy would come to serve under some very unique banners—usually red or black standards adorned with crude depictions of warfare
and death, although a few other background colors were occasionally used. Given the rudimentary means of communication available
throughout this era, as well as widespread illiteracy, flags were an
important means of creating unity and providing guidance in battle as
well as the focus of a unit's pride and self-esteem—plus, for sea-rovers
bent upon pillage and booty, a useful medium for instilling fear into
their intended victims.

ANCIENT PRACTICE

Because of their significance, even such an innocuous civilian group as
the Guild of Merchant Tailors of London owned dozens of ceremonial
flags, listing the following among an inventory compiled in 1609:

- one banner with the King's arms [James I];
- one with the city [of London] arms;

- one ancient and one new banner with the company's arms;
- two older ones with the late Queen's arms [Elizabeth I];
- two long streamers with the Guild's arms on a red background, two more on a blue background, and one on a green one;
- fifty trumpet-banners; etc.

The first 17th-century ensigns flown by independent West Indian privateers had generally adhered to ancient observance in such matters, being understood as intended to supplement the national colors of each ship's company rather than be flown alone.

For example, the dazed Spanish survivors who saw the Sieur de Grammont's *flibustiers* roaring triumphantly in the main square of Veracruz, celebrating their capture of that city at dawn on May 18, 1683, later related how these victors were cheering "the King of France with white flags and fleurs-de-lis, and a red one"[1]—the latter presumably being an individual commander's ensign and, as such, unfamiliar to the Spaniards. Even veteran military officers who studied this same multinational pirate force through spyglasses, as it came snaking out of that devastated city and trudging down Veracruz's sun-bleached shoreline a few days later, recorded that the column was led by "five French flags, four English, a green and a flowered one"[2]—once again, the latter two being unconventional banners, unrecognizable to these experienced European campaigners.

More than a dozen years earlier, Henry Morgan's throng of 1,200 buccaneers—drawn from virtually every country, race, and creed present in the Antilles—had likewise started their final push against Panama City at sunrise on January 28, 1671, by marching in battle array across a lush tropical plain and up the incline of Mata Asnillos Rise behind a bewildering array of "red and green banners and flags"[3] plainly visible to the 1,600 Spaniards waiting expectantly atop its crest.

Over the ensuing decades, most freebooters would continue to sail under their own national flags, plus personalized banners of their leaders. The English authorities tried to regulate this practice among its far-flung seamen, decreeing that private vessels could only fly a white flag and ensign adorned "with a red cross, commonly called St. George's Cross,"[4] plus an "ensign red with the like cross in a canton white at the upper corner thereof, next the staff."[5] Royal Navy warships alone were entitled to hoist "Their Majesties' jack, commonly called the Union Jack,"[6] with clearly marked variants being allowed to such privateer "ships as shall have commissions of letters-of-marque or reprisals against the enemy."[7] However, marauders often continued to roam under unauthorized Union Jacks and numerous other colors long after their wartime licenses had lapsed and the conflicts themselves been resolved.

THE BLOOD-RED PIRATE FLAG

For the entire second half of the 17th century, red remained the preferred background color for most individualized standards flown by freebooter commanders, in no small part because it conveyed such a palpable hint of malice. Ever since Roman times, blood-red banners had been threateningly unfurled before any battle where no quarter was to be given and therefore coincided with the buccaneers' desire to instill fear into their intended victims. And there were even occasions during the course of their Caribbean descents when such pitiless threats were actually put into action.

For example, Morgan had led a smaller band of his buccaneers in a stealthy approach against the unwary Panamanian town of Portobelo, bursting upon its residents at dawn on July 11, 1668, while they were still in bed. The 80-man Spanish garrison asleep inside Santiago de la Gloria citadel had held out for a couple of hours longer, refusing every call to surrender, until Morgan had angrily assembled a body of men for the unpalatable task of storming this fortress. His cutthroats had provided themselves with cover by harnessing a group of captives— including the town's *alcalde mayor,* two friars, plus several women and nuns—to act as a human shield for their assault party, which rushed through a hail of bullets to batter the citadel's gate with axes and torches. The defenders had only reluctantly opened fire, wounding both friars and killing an English freebooter—yet, amid all the din and confusion, failed to notice how another band of rovers was silently scaling up the far side of their fortress, undetected. A horrified Spanish survivor would later recall how, upon planting "their red flag on the castle walls"[8] as they carried Santiago de la Gloria, these buccaneers had proceeded to massacre 45 of its soldiers and left the remainder barely clinging to life, in a bloodbath according to the ruthless dictates of that age.

The Spaniards would also display similar scarlet insignias during armed confrontations against their hated enemy. When Captain Edward Stanley's tiny four-gun Royal Navy warship *Bonito* was driven by bad weather into seeking shelter off the southern Cuban coast in November 1684, while merely conveying dispatches to its Spanish authorities from Jamaica's governor, Stanley would later complain of being mistaken for a pirate and aggressively chased by a local *guardacosta*, whose galley bore down upon him "flying the Spanish flag with a red ensign"[9]—signaling an intent to kill everyone aboard.

In another instance confirming a red flag's special menace, a pirate raiding force that was fighting its way back across Nicaragua in May 1686 under Captains François Grogniet, Jean Rose, and Francis Townsley—retiring to regain their anchored ships, which were awaiting them off the Pacific coast, after having slipped ashore to sack the inland city of Granada—found 500 aroused militiamen barring their path at the town of Masaya. The chronicler Ravenau de Lussan, who was serving among these *flibustier* ranks, later wrote,

> They were flying the red flag, thus giving us to understand there would be no quarter. Upon seeing this, we hauled down our white [French] colors, and exposed a red flag like theirs.[10]

It was just such bloodthirsty banners which were to become known in English as the Jolly Roger, a euphemism believed derived from the French expression *joli rouge* or "happy red"—itself a sardonic reference to the cruel implications of any ensigns in that particular color.

And for this reason, of course, many pirate commanders would continue to embrace red for their personal emblems. Captain Edmond Cooke, for instance, allegedly flew a red flag striped with yellow and emblazoned with a white hand brandishing a sword when his band of marauders had penetrated into the Pacific Ocean along with John Coxon's company in April 1680. And in yet another example of a red flag being closely identified with 17th-century piracy, we have the official deposition given after Massachusetts's colonial sloop *Mary* had sortied from Boston on September 30, 1689 (O.S.), bearing 20 volunteer crewmen under Captain Samuel Pease to hunt down its former commander, Thomas Pound—once a licensed privateer, who had resumed operating offshore since the installation of King William as a Jacobin renegade.

Reaching Wood's Hole four days later, a boat had rowed out to inform Pease that the delinquents were cruising off nearby Tarpaulin Cove, and indeed their vessel was sighted shortly thereafter. The colonial sloop soon overhauled Pound's craft in a stiff south-southeasterly wind, and, as the distance between both vessels narrowed, Pease ordered the king's jack hoisted and a shot from *Mary*'s great gun fired across the renegades' forefoot—at which point it was observed through a glass how a crewman climbed Pound's mast and affixed "the red flag of piracy at the mainmast top."[11]

THE BLACK FLAG OF DEATH

Personalized flags with black backgrounds were to be a later affectation, adopted by pirate captains in the early 18th century and quickly proliferating to become the norm over the next couple of decades. The earliest recorded instance of the display of a black flag is believed to have occurred in July 1700, when Captain John Cranby of HMS *Poole* described the French corsair Emmanuel Wynne's ship as having been chased ashore at the Cape Verde Islands while fighting under "a sable ensign with crossbones, a Death's head, and an hour glass" (the latter to signify that the opponent's time was running out).

Prior to this date, black flags had normally only been flown as a symbol of mourning, raised and sustained for a fixed period of days in the aftermath to any particularly heartfelt loss. Yet by the time the War of the Spanish Succession or Queen Anne's War would conclude in 1713, most pirates had begun to use black backgrounds for their personal standards, supplemented by red ones as their battle flags.

There are many mentions in official records of such practice: for example, Captain James Macrae of the English East Indiaman *Cassandra* would describe the fearsome sight of Edward England's 32-gun

Bartholomew Roberts's personal pirate insignia, allegedly showing himself—sword in hand—standing atop "A Barbadian's Head" and "A Martinican's Head." (Author's Collection)

flagship *Fancy* bearing down upon his anchored merchantman on the morning of August 17, 1720 (O.S.), while lying off lonely Johanna Island near Madagascar, recalling later how this onrushing marauder was "flying a black flag at the main-topmast, a red flag at the fore-topmast, and the cross of Saint George at the ensign staff"—signifying a pirate ship manned mostly by an English crew, boring in with no intent of offering quarter. The memory remained so indelible that Mac-rae would also complain bitterly to his company directors of being abandoned at this terrible moment of peril by two other Indiamen, who weighed and "left us engaged with barbarous and inhuman enemies, with their black and bloody flags hanging over us, and no appearance of escaping being cut to pieces."[12]

Likewise, three years later, Captain Peter Solgard of the 20-gun HMS *Greyhound* would testify in open court at Newport, Rhode Island, that his warship had been mistaken for a trader and pursued by Ned Low's pirate sloops *Fortune* and *Ranger* off Long Island on June 10, 1723 (O.S.), detailing how, "when they came near, they hoisted black flags and fired each a shot, and soon afterwards they hauled down their black flags and hoisted red flags"[13]—at which point the battle became fully joined, ending with the unexpected result (for the unsuspecting rovers) of being beaten and one of their vessels taken, only Low making good his escape.

These black ensigns were often adorned with additional individu-alized symbols, usually representing some form of death—such as a skull, normally referred to in the 18th century as a death's head. Al-though the colorful expression "skull-and-crossbones" did not enter into common usage in the English language until much later on, a report submitted to London from Governor Walter Hamilton of the Antillean island of Antigua on December 14, 1716 (O.S.), described a recent spate of attacks perpetrated in those waters by Sam Bellamy—and specifically mentioned how his pirate sloop *Mary Anne* had run down a hapless pair of trading vessels near the Dutch island of Sabá while flying a large black flag emblazoned with "a Death's Head and Bones a-cross."[14]

Eleven months later, Hamilton would also describe an altogether different kind of pirate standard being flown by another rover, when he recorded the narrow escape of a little British sloop chased through the shoal waters of Saint Thomas in the Virgin Islands by a pirate ship of 18 or 20 guns, which had fired three times at its intended victim: "the first under British colors, which he [the pirate captain] lowered, and then hoisted a white ensign with the figure of a dead man spread in it."[15]

That same November 1717 (O.S.), the English merchantman *Montserrat* had been riding blissfully at anchor in the Lesser Antilles when two large ships and a sloop had come gliding into the same bay. An eager young officer aboard the merchantman named Thomas Knight, "thinking one did belong to Bristol,"[16] had himself rowed across in order to enquire whether these newcomers might be bringing out any mail from home. He was beckoned aboard, but suddenly "seeing Death Head in the stern"[17] as he drew near, Knight realized his mistake and tried to refuse—only to be compelled by growled pirate threats, soon finding himself stepping aboard Blackbeard's newly captured flagship, *Queen Anne's Revenge*.

And black flags were on display in great profusion that next spring, when the expedition bringing out Woodes Rogers to be installed as the Bahamas' first royal governor paused just outside its main harbor—the notorious pirate haunt of New Providence (modern Nassau)—at sunset on July 26, 1718 (O.S.). Unfamiliar with its waters, the Royal Navy sloops *Rose* and *Shark* had gingerly sounded their way around the western end of Hogg (today known as Paradise) Island, while Rogers's heavier ships remained tacking back and forth overnight, three miles farther out at sea.

Just as *Rose* was dropping anchor inside the harbor entrance at 6:30 P.M. that same evening, three warning shots were suddenly fired over the Royal Navy sloop by the large French prize of pirate captain Charles Vane, which was riding at anchor amid a cluster of vessels—all flying black flags. Vane then defiantly sent out a letter outlining his demands before allowing the royal governor to come ashore, and when no reply was received from Rogers by 2:00 A.M. on July 27, 1718 (O.S.), Vane aimed his French prize at the anchored pair of Royal Navy sloops and unleashed it in flames, causing both to cut their cables and sheer away to avoid the blazing inferno.

When Rogers's main squadron approached the western entrance at first light, they could see Vane and 90 diehard followers still stubbornly riding at anchor inside New Providence's harbor aboard the sloop *Katherine*, which his pirates had commandeered from their fellow rover Charles Yeats. As the governor's ships continued to forge closer into the western channel, Vane at last grudgingly got under way, to exit via its eastern channel—prompting Rogers to signal his pair of Royal Navy sloops to pursue, although he was obliged to report later to London how these bold pirates had "fled away in a sloop wearing the black flag, and fir'd guns of defiance when they perceived their sloop outsailed the two that I sent to chase them hence."[18]

Master John Shattock of Salem, Massachusetts, would have the misfortune of confirming Vane's choice of personal standard when his 40-ton brigantine *Endeavour* was intercepted by the pirate off Long Island in the Bahamian archipelago on October 23, 1718 (O.S.), while homeward bound from Kingston, Jamaica. Shattock later declared before a magistrate how *Katherine* "bore down on him, hoisted a black flag, and fired a shot at him."[19] Commanded "to hoist out his boat and come aboard him,"[20] *Endeavour*'s boat crew was furthermore threatened to have "a volley of small shot into them"[21] if they did not hurry, after which both master and crew were subjected to two days of beatings and brutality while their vessel was thoroughly ransacked.

And in yet another recorded instance of the display of such pirate standards, witnesses would recount how that very next summer, a dark-hulled vessel with a black flag fluttering from its masthead—Howell Davis's flagship *King James*—stood into the anchorage off the English slaving station of Anamaboe on the Gold Coast (modern Anomabu, Ghana), robbing three of its waiting English slavers and forcibly removing some prime seamen from among their crews, including the third mate of the merchant galley *Princess* out of London: Bartholomew Roberts.

Roberts would soon agree to become incorporated into the pirate ranks, and shortly thereafter succeed Davis in command, going on to excel as the last great rover chieftain, famous for his own distinctive emblems. Roberts's standard was to be seen by Lieutenant-General William Matthew, the governor of Saint Kitts, after Roberts's new flagship *Royal Fortune* and a consort had stood brazenly into that Antillean island's principal anchorage of Basseterre at 1:00 P.M. on September 27, 1720 (O.S.). Informed of this attack, the governor had galloped hastily to this scene on horseback, arriving an hour later to gaze impotently out from shore through a spyglass and behold how already "the pirates' ship and sloop with black flags, had cut out one ship—that was under sail actually then—and had set two more on fire."[22]

Over the next six months, Roberts would come to station himself on Saint Lucia and inflict such a heavy toll on peacetime merchant shipping bound to and from Martinique that its French governor had pleaded with his British neighbors for help. Cooperation from the governor of Barbados had then so incensed Roberts that he allegedly designed a special pirate jack that showed a figure of himself standing with a sword in his right hand and each foot atop a skull: one having the initials ABH written beneath it to signify "A Barbadian's Head" and the other AMH for "A Martinican's Head." A plate on his cabin door aboard *Royal Fortune* also supposedly bore this same design.

Eventually, Roberts had brought traffic in the Windward Islands to such a standstill by the spring of 1721 that he loaded all his plunder aboard two captured ships and struck out across the Atlantic for West Africa, where his cutthroat band would meet its doom less than a year later. While resting at anchor off Cape Lopez with his three vessels—flagship *Royal Fortune*, plus its lesser consorts *Great Ranger* and *Little Ranger*—a large sail was spotted out at sea on the morning of February 5, 1722 (O.S.) and eagerly assumed to be a rich passing slaver. Roberts therefore ordered his subordinate, Captain James Skyrme, to pursue with *Great Ranger*, which immediately weighed.

Sighting this vessel's departure, its distant prey turned away and ran before the wind, as if afraid, although its solitary pursuer managed to gradually overhaul. By 10:30 A.M. that same morning—Cape Lopez having fallen well below the horizon—Skyrme had closed up sufficiently to open fire with his bow chasers. And as the gap continued to narrow, *Great Ranger*'s decks could be seen lined with almost 100 cutlass-brandishing pirates, while above them streamed a bewildering array of flags—including, most prominently, a black standard. Yet the unwitting marauders were being lured to their death, for this large vessel was not a sparsely manned merchantman but rather the brand-new, 50-gun warship HMS *Swallow* of Captain Chaloner Ogle, sent to hunt down this pirate flotilla.

Half an hour later, the Royal Navy officer decided to spring his trap by abruptly bearing up to starboard, running out his guns, and letting fly with a crushing broadside. The pirates were appalled to discover that they had been drawn directly beneath the muzzles of a heavily armed man-of-war and fell into great confusion. A one-sided firefight ensued in which *Great Ranger* lost its main topmast and suffered 10 dead and 20 wounded, against no casualties aboard the warship. Finally, by 3:00 P.M. that same afternoon, the pirates had endured enough, and a desperately wounded Skyrme—one of his legs having been blown off—agreed to strike his colors. His last command was to order this black flag cast into the sea so that it could not be produced as evidence against him or any of his surviving followers in a court of law.

NOTES

1. Marley, *Sack of Veracruz: The Great Pirate Raid of 1683* (Windsor, Ontario: Netherlandic Press, 1993), 34.

2. Ibid., 54.

3. Nigel Cawthorne, *A History of Pirates: Blood and Thunder on the High Seas* (London: Booksales, 2005), 103.

4. Reginald G. Marsden, *Documents Relating to Law and Custom of the Sea*, vol. 1 (London: Navy Records Society, 1915), 163.

5. Ibid.

6. Ibid.

7. Ibid.

8. David F. Marley, *Pirates of the Americas*, vol. 1 (Santa Barbara, CA: ABC-CLIO, 2010), 256.

9. *Calendar of State Papers, Colonial Series, America and West Indies*, vol. 12 (London: Her Majesty's Stationery Office, 1899), 155.

10. Ravenau de Lussan, *Journal of a Voyage* (Cleveland: Arthur H. Clark, 1930), 132.

11. David F. Marley, *Pirates of the Americas*, vol. 2 (Santa Barbara, CA: ABC-CLIO, 2010), 740.

12. *The Gentleman's Magazine* 109 (London, 1811): 214.

13. Wilkins Updike, ed., *Memoirs of the Rhode Island Bar* (Boston: T. H. Webb, 1842), 268.

14. *Calendar of State Papers, Colonial: America and West Indies*, vol. 29 (London: Her Majesty's Stationery Office, 1930), 230.

15. *Calendar of State Papers, Colonial: America and West Indies*, vol. 30 (London: Her Majesty's Stationery Office, 1930), 148.

16. Ibid., 151.

17. Ibid.

18. Ibid., 373.

19. Colin Woodward, *The Republic of Pirates* (Orlando, FL: Harcourt, 2007), 305.

20. Ibid.

21. Ibid.

22. *Calendar of State Papers, Colonial: America and West Indies*, vol. 32 (London: Her Majesty's Stationery Office, 1933), 166.

11

DOCUMENTS

That race of wicked men.
—epithet from the Council of Trade and Plantations
in London, August 1700

DOCUMENT A.—RESOLUTION OF THE COUNCIL OF JAMAICA, FAVORING THE ISSUANCE OF PEACETIME PRIVATEERING LICENSES AGAINST SPANISH AMERICA, FEBRUARY 1666

*The early foreign footholds struggling to survive in the West Indies re-
lied on buccaneers for more than just their defense. These rovers also
provided a significant proportion of the economic life of these fledgling
outposts, bringing in prizes and booty that helped sustain their commercial livelihood. Whatever vexation might be experienced by Crown ministers in distant Europe, private officials in the Antilles still treasured
repeat visits from such freebooters as they returned from these piratical
depredations.*

*A prime example was to occur in February 1666, a year after the
Second Anglo-Dutch War had erupted back in Europe. English privateers
in the Caribbean had soon begun ignoring ministerial directives to attack
the Dutch, instead joining their French colleagues in descents upon their
traditional foes, the Spaniards—with whom London was at peace. Fearful that too strict an adherence to commissions and adjudications directed*

solely against the Dutch might alienate the mercurial rovers—so that they would shift their allegiance to Saint-Domingue and carry prizes there—Jamaica's merchants enjoined Governor Sir Thomas Modyford to allow Spanish raiding to continue, using the following arguments, which were read into the official minutes of a council meeting held at its inland capital of Santiago de la Vega on February 22, 1666 (O.S.):

Resolved: that it is to the interest of the island to have letters-of-marque granted against the Spaniard.

1. Because it furnishes the island with many necessary commodities at easy rates.
2. It replenishes the island with coin, bullion, cocoa, logwood, hides, tallow, indigo, cochineal, and many other commodities, whereby the men of New England are invited to bring their provisions, and many merchants to reside at Port Royal.
3. It helps the poorer planters, by selling provisions to the men-of-war.
4. It hath and will enable many to buy slaves and settle plantations, as Harmenson, Guy, Brimacain, and many others who have considerable plantations.
5. It draws down yearly from the Windward Islands many a hundred of English, French, and Dutch, many of whom turn planters.
6. It is the only means to keep the buccaneers on Hispaniola, Tortugas, and the South and North Cays of Cuba from being their enemies, and infesting their sea-side plantations.
7. It is a great security to the island that the men-of-war often intercept Spanish advices, and give intelligence to the Governor; which they often did in Col. D'Oyley's time and since.
8. The said men-of-war bring no small benefit to His Majesty and Royal Highness, by the 15ths and 10ths.
9. They keep many able artificers at work in Port Royal and elsewhere, at extraordinary wages.
10. Whatsoever they get, the soberer part bestow in strengthening their old ships, which in time will grow formidable.
11. They are of great reputation to this island and of terror to the Spaniard, and keep up a high and military spirit in all the inhabitants.
12. It seems to be the only means to force the Spaniards, in time, to a free trade, all ways of kindness producing nothing of good neighborhood; for though all old commissions have been called in and no new ones granted, and many of their ships restored, yet they continue all acts of hostility, taking our ships and murdering our

people, making them work at their fortifications and then sending
them into Spain, and very lately they denied an English fleet bound
for the Dutch colonies wood, water, or provisions.

For which reasons it was unanimously concluded, that the granting of
said commissions did extraordinarily conduce to the strengthening,
preservation, enriching, and advancing the settlement of this island.

Modyford agreed, writing to Whitehall to justify such an aggressive
regional policy because of the continual hostility met from Spanish
American authorities, adding that "it must be force alone that can cut
in sunder that unneighborly maxim of their government, to deny all
access of strangers."

London soon concurred as well, so that peacetime commissions
were resumed—unwittingly reinforcing many privateers' belief that
their actions were not necessarily constrained by Crown policies but
could be manipulated to suit their own interests.

Source: W. Noel Sainsbury, ed., *Calendar of State Papers, Colonial: America and
West Indies,* vol. 5 (London: Her Majesty's Stationery Office, 1880), 358.

DOCUMENT B.—BUCCANEER STRATEGIZING
DURING THE LATE 1660s, BY EXQUEMELIN

Around the year 1667, an impoverished French engagé *or indentured
servant, a 22-year-old Huguenot named Alexandre-Olivier Exquemelin, joined the* flibustiers *of Saint-Domingue to seek his fortune. Over
the next three and a half years, he served among their ranks and later
published a best-selling account of his adventures under such colorful commanders as Jean-David Nau l'Olonnais and Henry Morgan.
Among the many recollections contained in Exquemelin's book was the
following description of how roving bands of freebooters would coalesce
and decide among themselves upon a strategy for intercepting Spanish
vessels and shift their Caribbean hunting grounds according to seasonal
patterns:*

When they have stayed long enough in one place, they deliberate
where they shall go to try their luck. If any man happens to be familiar
with particular coasts where the merchantmen trade, he offers his services. The trading-ships cruise different places according to the season
of the year, for these regions cannot be reached at all times on account
of settled winds and currents. The people of New Spain and Campeche
do most of their commerce in ships sailing in winter from Campeche

to the coasts of Caracas, Trinidad, and Margarita, as the north-east trade winds do not permit this voyage in summer. When summer comes, they turn their vessels homewards again. The privateers, knowing the passage through which they must sail, lie in wait for them.

Source: Alexandre Olivier Exquemelin and John Esquemeling, *The Buccaneers of America* (London: George Allen, 1911).

DOCUMENT C.—LETTER FROM JAMAICA'S GOVERNOR TO HIS
SPANISH COUNTERPART AT HAVANA, COMPLAINING ABOUT
THE UNAVAILING EFFORTS AGAINST PIRACY, APRIL 1672

In the wake of Henry Morgan's spectacular sack of Panama, England had sought to rein in such blatant peacetime violations by appointing the pro-Spanish planter and businessman, Sir Thomas Lynch, as Jamaica's new royal governor, with special instructions to enact a much less aggressive policy against Spanish America. As part of this effort, Lynch had arrested his predecessor, Modyford, and sent him home to stand trial. He also recalled all privateer commissions and branded any renegades who continued to operate at sea as pirates.

Instead of welcoming these gestures, though, Spain had angrily increased its own colonial countermeasures, to the extent that an invasion of Jamaica actually came to be feared, while Spanish American ports remained as tightly closed as ever to English merchantmen. Therefore on April 5, 1672 (O.S.), Lynch—who was fluent in Spanish, having lived for a year in Salamanca—responded to the complaints of recent piratical attacks he had received from the governor of Cuba, Don Francisco Rodríguez de Ledesma, in the following bitter tones:

Since his letter by Capt. Don Juan Antonio, complaining of the taking and burning of La Villa de los Cayos by men pretended to be English, has written twice and acquainted him and the Governor of St. Jago that they were French pirates; and again declares that all subjects of his Majesty that do the like are pirates, and he may take and punish them as such, as Governor Lynch has done and shall do, as fast as they fall into his hands. Has a most particular inclination to serve the Spaniards, and amongst them himself, whom Sir Thomas has understood to be kind to our nation.

Considering this, and that the other neighboring Governors seem so little sensible of the King's great care to observe the Peace, and vast expense in clearing the Spanish coasts, makes this narration, that the Governor of the Havana and the Queen and Council at Madrid may know how candidly he has acted as a good friend and neighbor to the Spaniards. Relates how:

- he proclaimed the Peace, and sent back the Spanish prisoners to Cartagena, and sent the late Governor [Modyford] prisoner to England, "and shall do so the other chiefs of the fatal design of Panama";
- that he proposed to the Governor of Cartagena the redemption of the Spanish slaves at half their worth, set at liberty some *morenos*, "little to the people's satisfaction" [i.e., to the annoyance of Jamaica's planters], and sent them away at his own charge, "for which nobody has even thanked" him;
- that he furnished this Don Juan Antonio with everything for his voyage, and paid his pilot 700 pieces of eight, which he lost in August [1671] by a privateer;
- how about eight weeks since, he sent out a great ship of the King's and four other vessels with 500 men to take the pirates in the South Cays of Cuba, which took an English and a French ship, and offered the French ship to the Governor of St. Jago, which he refused, saying he durst not punish the French;
- how both were condemned to death at Jamaica, but the captains at the port and some of the Council begged a reprieve, as the Spaniards had refused to punish them, and there was no reason we should be the executioners; but resolves "to persist in doing what is just, though the Spaniards should continue insensible and the English offended";
- and how he has sent three times after a vessel belonging to Don Balthazar, the Marquis of Villa Alta's son, which was taken by an old brigantine and is now a pirate.

Complains that notwithstanding all this, the Governors of Cartagena and St. Jago, on pretence of fear of trade, had forbidden His Majesty's ships to come into their ports, and refused them provisions and water; and that the Governor of Campeche had detained money, plate, and negroes out of an English pink to the value of 12,000 pieces of eight, and referred the case to be tried at Madrid, "which to me, that have been there, seems worse than the taking it away." Confesses he did not know that the Spaniards' interest lay more in preserving their trade than their lives and countries, nor can he judge why they should not join with His Majesty's subjects in endeavoring to clear these coasts of these most pestilent pirates. If they can contribute nothing to it, they might at least give their thanks and good wishes towards it; but has given over expecting it, and supposes hereafter he shall be ordered to take other measures.

Judges the Governor of the Havana is more sensible, generous, and prudent, and therefore gives him this account of his actions and complaints, only begging an authentic attestation that the French that burned and sacked La Villa de los Cayos and carried away the women, did it under English colors and commission, for Sir Thos. must justify what he does as well to the French as to his King. Begs him to thank Senor Juan Delgado for furnishing the frigates with provisions for their money, and hopes he may be able to requite that civility.

Source: W. Noel Sainsbury, ed., *Calendar of State Papers, Colonial: America and West Indies*, vol. 7 (London: Her Majesty's Stationery Office, 1889), 345–46.

DOCUMENT D.—ENGLISH NEWSPAPER ACCOUNT
OF THE SACK OF VERACRUZ, 1683

The breathtakingly audacious seizure of the main Mexican seaport of Veracruz, destination for Spain's legendary transatlantic plate fleets, by fewer than a thousand pirates under Laurens de Graaf and the Sieur de Grammont in May 1683 created a sensation on both sides of the Atlantic. Rumors spread like wildfire, eventually being supplanted in this era of slow long-distance communication by more measured official reports—such as the following account, which reached London from Jamaica six months after the event and was duly published in the Thursday, November 1, 1683 (O.S.) issue of the London Gazette. *Even then, this article was still not entirely accurate in all its details:*

Jamaica, August 12, 1683 [O.S.]. The 24th of the last month, the master of a sloop brought hither the news of the privateers having taken La Vera Cruz, whereof we have since these particulars: They rendezvoused at Cape Catoche (the south cape of the Bay of Mexico) the 7th of April last. They were Van Horne [Nicolaas van Hoorn], a Hollander, in an English ship of 50 guns, who was Admiral; Laurence [de Graaf], a Hollander, in a prize of 26 guns, Vice-Admiral; Christian, a Hollander, in Van Horne's Patache of 40 guns; Mitchel [Michiel Andrieszoon], a Frenchman, in a prize of Laurence's of 26 guns; Yanchy [Jan "Jantje" Willems], a Hollander, in a prize of 16 guns; Blot, a Hollander, in a prize of 8 guns; Jacob Hall, a Bermudian, of 8 guns; [George] Spurre, an Englishman, in a sloop of Jamaica; and a Barco Longo of Laurence's. These vessels had betwixt 900 and 1,000 men, most French and Dutch, and some few English.

On the 8th of May, they came on the coast of La Vera Cruz and lay by, and they put the men that were to land on board Yanchy and Christian, then stood off; the 9th these two ships stood in, and in the night the Spaniards in the castle and on shore, made fires to pilot them in, taking them to be two of the Flota [i.e., the anticipated annual plate fleet], so they came to an anchor, and landed before one o'clock in the morning two miles from the town, 774 men. Van Horne had the body, as General, and was to attack the Plaza, where they expected the Court of Guard, but found only four men. Laurence commanded the Forlorn, and with it attempted the two forts, the one of 12, the other of 8 guns, both closed forts, but they found them open and the sentinels asleep; so with loss of one man killed by the Spaniards, and three by the mistake of the French, by break of day they were masters of the forts and town; and had they, as Laurence advised, sent at the same time two cannons and 50 men, they had without doubt surprised the castle, which stands in the sea 3-quarters of a mile and has 70 guns mounted.

But the Pyrates thinking it more safe and profitable to plunder the town, set guards at the streets' ends, and sent parties to break open the houses, where they found everybody as quiet as their graves, and for three days they did nothing but break houses, plunder them, and drag the miserable inhabitants to the Cathedral, and though in this time they got abundance of plate, jewels, etc., and about 350 bags of cochenille, each containing 150 or 200 L. [pounds] as they say; yet were they not satisfied, but put considerable people to ransom, and threatened to burn the Cathedral and prisoners, which were about 5,700, if they did not immediately discover all they had; so that the 4th day they got more than the other three, and had 70,000 pieces of eight for the Governor Don Luis de Cordova's ransom, which Spurre found hid among grass in a stable.

The Pyrates feared the Flota, which had been two days in sight, consisting of twelve great ships, and likewise apprehended succors might come to the Spaniards from Los Angeles (a city thirty leagues from La Vera Cruz) so they left the town and carried their prisoners and plunder to a cay where their ships rode, called Los Sacrificios from a famous Indian temple that was there. Here they stayed eight days to receive ransoms, and to divide what they got, which they generally say was about 800 Pieces of Eight a share in plate and money, and they made about 1,200 shares for men and ships; and Van Horne had about 80 shares for himself and two ships; and here Laurence and he quarreled and fought, and Van Horne was wounded in the wrist, nobody thinking it mortal.

They all embarked, and Van Horne proposed to attack the Flota, and engaged to board the Admiral, but Laurence would not, and so away they went with about 1,000 Negroes and Mulattoes: about 15 days after Van Horne died, his wound having gangrened, and was thrown into the sea off Cape Yucatan, leaving his son a youth of ten or twelve years old, they say, to the value of 20,000 £. on board, and his lieutenant, Gramont, took upon him the command of the ship, and intended for Petit Guave. Laurence and the rest have been off of this Island [Jamaica], and are gone to Guantanamo, a port on the south side of Cuba. Spurre is dead, and 3 or 400 more, and our Governor is endeavoring to seize his sloop.

The preceding has had its spellings, punctuation, and capitalizations slightly modified to conform to modern usage, and a more abbreviated version of this same report—which had apparently been brought into Port Royal by a fishing sloop from the Cayman Islands on July 24, 1683 (O.S.)—can be found in Governor Sir Thomas Lynch's letter addressed only two days afterward to Sir Leoline Jenkins, reproduced in W. Noel Sainsbury (ed.), *Calendar of State Papers, Colonial: America and West Indies*, Vol. 11 (London: Her Majesty's Stationery Office 1898), 457–58.

Source: London Gazette, November 1, 1683.

DOCUMENT E.—ACCOUNT OF THOMAS POUND'S CAPTURE, 1689

The deposal of James II from England's throne during the winter of 1688–1689 in favor of the Protestant champions William and Mary, had resulted in certain upheaval and reversals of fortune in North America. Thomas Pound, captain of Massachusetts's colonial sloop Mary *under the old regime, was to provide one such case. Relieved of his command and left unemployed when it was subsequently learned in early August 1689 that the former king had landed in Ireland with a French army to attempt to recoup his throne, Pound and a half dozen colleagues had quietly departed Boston as passengers aboard a small vessel, only to seize it and initiate a self-proclaimed "privateering" campaign.*

Regarded as outright pirates by the commonwealth's new royal authorities, Pound's old sloop Mary *was sent out less than two months later under its new commander, Samuel Pease, to hunt down these renegades. The following deposition was given by the Williamite adherent, Lieutenant Benjamin Gallop, after a bloody encounter with the defiant Pound off Tarpaulin Cove:*

We whose names are hereto subscribed, being of the company late belonging to the sloop *Mary*, Cap'n Samuel Pease commander, set forth at Boston within the Colony of the Massachusetts Bay, with commission from the Govern'r and Council of the said colony bearing date the 30th day of September last past [i.e., September 30, 1689, O.S.], before the date of these . . . to surprise and (in case of their making resistance) by force of arms to take Thomas Hawkin and Thomas Pound, who with a number of armed men joined with them, had piratically seized several vessels belonging to Their Majesties' subjects of this colony and other parts of the country, &c.

In prosecution of which said design, setting sail from Boston upon Friday the fourth of October 1689 [O.S.], being off of Wood's Hole, we were informed there was a pirate at Tarpaulin Cove, and soon after we espied a sloop on ahead of us, which we supposed to be the sloop wherein said Pound and his company were. We made what sail we could, and soon came near up with her, spread our King's jack and fired a shot athwart her fore-foot, upon which a red flag was put out on the head of the said sloop's mast. Our Cap'n ordered another shot to be fired athwart her fore-foot, but they not striking, we came up with them.

Our Cap'n commanded us to fire at them, which we accordingly did, and called to them to strike to the King of England. Pound standing on the quarterdeck with his naked sword flourishing in his hand, said: "Come on board, you dogs, and I will strike you presently," or words to that purpose, his men standing by him upon the deck with guns in their hands; and he taking up his gun, they discharged a volley at us, and we at them again, and so continued firing one at the other for some space of time, in which engagement our Cap'n Samuel Pease was wounded in the arm, in the side, and in the thigh.

But at length bringing them under our power, we made sail towards Rhode Island, and on Saturday the fifth of said October [October 5, 1689, O.S.], got our wounded men on shore there, and procured surgeons to dress them. Our said Captain lost much blood by his wounds and was brought very low, but on Friday after, being the eleventh day of the same October, being brought on board the vessel intending to come away to Boston, was taken with bleeding afresh, so that we were forced to carry him on shore again to Rhode Island, and was followed with bleeding at his wounds, and fell into fits, but remained alive until Saturday morning, the twelfth of October aforesaid, when he departed this life.

John Sicklerdam: The prisoner now at the bar was one of the said sloop's company, with whom we were engaged as aforesaid, by which company our said Cap'n Samuel Pease was shot and wounded, of which wounds he languished and died as aforesaid. We further add that the said flag was put out at the head of said sloop's mast, before we fired at them.

Boston, 14° January, 1689 [1690 N.S.], sworn in Court of Assistants. Attested: Isaac Addington, Secr'y

Ben Gallop
Colburn Turell
Abraham Adams
Daniel X Langly,
his mark

Remarkably, although Pound and his surviving confederates were found guilty of piracy, they were not immediately executed. Rather—given the peculiar circumstances motivating their cruise—they were sent to England for final adjudication. And once there, Pound eventually succeeded in obtaining a pardon and being set at liberty, even securing command of another ship.

Source: New England Historical and Genealogical Register, vol. 2 (Boston, 1848), 393. Spelling and punctuation have been slightly modernized.

DOCUMENT F.—ACT FOR THE MORE EFFECTUAL SUPPRESSION OF PIRACY, 1698

At the conclusion of King William's War in September 1697, the authorities in London moved to address the problem of pernicious commerce raiding, which habitually persisted even after the declaration of any general peace. All too often, rovers would continue their depredations while either feigning ignorance of the treaty by switching allegiance to a foreign flag or simply as brazen renegades. The 160-year-old statutes governing the prosecution of pirates had long since become outdated and were too restricted in scope, because English commercial traffic had now expanded well beyond European waters, where such laws had originally been intended to be applied. The impracticality of continuing to remit prisoners home from overseas colonies and outposts scattered all around the globe, merely to be tried before English justices, represented a significant handicap toward any effective remedy of this problem.

The result would be the drafting of a new "Act for the More Effectual Suppression of Piracy," which was to be concluded one year later and be passed by both houses of Parliament by 1700, going into full effect the next year. On April 2, 1701 (O.S.), the Council of Trade and Plantations in London took delivery of 50 copies of this new act, along with samples of the proper sort of commissions that were to be issued for legally trying pirates in overseas jurisdictions by colonial officials, for distribution worldwide. As shall be seen, this act also encompassed mutineers and deserters as well as masters who deliberately marooned unwanted mariners.

> *Over the next two centuries, thousands of pirates would be tried under this particular statute, including "Calico Jack" Rackham and many other famous names. For example, the trial of 36 of Ned Low's confederates from the pirate sloop* Ranger *opened on July 10, 1723 (O.S.) in Newport, Rhode Island, with the reading aloud of this commission in open court—after first "commanding silence upon pain of imprisonment" from all those present in the courtroom. The act appears in its entirety here:*

I. Reasons for passing this Act; Piracies, &c., may be enquired of at Sea, or upon Islands, and by Commission under the Great Seal or Admiralty Seal; Power of Commissioners; Information to be upon Oath; Court to consist of Seven at least.

Whereas by an Act of Parliament made in the twenty-eighth year of the reign of King Henry the Eighth it is enacted that treasons, felonies, robberies, murders, and confederacies committed on the sea shall be enquired of, tried, and determined according to the common course of the laws of this land used for such offences upon the land within this realm, whereupon the trial of those offenders before the Admiral or his Lieutenant or his Commissary hath been altogether disused;

And whereas that since the making of the said Act, and especially of late years, it hath been found by experience that persons committing piracies, robberies, and felonies on the seas in or near the East and West Indies, and in places very remote, cannot be brought to condign punishment without great trouble and charges [i.e., expenses] in sending them into England to be tried within the realm, as the said statute directs, insomuch that many idle and profligate persons have been thereby encouraged to turn pirates and betake themselves to that sort of wicked life, trusting that they shall not or at least cannot easily be questioned for such their piracies and robberies, by reason of the great trouble and expense that will necessarily fall upon such as shall attempt to apprehend and prosecute them for the same;

And whereas the numbers of them are of late very much increased and their insolencies so great, that unless some speedy remedy be provided to suppress them by a strict and more easy way for putting the ancient laws in that behalf in execution, the trade and navigation into remote parts will very much suffer thereby;

Be it therefore declared and enacted by the King's most Excellent Majesty, by and with the advice and consent of the Lords spiritual and temporal, and Commons in this present Parliament assembled, and by the authority of the same that all piracies, felonies, and robberies committed in or upon the sea or in any haven, river, creek, or place where the Admiral or Admirals have power, authority, or jurisdiction, may be examined, inquired of, tried, heard, and determined and adjudged according to the directions of this Act, in any place at sea or upon the land in any of His Majesty's islands, plantations, colonies, dominions, forts, or factories to be appointed for that purpose by the King's commission or commissions under the Great Seal of England, or the seal of the Admiralty of England directed to all or any of the Admirals, Vice-Admirals, Rear-Admirals, Judges of Vice-Admiralties, or Commanders of any of His Majesty's ships of war, and also to all or any such person or persons, officer or officers by name, or for the time being as His Majesty shall think fit to appoint;

Which said commissioners shall have full power jointly or severally by warrant under the hand and seal of them, or any one of them, to commit to safe custody any person or persons against whom information of piracy, robbery, or felony upon the sea shall be given upon oath (which oath they or any one of them shall have full power and are hereby required to administer), and to call and assemble a Court of Admiralty on shipboard or upon the land when and as often as occasion shall require, which Court shall consist of seven persons at the least.

II. Three may call together a Court of Seven

And if so many of the persons aforesaid cannot conveniently be assembled, be it further enacted by the authority aforesaid that any three of the aforesaid persons (whereof the President or chief of some English factory; or the Governor, Lieutenant-Governor, or member of His Majesty's Councils in any of the plantations or colonies aforesaid; or commander of one of His Majesty's ships, is always to be one), shall have full power and authority by virtue of this Act to call and assemble any other persons on shipboard or upon the land to make up the number of seven.

III. What Persons may sit and vote in such Court

Provided that no persons but such as are known merchants, factors, or planters; or such as are Captains, Lieutenants, or Warrant Officers in any of His Majesty's ships of war; or Captains, Masters, or Mates of some English ship, shall be capable of being so called, and sitting and voting in the said Court.

IV. Court may issue Warrants for Persons accused, and Attendance of Witnesses, and examine upon Oath, and give Sentence of Death, Persons convicted to suffer accordingly.

And be it enacted by the authority aforesaid, that such persons called and assembled as aforesaid shall have full power and authority according to the course of the Admiralty to issue warrants for bringing any persons accused of piracy or robbery before them to be tried, heard, and adjudged; and to summon witnesses and to take informations and examinations of witnesses, upon their oath; and to do all things necessary for the hearing and final determination of any case of piracy, robbery, and felony; and to give sentence and judgment of death, and to award execution of the offenders convicted and attainted as aforesaid, according to the civil law and the methods and rules of the Admiralty. And that all and every person and persons so convicted and attainted of piracy or robbery, shall have and suffer such losses of lands, goods, and chattels as if they had been attainted and convicted of any piracies, felonies, and robberies according to the aforementioned statute made in the reign of King Henry the Eighth.

V. Proceedings upon assembling of Court.

Provided always and be it further enacted by the authority aforesaid, that so soon as any court shall be assembled as aforesaid, either on shipboard or upon the land, the King's commission shall first be openly read; and the said court then and there shall be solemnly and publicly called and proclaimed, and then the President of the Court shall in the first place, publicly in open court, take the following oath, vizt.:

Oath of President:

> I, A. B., do swear in the presence of Almighty God, that I will truly and impartially try and adjudge the prisoner or prisoners which shall be brought upon his or their trials before this court, and honestly and duly on my part put His Majesty's commission for the trying of them in execution, according to the best of my skill and knowledge; and that I have no interest, directly or indirectly, in any ship or goods for the piratically taking of which any person stands accused, and is now to be tried, so help me God.

Who is to administer the same to every person sitting and voting upon the trial; Register to read the articles against the prisoner; prisoner to plead; proceedings where prisoner pleads not guilty; prisoner may bring witnesses for his defense, and may be heard; President to collect the votes of the court; judgment to be given in presence of the prisoner; execution.

And he having taken the oath in manner aforesaid, shall immediately administer the same oath to every person who shall sit, and have and give a voice in the said court upon the trial of such prisoner or prisoners as aforesaid; and immediately thereupon the said prisoner or prisoners shall be formally brought before them, and then the

Register of the said court shall openly and distinctly read the articles against such prisoner or prisoners upon which they or any of them is to or are to be tried, wherein shall be set forth the particular fact or facts of piracy, robbery, and felony, with the time and place when and where, and in what manner it was committed.

And then each prisoner shall be asked whether he be guilty of the said piracy and robbery or felony, or not guilty, whereupon every such prisoner shall immediately plead thereunto guilty or not guilty, or else it shall be taken as confessed and he shall suffer such pains of death, loss of lands, goods, and chattels, and in like manner as if he or they had been attainted or convicted upon the oath of witnesses or his own confession, but if any prisoner shall plead not guilty, witnesses shall be produced by the Register and duly sworn and examined openly *viva voce* in the prisoner's presence. And after a witness hath answered all the questions proposed by the President of the court and given his evidence, it shall and may be lawful for the prisoner to have the witness cross-examined, by first declaring to the court what questions he would have asked; and thereupon the President of the court shall interrogate the witness accordingly, and every prisoner shall have liberty to bring witnesses for his defense, who shall be sworn and examined upon oath as the witnesses were that testified against him; and afterwards the prisoner shall be fairly heard, what he can say for himself, all which being done the prisoner shall be taken away and kept in safe custody, and all other persons except the Register shall withdraw from the said court.

And then the court shall consider of the evidence which hath been given, and debate the matters and circumstances of the prisoner's case, and the President of the court shall collect all the votes of the persons who do sit and have voices in the said court, beginning at the junior first, and ending with himself; and according to the plurality of voices, sentence and judgment shall be then given and pronounced publicly in the presence of the prisoner or prisoners, being called in again; and according to sentence and judgment, the person or persons attainted shall be executed and put to death at such time, in such manner, and in such place upon the sea or within the ebbing or flowing thereof, as the President or the major part of the court, by warrant directed to a provost marshal (which the President or said major part shall have power to constitute), shall appoint.

VI.   *What Persons may be Register; Oath of Register; His Duty.*

And be it further enacted by the authority aforesaid, that some person being a public notary shall be Register of the court; and in case of his absence, death, or incapacity, or for want of a person so qualified, the President of the court shall and may appoint a Register, giving him an oath which he is hereby empowered to administer, duly, faithfully, and impartially to execute his office; which Register shall prepare all warrants and articles, and take care to provide all things requisite for any trial according to the substantial and essential parts of proceedings in a Court of Admiralty, in the most summary way; and shall take minutes of the whole proceedings and enter them duly in a book, by him to be kept for that purpose, and shall from time to time as opportunity offers, transmit the same with the copies of all articles and judgments given in any such cases in any court whereof he shall be Register, unto the High Court of Admiralty of England.

VII. *Natural born Subjects committing Acts as herein mentioned, deemed, and upon Conviction, to suffer according to Stat. 28 Hen. VIII. c. 15.*

And be it further enacted by the authority aforesaid, that if any of His Majesty's natural born subjects or denizens of this kingdom shall commit any piracy or robbery, or any act of hostility against other His Majesty's subjects upon the sea, under color of any commission from any foreign prince or state, or pretence of authority from any person whatsoever, such offender and offenders and every of them shall be deemed adjudged and taken to be pirates, felons, and robbers; and they and every of them being duly convicted thereof according to this act, or the aforesaid statute of King Henry the Eighth, shall have and suffer such pains of death, loss of lands, goods, and chattels as pirates, felons, and robbers upon the seas ought to have and suffer.

VIII. *Commanders of Ships, &c. turning Pirate, &c., or attempting to corrupt other Commanders &c.; to suffer as Pirates.*

And be it further enacted that if any commander or master of any ship, or any seaman or mariner, shall in any place where the Admiral hath jurisdiction, betray his trust and turn pirate, enemy, or rebel and piratically and feloniously run away with his or their ship or ships, or any barge, boat, ordnance, ammunition, goods, or merchandizes; or yield them up voluntarily to any pirate;

Or shall bring any seducing messages from any pirate, enemy, or rebel; or consult, combine, or confederate with, or attempt or endeavor to corrupt any commander, master, officer, or mariner to yield up or run away with any ship, goods, or merchandizes, or turn pirate or go over to pirates; or if any person shall lay violent hands on his commander, whereby to hinder him from fighting in defense of his ship and goods committed to his trust; or that shall confine his master, or make or endeavor to make a revolt in the ship;

Shall be adjudged, deemed, and taken to be a pirate, felon, and robber; and being convicted thereof, according to the directions of this act, shall have and suffer pains of death, losses of lands, goods, and chattels as pirates, felons, and robbers upon the seas ought to have and suffer.

IX. Persons aiding Pirates, &c., who shall thereupon act; adjudged Accessories.

And whereas several evil disposed persons in the Plantations and elsewhere, have contributed very much towards the increase and encouragement of pirates by setting them forth and by aiding, abetting, receiving, and concealing them and their goods; and there being some defects in the laws for bringing such evil disposed persons to condign punishment:

Be it enacted by the authority aforesaid, that all and every person and persons whatsoever, who after the twenty-ninth day of September in the year of our Lord one thousand seven hundred, shall either on the land or upon the seas, wittingly or knowingly set forth any pirate, or aid and assist or maintain, procure, command, counsel, or advise any person or persons whatsoever to do or commit any piracies or robberies upon the seas, and such person and persons shall thereupon do or commit any such piracy or robbery, then all and every such person or persons whatsoever, so as aforesaid setting forth any pirate or aiding, assisting, maintaining, procuring, commanding, counseling, or advising the same, either on the land or upon the sea, shall be and are hereby declared and shall be deemed and adjudged to be accessory to such piracy and robbery done and committed.

X. Persons concealing Pirates, &c., or Vessels, &c., taken by such, adjudged Accessories; tried and to suffer as Principals, under Stat. 28 Hen. VIII. c. 15; the said Statute in force.

And further that after any piracy or robbery is or shall be committed by any pirate or robber whatsoever, every person and persons who knowing that such pirate or robber has done or committed such piracy and robbery, shall on the land or upon the sea receive, entertain, or conceal any such pirate or robber, or receive or take into his custody any ship, vessel, goods, or chattels which have been by any such pirate or robber piratically and feloniously taken; shall be and are hereby likewise declared, deemed, and adjudged to be accessory to such piracy and robbery.

And that after the said nine-and-twentieth day of September, all such accessories to such piracies and robberies shall and may be enquired of, tried, heard, determined, and adjudged after the common course of the laws of this land, according to the said statute made in the twenty-eighth year of King Henry the Eighth, as the principals of such piracies and robberies may and ought to be, and no otherwise; and being thereupon attainted shall suffer such pains of death, losses of lands, goods, and chattels, and in like manner as the principals of such piracies, robberies, and felonies ought to suffer according to the said statute of King Henry the Eighth, which is hereby declared to be and continue in full force, anything in this present act contained to the contrary notwithstanding.

> XI. *When Officers and Seamen killed or wounded in defending Ship, which shall be brought to Port, Judge of the Admiralty, &c., may levy £2 per Cent. upon the Owners, &c., for Benefit of such Officers and Seamen, or their Widows and Children, as herein mentioned.*

And forasmuch as it will also conduce to the suppressing of robberies on the sea, if due encouragement be given and rewards allowed to such commanders, masters, and other officers, seamen, and mariners as shall either bravely defend their own ships or take, seize, and destroy pirates, sea-rovers, and enemies:

Be it further enacted by the authority aforesaid that when any English ship shall have been defended against any pirates, enemies, or sea rovers by fight and brought to her designed port, in which fight any of the officers or seamen shall have been killed or wounded, it shall and may be lawful to and for the judge of His Majesty's High Court of Admiralty; or his surrogate in the port of London; or the mayor, bailiff, or chief officer in the several out-ports of this kingdom, upon the petition of the master or seamen of such ship so defended as aforesaid, to call unto him four or more good and substantial merchants, and such as are no adventurers or owners of the ship or goods so defended, and have no manner of interest therein:

And by advice with them to raise and levy upon the respective adventurers and owners of the ship and goods so defended, by process out of the said court, such sum or sums of money as himself and the said merchants by plurality of voices shall determine and judge reasonable, not exceeding two pounds per cent[um] of the freight and of the ship and goods so defended, according to the first costs of the goods; which sum or sums of money so raised shall be distributed among the captain, master, officers, and seamen of the said ship, or widows and children of the slain, according to the direction of the judge of the said court; or his surrogate in the port of London; or the mayor, bailiff, or chief officer in the several out-ports of this kingdom, with the approbation of the merchants aforesaid, who shall proportion the same according to their best judgment unto the ship's company as aforesaid, having special regard unto the widows and children of such as shall have been slain in that service, and such as have been wounded or maimed.

XII. Rewards to Informers, of Conspiracy to destroy or run away with Ship.

And for the better and more effectual prevention of combinations and confederacies for the running away with, or destroying of any ship, goods, or merchandizes:

Be it further enacted by the authority aforesaid that a reward of ten pounds for every ship or vessel of one hundred tons or under, and fifteen pounds for every ship or vessel of a greater burden, shall be paid by the captain, commander, or master of every ship or vessel wherein any such combination or confederacy shall be set on foot for the running away with, or destroying any such ship, or the goods and merchandizes therein laden; to such person as shall first make a discovery thereof, upon due proof of such combination or confederacy, the same to be paid at the port where the wages of the seamen of the said ship are or ought to be paid, after such discovery and proof made.

XIII. Continuance of Act.

Provided also: that this Act shall be in force for seven years, and to the end of the next session of Parliament after the expiration of the said seven years, and no longer.

XIV. Jurisdiction of Commissioners for Trial of Pirates under Stat. 28 Hen. VIII. c. 15. and this Act, in determining Offences; and issuing Warrants; Governors of Plantations, &c. to assist Commissioners and their Officers.

And for the more effectual prosecution and punishment of piracies, felonies, and robberies upon the sea, and of all other offences aforementioned, be it declared and enacted by the authority aforesaid that the commissioners appointed or to be appointed by the aforementioned statute of King Henry the Eighth, or the commissioners for trial of pirates appointed by this Act, shall from and after the said nine-and-twentieth day of September, one thousand seven hundred, have the sole power and authority of trying, hearing, and determining the said crimes and offences within all or any of the colonies and plantations in America governed by proprietors, or under grants or charters from the Crown, and of bringing the offenders to condign punishment;

And shall and may issue forth their warrant or warrants for the seizing and apprehending of any pirates, felons, or robbers upon the sea, or their confederates or accessories being within any of the said colonies and plantations, in order to their being brought to trial within the same or any other plantation in America according to this Act, or sent into England to be tried there;

And that all and every Governor and governor's person, and persons in authority in the said colonies and plantations governed by proprietors or under charters as aforesaid, shall assist the commissioners and their subordinate officers in doing their duty, and also in the execution of such warrants and otherwise; and shall deliver up to such commissioner or commissioner's officer or officers, any pirates, felons, and robbers upon the sea, and their confederates and accessories, in order to their being tried or sent into England as aforesaid, any letters, patents, grants, or charters of government in and about the said plantations, or other usages heretofore had or made to the contrary notwithstanding.

   XV. Governors not obeying this Act, Penalty.

And be it hereby further declared and enacted, that if any of the Governors in the said plantations, or any person or persons in authority there, shall refuse to yield obedience to this Act, such refusal is hereby declared to be a forfeiture of all and every the charters granted for the government or propriety of such plantation.

   XVI. How Commissions for Trial of Offences within the Cinque Ports to be
   directed; and how Trials thereupon to be had.

Provided always and be it enacted by the authority aforesaid, that whensoever any commission for the trial and punishment of the offences aforesaid, or any of them, shall be directed or sent to any place within the jurisdiction of the Cinque Ports, that then every such commission shall be directed unto the Lord Warden of the Cinque-Ports for the time being, or to his lieutenant and unto such other persons as the Lord High Chancellor or Keeper of the Great Seal of England, for the time being, or commissioners for the custody of the Great Seal shall name and appoint;

And likewise that every inquisition and trial to be had by virtue of such commission so directed, and sent to any place in the said Cinque-Ports shall be made, and had by the Inhabitants of the said Cinque-Ports or the members of the same, anything in this Act to the contrary [thereof] notwithstanding.

XVII.   Seamen, &c., deserting; Penalty.

And for the prevention of seamen deserting of merchant ships abroad, in parts beyond the seas, which is the chief occasion of their turning pirates, and of great detriment to trade and navigation in general:

Be it enacted by the authority aforesaid that all such seamen, officers, or sailors who shall desert the ships or vessels wherein they are hired to serve for that voyage, shall for such offence forfeit all such wages as shall be then due to him or them.

XVIII.   After 29th Sept. 1700, Masters of Merchant Ships forcing Men on Shore, &c.; Punishment.

And be it further enacted by the authority aforesaid, that in case any master of a merchant ship or vessel shall after the nine-and-twentieth day of September, one thousand and seven hundred, during his being abroad, force any man on shore or willfully leave him behind in any of His Majesty's plantations or elsewhere, or shall refuse to bring home with him again all such of the men which he carried out with him, as are in a condition to return when he shall be ready to proceed in his homeward-bound voyage;

Every such master shall being thereof legally convicted, suffer three months' imprisonment without bail or mainprize.

Source: John Raithby, ed., *Statutes of the Realm,* vol. 7, *1695–1701* (London, 1820), 590–94.

DOCUMENT G.—BARTHOLOMEW ROBERTS'S THREATENING
LETTER TO THE GOVERNOR OF SAINT KITTS, 1720

Shortly after noon on September 27, 1720 (O.S.), two vessels stood boldly into the West Indian island of Saint Kitts's peaceful anchorage of Basseterre and attacked. By the time Governor William Matthew could arrive overland on horseback an hour later, he realized that it was too late. Already, "the pirates' ship and sloop with black flags, had cut out one ship—that was under sail actually then—and had set two more on fire." A few belated salvoes were being fired off by the shore batteries as the raiders glided easily out of range.

After nightfall, a boat reappeared from out at sea to release a few prisoners as well as bearing a plea from the captive merchant Master Henry Fowles for a number of sheep and goats to be prepared to ransom his ship—plus the following letter from the audacious pirate captain himself, addressed personally to the governor:

Royal Fortune, Sept. 27th, 1720 [O.S.].

This comes expressly from me to let you know that had you come off, as you ought to 'a done, and drank a glass of wine with me and my company, I should not [have] harmed the least vessel in your harbor. Farther, it is not your guns you fired that affrighted me, or hindered our coming on shore, but the wind not proving to our expectation, that hindered it.

The *Royal Rover* you have already burnt and barbarously used some of our men, but we have now a ship as good as her, and for revenge you may assure yourselves, here and hereafter, not to expect anything from our hands but what belongs to a pirate. As farther, gentlemen, that poor fellow you now have in prison at Sandy Point is entirely ignorant and what he hath, was gave him, and so pray make conscience for once, let me beg you, and use that man as an honest man and not as a C [criminal?]. If we hear any otherwise, you may expect not to have quarters to any of your Island.

Yours, Bathll. Roberts.

The next morning, a boatload of pirates deposited the captive Fowles ashore; then at 11:00 A.M., Roberts's consort sloop approached to receive the anticipated ransom. Instead, Governor Matthew ordered the reinforced batteries to open fire once more, loosing two salvoes and striking the pirate vessel several times before it retreated out of range. An angry Roberts would spend the next six months ravaging merchant traffic in the Windward Islands, bringing movement to almost a complete standstill before finally disappearing over the horizon toward Africa in the spring of 1721.

Source: Cecil Headlam, ed., *Calendar of State Papers, Colonial: America and West Indies*, vol. 32 (London: Her Majesty's Stationery Office, 1933), 169.

DOCUMENT H.—BOSTON NEWSPAPER REPORT OF PIRATICAL ASSAULTS OCCURRING IN THE WEST INDIES, JANUARY 1722

Almost three centuries ago, just as today, lurid accounts of attacks far from home were reported in America's earliest newspapers and read by

*every segment of society. The following excerpt is taken from the May 7,
1722 (O.S.), edition of the* Boston News-Letter, *describing the misfortune that four months previously had befallen the merchant captain
Benjamin Edwards—whose large brick home stood at Back Street (modern 104 Salem Street) in the North End of Boston—at the hands of pitiless George Lowther and his gang of cutthroats off the Honduran coast:*

Boston, On the 10th of January last, the ship *Gray-hound* of this port,
Capt. Benjamin Edwards commander, in the bay of Hundoras [*sic*], was
attacked by the *Bumper* galley, then call'd the *Happy Delivery*, a ship
of 250 tons, having on board 80 or 90 pirates, commanded by George
Lowder; she had a consort sloop of 30 tons and 25 men, who after a
stout resistance made, was taken and barbarously handled by them.
They also took seven other vessels, two of them brigantines belonging
to Boston; one they sunk, and the other they burnt. Capt. Hamilton's
sloop of Jamaica, they carried with them, another of Virginia they emp-
tied and gave her to the Master; Capt. Ayre's sloop *Connecticut* they
burnt. The other was a Rhode Island sloop of about 80 tons.

The said pirate forced away from Capt. Edwards the following
mariners, viz.:

Christopher Atwell, Chief Mate, aged about 26, much pock-broken, born
in the West of England.

Charles Harris, second Mate, aged about 25, small stature, born in
London.

Henry Smith, carpenter, aged about 25 years, born in Boston.

Joseph Willis, aged 18 years, apprentice to the Capt., born in London.

David Lindsay, aged 50 years, born in Scotland;

and they burnt his ship.

*Such roving desperadoes often coerced skilled seamen into their
service to help sail their vessels, although without necessarily welcoming them into their criminal ranks. And despite his harrowing mistreatment and financial losses, Captain Edwards succeeded in regaining
Boston, eventually dying a wealthy man in 1751.*

Source: Boston News-Letter, May 7, 1722.

DOCUMENT I.—NED LOW'S PIRATE ARTICLES, 1723

*At 8:00 A.M. on July 11, 1723 (O.S.), 36 crewmen of Captain Ned Low's
consort sloop* Fortune *were brought to trial for piracy, robbery, and
felony before New England's lieutenant-governor William Dummer*

in Newport, Rhode Island. Several of the accused said that they had been "forced men," pressed into service off merchantmen by the pirates, yet had never actually joined their company by signing Low's articles. One acquitted prisoner, John Kencate—taken in September 1722 from the galley Sycamore *in the Cape Verde Islands, to act as the pirates' surgeon—recalled the articles themselves as follows, "to the best of his remembrance, having often seen them whilst with Low":*

1st. The captain shall have two full shares; the master a share and a half; the doctor, mate, gunner, carpenter, and boatswain, a share and a quarter.

2d. He that shall be found guilty of striking or taking up any unlawful weapon, either aboard of a prize or aboard the privateer, shall suffer what punishment the Captain and majority of the company shall think fit.

3d. He that shall be found guilty of cowardice in time of any engagement, shall suffer what punishment the captain and the majority of the company shall think fit.

4th. If any jewels, gold, or silver, is found on board a prize, to the value of a piece of eight, and the finder does not deliver it to the quartermaster in twenty-four hours' time, shall suffer what punishment the Captain and majority of the company shall see fit.

5th. He that shall be found guilty of gaming, or playing at cards, or defrauding or cheating one another to the value of a royal of plate, shall suffer what punishment the Captain and a majority of the company shall think fit.

6th. He that shall be guilty of drunkenness in the time of an engagement, shall suffer what punishment the Captain and majority of the company shall think fit.

7th. He that hath the misfortune to lose any of his limbs; in the time of an engagement in the company's service, shall have the sum of six hundred pieces of eight, and be kept in the company as long as he pleases.

8th. Good quarters to be given when craved.

9th. He that sees a sail first, shall have the best pistol, or small arm aboard of her.

10th. And lastly, no snapping of arms in the hold.

Ten of the accused were duly spared, the remainder being hanged eight days later at Bull's Point, and buried "within the flux and reflux of the sea."

Source: Wilkins Updike, ed., *Memoirs of the Rhode Island Bar* (Boston: T.H. Webb, 1842), 292–93.

GLOSSARY

Both their discourses and actions, plainly showed the wickedness
of their designs.

> —Governor Alexander Spotswood of Virginia,
> deriding the supposed retirement of Blackbeard
> and his piratical minions, 1719

In both literature and film, the language attributed to pirates has
always added to their allure. Seventeenth-century accents and expressions, exotic place names and foreign patois have been further embel-
lished with nautical terms, producing a unique pattern of speech and
much colorful phrasing. Some authentic terms have endured into our
modern era, while those that may have fallen into disuse still retain
their appeal.

Abraham's Cay—a lawless pirate harbor on the Nicaraguan coast, concealed
at the mouth of what the Spaniards had long ago labeled the *Escondido*
(Hidden) River, and which is today better known as Bluefields. Apparently
this remote outpost was first claimed and settled by the Dutch rover Abraham Albertszoon Blauveldt, whose New York–based brother Willem may
have also given the family surname to Bluefields, Jamaica.

account—an English slang expression for piracy, more commonly used with
a verb—such as in going or sailing on the account—and doubtless derived

from the fact that lawless rovers served without any wages against an eventual distribution of whatever ill-gotten booty was obtained.

advice boat—a term for any vessel bearing dispatches or special warnings, originally derived from the Spanish verb *avisar,* which means to advise or forewarn. Historically, whenever a fleet was scheduled to depart a Spanish port, it was customary to send an *aviso* on ahead to scout for enemies and give advance notice at its intended destination. From the Spanish, this word had passed directly into English usage.

almiranta—generic Spanish term for any vice-flagship, either in a naval formation or a commercial fleet; originally derived from the Arabic title *al-amir* (the emir). See full description under *capitana* below.

apostles—military slang for the 12 charges usually carried in 17th-century bandoliers or cartridge belts, the recital of which names helped combatants to keep count of their expended rounds during the heat of battle.

Armada de Barlovento—Spanish name that means Windward Fleet, the designation of a permanent naval squadron assigned to patrol the Caribbean Sea against foreign enemies, pirates, and smugglers as well as to deliver Crown payrolls and supplies to island outposts—often with mixed success during the 17th century.

Armada del Mar del Sur—Spanish squadron based out of Callao, Peru, whose principal mission was to convey consignments of raw silver from the Andean mines of Potosí into Lima for minting, then on to Panama City so that the minted bars and coins could be dispatched across the Atlantic to the royal exchequer in Madrid. In carrying out these duties, the armada often evaded or clashed with pirate marauders during the 1680s.

armadilla—generic Spanish term for any small flotilla of warships, being the diminutive form of the word *armada,* which signifies a fleet of warships. Formations that sporadically sortied from major ports such as Cartagena or Campeche to chase away nearby pirate groups, were commonly called *armadillas.*

arribada—generic Spanish legal term for any unauthorized arrival off a coast, or entry into port, punishable by seizure of the offending vessel and its contents.

asiento—misunderstood in English as the name of the monopoly for supplying African slaves into Spanish America, although this term was generally applied to any contract entered into by the Spanish Crown or its dependencies for obtaining specific goods or services, countless such arrangements or *asientos* being signed every year for a wide variety of items, ranging from gunpowder to ships' biscuits.

aviso—generic Spanish word for any dispatch vessel or mail boat; see *advice boat* above.

azogue—Spanish term for quicksilver or mercury, a vital ingredient for refining the silver ores mined throughout its American empire. This product had to be transported by sea and thus sometimes fell prey to enemy privateers or pirates and was ransomed at extortionate prices.

Bab-el-Mandeb—Arabic name given to the narrow and difficult strait leading into the Red Sea, meaning the Gate of Tears, which was to be prowled during the late 17th century by such North American pirates as Captains Thomas Tew and William Kidd.

Banda del Norte—Spanish name for the northern coastline of Hispaniola, which Spain had abandoned and was to be gradually occupied during the late 17th century by French buccaneers and settlers, expanding out of their offshore pirate stronghold on Tortuga Island.

barco luengo or *longo*—Spanish name that literally means long boat, yet in fact referred to a particular type of galliot or oared sailing vessel commonly used throughout the West Indies. Because of their shallow draft and combined means of propulsion, *barcos luengo* were ideally suited for service in shallow waters and thus were favored by pirates and their coast guard opponents alike. From the Spanish, this expression had entered the English language with many different spellings.

Bay of Campeche—English name for the broad Mexican bay whose real name is the Laguna de Términos, occupied as of the mid-17th century by foreign logwood poachers and visiting pirates. The name *Campeche* was often written phonetically as Campeachy by English interlopers, while the long barrier island enclosing the Laguna's waters—modern Isla del Carmen—was then known as Isla Triste or Sad Island, often reduced to Trist or Tris.

Bayman or Baymen—nickname for foreign interlopers who lived in or frequented the Bay of Campeche.

bilbo or bilboes—17th-century nickname for any rapier or fine, flexible thrusting sword, supposedly derived from the name of the Spanish port of Bilbao, where many such tempered blades were bought. Bilboes, on the other hand, referred to a long iron bar with shackles used to confine the feet of prisoners.

Biscayan privateers—squadron of corsairs specifically raised in northeastern Spain during the late 17th century to combat the wave of pirates and smugglers running rampant throughout the West Indies. Their small squadron reached the Caribbean by late 1686, operating for a half dozen years, to little effect.

black dog—English slang expression for a counterfeit silver coin, especially a shilling, during the early 18th century.

blue officers—French nickname for nonaristocratic officers of privateer or merchant backgrounds who were admitted into the navy on a temporary and unpaid basis during wartime in the late 17th and early 18th centuries; they were openly resented by high-born officers of the Grand Corps, the self-styled *rouges* or "reds."

caper—English and French spelling of the Dutch word *kaper,* meaning a privateer; see full description under *kaper* below.

capitana—generic Spanish term for any flagship, either in a naval or a commercial fleet, while *almiranta* is applied to a vice-flagship—seemingly reverse the usual order whereby captains are subordinate to admirals. However, when these expressions first gained currency in medieval Spain, it was customary for fleets to be commanded by a *capitán general,* while the designation *almirante* was later adapted from the Arabic *al-amir* or the emir.

careen—nautical expression meaning to tilt a stationary vessel in shallow water or on a beach to expose its underside for cleaning or repairs; originally derived from the Latin word *carina,* for ship's keel. Pirate commanders, who seldom enjoyed the luxury of a protected harbor, had to careen their ships with great care in isolated bays.

cassava—a slender, erect shrub native to tropical America and the West Indies whose tuberous roots were harvested during the 17th century to provide sustenance for slaves and indentured servants, usually in the form of bread or tapioca. Because of this lowly association, cassava came to have a negative connotation as a food source.

charter party—English name for any covenant drawn up by freebooters prior to a cruise, predetermining a fair division of spoils at its conclusion; derived from the French commercial expression *charte-partie*—literally, a split charter—entered into whenever two or more merchants agreed to share cargo space in a single hired vessel.

cincuentena—Spanish militia cavalrymen on Santo Domingo organized into volunteer companies of 50 irregular riders apiece—in Spanish, *cincuenta,* hence their nickname. The French *boucaniers* who shared Hispaniola and often had to hunt wild cattle singly or in small bands, dreaded falling into the *cincuentenas'* hands and told lurid tales about their cruelty.

clipped money—coins illegally reduced in weight by filing, shaving, or clipping metal from around their edges, thereby deceitfully reducing their value, the resultant shards being melted down for resale.

cocket—a written certificate issued by a custom house to a departing ship confirming that its cargo had been duly registered for a specific destination and the appropriate duties paid; as such, an important paper for later establishing the legitimacy of a vessel's voyage.

commission port—legal designation of the seaport at which a privateer received his commission and posted a bond for his good conduct during his forthcoming cruise and into which all his prizes had to be sent for adjudication, a measure designed to hold rovers accountable for the actions they perpetrated during their forays.

corsair—synonym for privateer. Especially in Spanish, *corsario* meant an individual or vessel officially licensed to commit hostilities at sea. The Spanish also referred to privateering as *andar a corso* or to a privateering commission as a *patente de corso.*

Crab Island—English name for Vieques Island, lying eight miles east of Puerto Rico, and which is still noted today for its large land crabs.

Cross of Burgundy—17th-century name for the Spanish flag, which had long featured a red *raguly saltire* cross on a white background, ever since the 1530 coronation of Spain's Hapsburg monarch Charles V as Holy Roman Emperor.

Darien colony—short-lived Scottish settlement established on the northeastern shores of Panama in November 1698, when 1,200 colonists disembarked from five ships; despite fending off an overland Spanish assault, they nonetheless quickly succumbed to disease, lack of profits, and internal strife, and the survivors withdrew by the next summer.

daudorus—a Scottish euphemism for a thrashing or beating, apparently derived from the ancient verb "to daud" or to beat.

Dead Man's Island—see *Isla del Muerto* below.

Devil's Torrent—translation of the Spanish term *Raudal del Diablo*, given to a whitewater section of the San Juan River in Central America where the Fortress of the Limpia, Pura e Inmaculada Concepción (modern El Castillo) was erected from 1673 to 1675 to prevent penetrations upriver by West Indian pirates.

dogger—a 17th-century nautical expression equivalent to tender, signifying an auxiliary vessel manned out of a larger ship; its modern application is quite different, referring to a specific type of North Sea fishing vessel— usually two-masted and with a bluff bow—whose name has derived from the Dutch word *dogger-boot* or codfish boat.

doubloon—English word for the largest of Spanish gold coins in circulation during the late 17th and early 18th centuries; derived from its original name of *doblón*, signifying an *escudo* or piece of currency worth double its face value.

dry gripes—English nickname for a stomach malady associated with the Caribbean, sometimes called the West-India dry gripes, which was actually a form of lead poisoning brought on by the common practice of distilling rum through lead pipes. Also known as the dry bellyache, because it was characterized by extremely painful intestinal cramps, yet no diarrhea, only constipation.

Dry Tortugas—17th-century English nickname for the shoals at the west end of the Florida Keys, so called to distinguish them from Salt Tortuga off Venezuela and the French island of Tortuga off Hispaniola.

ducat—English name for a mid-sized Spanish gold coin known as a *ducado* and worth 11 reals; the next smallest such coin was the *escudo*, worth 10 reals, followed by the silver peso worth eight reals.

duck cloth—a hardy type of linen or canvas with many shipboard uses; its peculiar name originally derived from the generic Dutch word for cloth: *doek*.

ducking—a type of nautical punishment in which a malefactor was hoisted up to the tip of a yardarm and then dropped repeatedly into the sea, plunging painfully beneath the surface and bobbing back up again, like a duck.

enfants perdus—17th-century French military slang that means the lost children and was used to describe any vanguard, assault force, or other advance unit in battle; the English equivalent was the forlorn.

engagé—a French indentured servant, usually a young man brought out from Europe to work off a payment in the Americas; often exploited or abused, this became a deeply resented position in the West Indies and fed a steady stream of embittered recruits into freebooter ranks.

filibuster—a synonym for privateer, likely derived from the Dutch word *vliebooter*, a once-derisive nickname for sailors who only plied as far as the nearby island of Vlieland in tiny craft. During the 16th century, though, it became an expression of pride among rebel Dutch seamen, while flyboat came to mean any fast-sailing vessel used for warlike purposes or voyages of discovery. The term came to be applied to West Indian seaborne raiders, particularly among the French, who spelled it as *flibustier*. Much later, it would develop an additional meaning in the United States, after a 19th-century Congressman accused an opponent of acting as a filibuster by halting all business through continuous speaking.

flag of truce—in addition to its obvious meaning—a white standard displayed to request a military parley during a lull in fighting—this term was also applied to any vessel delegated to visit a hostile coast or port during wartime, most often to transact a prisoner exchange.

flibustier—see "filibuster" above

flip—English nickname for a mixed alcoholic drink similar to punch, very popular among West Indian seamen and made chiefly with hot watered-down beer and brandy and sometimes sweetened and spiced.

flota—common Spanish name for the annual plate fleets sailing to and from the main Mexican seaport of Veracruz, while Spain's other great convoys—which serviced the Colombian port of Cartagena and Portobelo in Panama—were known as the *galeones*.

flute—originally, a distinct type of Dutch cargo vessel developed during the early 17th century with radically tapered upper works so as to only require small crews for moving large shipments of goods; the name later became the general designation for most lightly armed naval transports, especially in France's royal navy.

Flying Gang—nickname for the gang of hoodlums who controlled the waterfront at lawless Nassau from 1715 to 1718, extorting payments from visiting masters as its self-anointed customs officers prior to the restoration of proper Crown rule.

forban—French synonym for an outright pirate or lawless sea rover, as opposed to a licensed *corsaire* or *flibustier*.

forlorn, the—17th-century English military slang for any advance unit or vanguard, the French equivalent being *les enfants perdus.*

freebooter—general term for any individual performing military or naval service without salary but rather for shares of plunder or prize money alone; believed derived from the Dutch *vrijbuiter,* which probably entered the English language during the frequent wars in the Low Countries of the late 16th and early 17th centuries.

French King, to have seen the—curious English slang expression dating from the mid-17th century, meaning to be drunk.

galeones—the name commonly applied in Spain to the annual transatlantic plate fleets that sailed to the Colombian port of Cartagena and Panamanian terminus of Portobelo for the silver output from South America, while formations traveling to and from Mexico were referred to as the *flotas* (see above).

Gardens of the Queen—name originally given by Christopher Columbus to the maze of beautiful tropical islands off southern Cuba, in honor of Queen Isabella of Spain; these were never populated by Spaniards because of their shallow and reef-lined approaches, so they became a favorite haunt of foreign smugglers and pirates. English officials and seafarers usually referred to them as the south cays of Cuba.

gibbet—iron cage made in the size and shape of a human body to publicly exhibit executed criminals as a warning to others; many pirates ended their days in this device, such as Captain William Kidd, whose body was to be displayed along the banks of the Thames River for several months after his execution in May 1701.

gobernador de tercio—official title of the Spanish officer in command of the marine regiment serving aboard Spain's West Indian squadron, the Armada de Barlovento, who flew his flag aboard a separate ship consequently known as the *gobierno.*

Golden Island—an offshore pirate haunt lying amid reef-lined waters near modern Punta Escocés, about 150 miles east of Portobelo along Panama's northeastern coastline, which was used by buccaneers during the 1680s to hide their ships and march across the isthmus to attack Spanish vessels plying the Pacific Ocean.

guardacostas—Spanish term literally meaning coast guards, applied equally to both such corsairs or their vessels, who were commissioned in increasing numbers during the 18th century by Spanish American officials to operate in regional waters; English seafarers repeatedly complained of their arbitrary seizures and harsh conduct, hardened by generations of pitiless warfare against cruel pirates—to which was added a single-minded pursuit of profit, for, like their rover foes, most *guardacostas* only received shares from any captures they made, not regular wages.

Half-Way Tree—a crossroads in Jamaica, northwest of Kingston, so named because during rotations of British troops between Port Royal and the inland capital of Spanish Town, they were allowed to rest beneath an ancient cottonwood tree that grew at this spot during their marches across that warm expanse.

harnessed—slang English expression, meaning bearing arms. For example, witnesses testified during the trial at Newport, Rhode Island, of the pirate sloop *Ranger*'s survivors in July 1723 that most of its crewmen "were harnessed, that is armed with guns," which contributed toward the death penalty being handed down for those convicted.

Hispaniola—English name for the island today shared between Haiti and the Dominican Republic, which Christopher Columbus had first christened in December 1492 as the Isla Española or Spanish Island, because its appearance so strongly reminded him of the coasts of Spain. This name was retained throughout the colonial era, passing phonetically from Spanish into English.

hogshead—large wooden barrel used to transport bulk cargo in ship holds, usually liquids such as beer or wine or commercial produce such as sugar, molasses, or tobacco. It is believed that this curious name may have been a corruption of the Dutch term for such a large cask, *oxhooft*. During the 17th and 18th centuries, hogsheads varied considerably in size, depending upon region.

hornpipe—a sailor's dance, popular since the 16th century, whose name derived from the single-reed woodwind commonly played as its musical accompaniment. Dance steps mimicked shipboard activities, such as clapping hands to the forehead as if peering out to sea, lurching as if experiencing heavy weather, and so on.

inch of candle—method of setting a time limit by marking a line upon a lit candle, commonly used during auctions of prize vessels brought into Port Royal, Jamaica. After receiving the highest bid, a candle would be lit and scored an inch from the top; if no higher amount was offered before the flame burned down past this mark, the sale became final.

indigo—a valuable bluish-purple powder produced by certain tropical plants that was a coveted commercial dye in Europe and so made a tempting prize for privateers and pirates.

interloper—in the late-17th-century Caribbean, a term specifically applied to any unsanctioned merchant visitor who brought goods or slaves into the region without a license in hopes of smuggling them ashore for sale, in contravention of the existing monopolies.

in the gun—slang English expression, meaning to be tipsy or slightly inebriated.

Isla del Muerto—Spanish name meaning Dead Man's Island. At least six spots still bear this grim name today, although none are directly associated with piracy.

Isle of Ash—English mispronunciation of Ile-à-Vache, the French name for Cow Island, a favorite pirate gathering spot and lookout point off the southwestern tip of Haiti.

Jolly Roger—English euphemism for a pirate flag, although dating from the Victorian era and believed to be derived from the French expression *joli rouge,* a jocular reference to the blood-red standards that had been flown whenever no quarter was to be given.

kaper—the Dutch word for privateer, meaning a ship outfitted with a government commission to conduct hostilities during wartime as well as the crewmen who served aboard it. The term passed into both French and English, although almost always written as caper, and gradually faded from use as Dutch privateering activity went into a steady decline during the last quarter of the 17th century.

keelhauling—a brutal form of nautical punishment in which the condemned was dangled from the tip of a ship's yardarm with a weighted line tied to his feet, the other end passing under the hull and up to the opposite end of the yardarm. The prisoner was then dropped into the sea and the line hauled in, so as to be tugged beneath the ship in suffocating agony over its sharp barnacles, emerging—barely conscious and hanging upside down— on the far side.

kilduijvel **or kill-devil**—a 17th-century Dutch euphemism for rum, supposedly because it could still the Devil in man.

laars—the Dutch name for a cat-o'-nine-tails, the whip of unraveled heavy rope used to administer floggings aboard ships.

landlubber—originally an English insult meaning a pilfering tramp or vagrant—also rendered as land leaper, land loper, land pirate, and land rat—and being understood as such throughout the 17th and 18th centuries. It was not until much more recent times that it became a contemptuous expression used among sailors for any inexperienced hand.

league—a measurement of distance roughly equivalent to three miles, although varying widely by nationality throughout the 17th and 18th centuries. English nautical leagues were gauged at 20 for every degree of latitude, roughly equivalent to 6,000 total yards, each league being furthermore subdivided into three nautical miles.

let-pass—the simplest form of license issued to vessels in the West Indies, identifying its commander and requesting that he be allowed to proceed— that is, be let past—toward a particular destination. Rapacious privateer captains sometimes used such innocuous documents to justify their depredations, while Spanish officials objected to let-passes being issued for such places as Honduras or the Bay of Campeche, which they regarded as lying within their territory and thus off limits to foreigners.

letter of marque—another name for a privateering commission, apparently distinct in that crewmen were to receive regular wages in addition to shares from any captures, as opposed to traditional privateersmen, who served for booty alone. During the 17th and 18th centuries, this term was sometimes misspelled as *letter of mart.*

letter of reprisal—special type of privateering commission issued during peacetime to redress a particular wrong that could not be satisfied through a proper legal recourse. In essence, a letter of reprisal allowed an aggrieved party to seek restitution through the indiscriminate capture of foreign vessels without constituting an official declaration of war nor allowing the bearer to accumulate more than a set amount in prize money.

light money—English euphemism for coins that had been clipped or filed around their edges, making them worth less by weight than their purported face value, a frequent problem during the 17th and 18th centuries.

the Line—nickname for the ancient boundary agreed between Spain and Portugal, dividing their claims to the newly discovered Americas about 1,100 miles west of the Cape Verde and Azores Islands; Oliver Cromwell's decision to send a major peacetime expedition to conquer a West Indian colony in 1654 had been spurred by Spanish captures of English vessels in those waters, which Spain refused to compensate "on the ground that beyond the Line, trade and jurisdiction alike are the exclusive prerogatives of His Catholic Majesty."

logwood or dyewood—dark red tropical tree native to the West Indies, harvested to produce a black or brown dye that became highly prized in Europe for tinting cloth, because—in the words of the pirate chronicler Alexandre-Olivier Exquemelin—it does "not fade like ours."

lubber—see *landlubber.*

Madagascar—a huge island that lies about 250 miles off the southeast coast of Africa, beside the trade route leading around the Cape of Good Hope into the Indian Ocean, and whose innumerable coves and ready provisions made it a notorious pirate lair during the late 17th and early 18th centuries.

Main—contracted form of the geographic term the Spanish Main, for the stretch of coastline extending from Venezuela to Panama; see *Spanish Main* below.

mal de Siam—a late-17th-century French nickname for yellow fever, translated literally to mean the Siamese disease, because, according to the chronicler priest Jean-Baptiste Labat, it had been introduced into Martinique by the crew of the royal vessel *Oriflamme* while homeward bound from their voyage to Bangkok and Brazil.

Mar del Sur—Spanish name for the Pacific Ocean, literally meaning the South Sea. This curious designation had come about during the initial wave of conquests, when the first conquistadors had encountered the Gulf of Mexico, followed by others a few years later probing the Pacific, so that these two bodies of water became temporarily identified as the North Sea and South Sea. Although the former soon reverted to its current name, the Pacific would remain known as the *Mar del Sur* for decades thereafter.

maroon—an expression originally derived from the Spanish adjective *cimarrón*, which is generally used to denote anything wild, rogue, or untamed, but came to be specially applied to *negros cimarrones* or runaway slaves, who often fled their masters and sought refuge in torrid coastal zones. Buccaneers and other foreign seamen who chanced upon these isolated havens assumed that residents had been driven there—"marooned"—for rebelliousness, so the term came to be misinterpreted in English as deliberately abandoning someone on a desolate island or beach as punishment.

Maroon Islands—nickname for the Bahamian archipelago during the late 17th and early 18th centuries, when its waters abounded with corsairs and most islands lay deserted, so that transient ships were often intercepted and hapless crewmen abandoned ashore.

matross—17th-century English expression for a gunner's mate, doubtless derived from the Dutch word *matroos*, which simply means sailor.

moidore—term that had originally entered the English language from the Portuguese expression *moeda d'ouro*, literally meaning a coin of gold but which came to be applied to any finely wrought piece of gold currency during the 18th century.

morro—a generic Spanish word for any large harbor castle or coastal fortification; the term originated during medieval times, when many such defenses were erected in Spain to guard against seaborne descents by fierce North African Moors.

mum—a strong ale popular during the 17th century made from wheat and oat malts and flavored with herbs. Originally developed in Brunswick in Germany, its name was also spelled as *mumme* and *mom*.

out of the sea—expression used by English pirates whenever challenged by a ship as to where they were coming from.

Para—Dutch nickname for the city of Paramaribo, capital of their South American colony of Suriname, whose river approaches were guarded by Fort Zeelandia.

partridge—English nickname for clusters of small rounds fired from cannons, a term that would later become more widely known as grapeshot because of the approximate size of each individual ball. Apparently the expression *partridge* had derived during the 17th century from the scattering buckshot commonly used in hunting such birds.

patache—generic Spanish term used to describe any smaller vessel that served as a consort to a larger ship, or as a fleet auxiliary, rather than the designation of a specific type of craft. Over the centuries, this expression had passed verbatim into both the English and French languages, although often misspelled.

pedrero—Spanish name for a swivel gun, a term derived from the word *piedra* (stone), the most common type of ball fired by the earliest guns, when gunpowder was first being introduced during medieval times. Light warships such as galliots, which patrolled near Caribbean shorelines, were often armed with only *pedreros*—a term that would be misspelled many different ways in English.

picaroon—Anglicized version of the Spanish word *picarón*, meaning a great rogue or great rascal, which, in the 17th century—prior to the standardization of accents in the Spanish language—was commonly written as *picaroon* and as such passed directly into the English language, being applied to thieves and pirates alike.

pichelingue—Spanish nickname for any Dutchman, a term believed to have evolved from a garbling of the name of the great Zeeland seaport of Vlissingen or Flushing, from where so many Dutch ships had sailed for the New World.

piece of eight—English name for the silver Spanish coin known as a *peso de ocho reales*, meaning a peso worth eight reals, which were produced in such vast quantities at the royal mints of Mexico City and the Peruvian capital of Lima that they came to circulate all around the world, as far as the Philippines and China. A commonly accepted form of currency in England's colonies, they were valued at four and a half shillings or four shillings sixpence apiece.

pipe—in 17th-century nautical terms, a large and long wooden barrel used for transporting bulk cargo in the hold of a ship, usually liquids such as beer or wine.

piragua—Spanish American name for a crude type of coastal craft or riverboat made from a hollowed-out log. The original expression appears to have been the Carib word for dugout canoe; such boats were made by felling a soft cotton or cedar tree, then hollowing out its core with fire and axes. Many piraguas were quite large, measuring almost 40 feet long, and capable of traveling swiftly with the aid of simple masts and numerous paddlers. Their ability to work through shallow waters and land easily on any beach made them popular with pirates.

pistole—generic English term signifying any foreign gold coin, especially of Spanish or French manufacture, worth more than a pound sterling. For example, the corrupt private governor of the Bahamas, Elias Haskett, was accused in 1701 of refusing a £50 bribe to free the confined mulatto privateer Read Elding, instead angrily "swearing that if Elding did not send him 50 pistols (£67, 10 shillings), he should not be released."

pistol-proof—slang expression among English buccaneers or fighting men, for anything invincible or outstanding; supposedly derived from being impervious to close-quarter gunfire, when handheld pistols were used at point-blank range.

plate fleet—convoy sent annually from Seville or Cadiz across the Atlantic for the king of Spain's American *plata* or silver, hence its name. By the late 17th century, such sailings were becoming less and less frequent.

puerto real—generic Spanish nautical expression meaning port royal, which, during the 17th century was used by seamen to describe any large, deep-water anchorage. The favorite buccaneer anchorage hidden on the southern face of Roatán Island, today known as Coxen's Hole, also went by the name of Puerto Real.

punch house—English nickname for any low drinking establishment, the term originating because punch or some other such alcoholic concoction was routinely sold there, although eventually the term came to mean a brothel as well.

purchase—English euphemism for booty or loot, much used among privateersmen and pirates. In particular, the phrase "no purchase, no pay," was employed to advise any prospective recruits before a cruise that if no prize money—that is, purchase—resulted, there could be no pay for the men, who otherwise received no regular wages.

rack—in nautical terminology during the late 17th and early 18th centuries, a synonym for wreckage," as in the more universal expression "rack and ruin."

Red Seamen—English nickname for rogue privateers, many from North America, who used the pretext of attacking French interests in Asia to capture hapless native merchantmen and slip home to dispose of their exotic booty, far from the scene of these crimes.

round robin—pirate practice of signing names in a circle so that no one single name would be more prominent.

Sainte-Barbe or Santa Bárbara—French and Spanish expression, respectively, for a powder room or magazine, derived from the Catholic observance of Saint Barbara as the patron saint of all those who work with explosives, such as gunners or miners, a votive image being commonly displayed on the door.

salmagundi—a communal stew or ragout dish made with a mixture of meats, to which vegetables and other items might be added, the whole being highly seasoned and highly popular among West Indian buccaneers; spelled *salmigondis* in French.

Salt Tortuga—English nickname for sun-bleached Isla Tortuga, an island that lies off the northern shores of Venezuela, where turtle meat could be slaughtered and cured from the local salt pans, and thus—according to the buccaneer chronicler William Dampier—so called "to distinguish it from the shoals of Dry Tortuga, near Cape Florida, and from the isle of Tortuga by Hispaniola."

santo y seña—Spanish system of passwords, based upon the Church calendar, whereby any stranger approaching after nightfall would be challenged with a saint's name shouted out at random by a sentry, the correct response being the place name associated with each particular saint: for example, to a cry of "Santa Rosa?" the proper reply must be "Lima!" This system had been introduced with foreign pirates in mind, especially the heretic English or Dutch.

sargento mayor—17th-century Spanish military rank, much more senior than its present-day English equivalent would imply, a sargento mayor serving as second in command to any military governor of a large city or commander of a royal garrison.

Sir Cloudesley—jocular English name for a drink made of small beer and brandy, often with sweetening, spices, and nearly always lemon juice added, named in honor of the famous mariner Sir Clowdisley Shovell—both for his services against the Barbary corsairs, as well as his unusual and dreamy first name.

situados—payrolls and subsidies dispatched annually from the viceroyalties of Mexico and Peru to other, less wealthy Spanish American colonies, and which were often targeted by pirates.

skull and crossbones—not an expression current during the 17th and early 18th centuries, instead the usual term for the dread symbol displayed by pirates being the death's head.

snow—name for a type of two-masted brig or brigantine, with a distinctive half-mast located just behind its mainmast; originally called a *snaauw* in Dutch, this design fell into disuse as the 18th century progressed.

Somers Island—early English name for Bermuda, sometimes misspelled as Summers Island, although this curious name originated from the shipwreck of Sir George Somers's expedition, while bound toward Virginia.

South Sea—name originally applied to the Pacific Ocean by its first Spanish explorers and conquistadors during the 16th century, as they pushed south from the Caribbean and Gulf of Mexico to discover this vast new body of water; the presence of the wealthy viceroyalty of Peru due south of Panama doubtless did much to perpetuate the name *Mar del Sur* throughout the colonial era, which then passed directly from the Spanish language into English.

Spanish Main—curious name for the stretch of Caribbean coastline encompassing northern Panama, Colombia, and Venezuela, devised during the early 16th century when the first Spanish explorers erroneously assumed that they were charting portions of Asia's *Tierra Firme* or "Mainland." Even after further exploration had revealed it to be part of a vast new continent, it remained customary to refer to this expanse of coastline in Spanish circles as the Mainland, from whence this expression passed into English as the Spanish Main.

state ship—mid-17th-century designation for vessels of England's navy after the execution of King Charles I in January 1649 and creation of Sir Oliver Cromwell's protectorate had rendered the honorific term His Majesty's Ship irrelevant, until the monarchy was restored in 1660.

states' ship—designation for vessels owned or operated by the Dutch states-general.

Sunday keeping—Puritan religious observance, meaning to refrain from work on the Sabbath.

sure as a gun—slang English expression, meaning something that is known or can be accepted with complete certainty or accuracy.

swing—a euphemism for hanging; the retiring governor Alexander Spotswood wrote in June 1724 of the perils of his taking passage home to England through pirate-infested waters, as they had sworn to avenge his "making so many of their fraternity to swing in the open air of Virginia."

tattoo—word derived from the Tahitian language, first recorded in Western writing during James Cook's visit to that Pacific island in July 1769. The practice of tattooing did not become popular among European sailors until the late 18th century, long after the golden age of piracy.

tenths—during the 17th century, the percentage due to the king of England from the value of any enemy ships captured by privateers, after being adjudicated as legitimate prizes before a court of law.

tipple—English slang for liquor or any alcoholic drink.

Tortille—French nickname for Isla Tortuga, a sun-bleached island off northern Venezuela, where rovers often visited to gather salt and harvest turtles.

trepan—a slang English expression, used throughout the 17th and 18th centuries as either a noun or verb to denote any deception or trap intended to ensnare, ambush, or take someone by surprise.

Tris or Trist—English contraction of the Spanish term *Isla Triste* (Sad Island), which was the original name of the long barrier island enclosing Mexico's Laguna de Términos, occupied throughout the late 17th and early 18th centuries by foreign logwood cutters and transient pirates. Its modern name is Isla del Carmen.

waggoner—17th-century English term for a sea atlas, or any book combining sea charts and written sailing instructions; named after the famous Dutch cartographer Lucas Janszoon Waghenaer, who had published the first such printed atlas in 1584 under the title *Spiegel der Zeevaerdt,* translated into English four years later as *The Mariner's Mirror.*

Wild Coast—17th-century Dutch name for the stretch of Atlantic shoreline extending along the northeastern edge of South America, running from the Gulf of Paria to the Amazon River, and once home to the legendary El Dorado.

woolding—torture sometimes employed by Morgan's pirates to extract information from captives, described by John Style in January 1670 as tying a cord around a prisoner's head "and with a stick twisting it, till the eyes start out."

BIBLIOGRAPHY

EYEWITNESS CHRONICLERS

Atkins, John. *A Voyage to Guinea, Brazil, and the West Indies in His Majesty's Ships the* Swallow *and* Weymouth. Northbrook, IL: Metro Books, 1972 reedition of 1735 original.

> Account written by a naval surgeon of a two-year peacetime cruise to help put down piracy off West Africa, which began with a departure from Spithead in February 1721. During their patrol, some 270 pirates were captured and brought to trial, after which these Royal Navy vessels proceeded to Brazil and the West Indies, where they were dismasted by a hurricane while lying at Port Royal.

Barnard, John, Rev. *Ashton's Memorial: An History of the Strange Adventures and Signal Deliverances of Mr. Philip Ashton.* Salem, MA: Peabody Museum, 1976 reedition of a 1725 original, edited by Russell W. Knight.

> Ashton was a young fisherman from Marblehead, Massachusetts, who had been pressed into service aboard the pirate flagship of cruel Captain Ned Low in June 1722. He succeeded in escaping onto the island of Roatán during a layover nine months later and was eventually rescued by a merchant vessel and carried home by May 1725, where the local minister recorded his miraculous deliverance.

Cockburn, John. *A Journey over Land, from the Gulf of Honduras to the Great South-Sea.* Gale Ecco online reeedition of 1735 original, published in London by C. Rivington.

Narrative of the misfortunes suffered by a half dozen English sailors who were detained as pirates by a Spanish *guardacosta* and deposited at Puerto Caballos in 1730, subsequently escaping from jail in San Pedro Sula and eventually traversing the Isthmus of Panama.

Dampier, William. *A New Voyage Round the World.* New York: Dover, 1968 re-edition of 1697 original.

As an adventurous 23-year-old, Dampier had first sailed in February 1676 to live among the buccaneer camps in Mexico's Bay of Campeche for two years, then around Christmas 1679 joined the pirate crew of Captain Richard Sawkins, spending the next dozen years roaming the Pacific Ocean and Far East. Finally returning to England aboard an East Indiaman in September 1691, he published this account of his travels six years later, which included many firsthand descriptions of pirate life.

Du Tertre, Jean-Baptiste. *Histoire générale des Antilles habitées par les François.* 4 vols. Paris: Thomas Jolly, 1667–1671.

Originally a young soldier from Calais serving in Flanders, Du Tertre changed his first name from Jacques to Jean-Baptiste upon joining the Dominican Order in 1633, and seven years later was sent as a missionary to the primitive French Antilles. Du Tertre would publish numerous firsthand accounts describing the life of its pioneer inhabitants, including several early buccaneers.

Exquemelin, Alexandre-Olivier. *The Buccaneers of America.* Translated from the Dutch by Alexis Brown, with an introduction by Jack Beeching. London: Penguin, 1969.

Best-selling book written by a young Huguenot who had served among the buccaneers during the late 1660s before emigrating to Amsterdam and graduating as a member of the Dutch Surgeons' Guild in 1679.

Guijo, Gregorio M. de. *Diario, 1648–1664.* Mexico City: Editorial Porrúa, 1952; and Robles, Antonio de. *Diario de sucesos notables (1665–1703).* Mexico City: Editorial Porrúa, 1972.

A continuous record written by successive Mexican diarists, briefly recording newsworthy events from that era, including numerous piratical assaults.

Howse, Derek, and Norman J. W. Thrower, eds. *A Buccaneer's Atlas: Basil Ringrose's South Sea Waggoner. A Sea Atlas and Sailing Directions of the Pacific Coast of the Americas 1682.* Berkeley: University of California Press, 1992.

Facsimile reproduction of the Spanish chart book captured in the Pacific Ocean by Captain Bartholomew Sharpe, who, after his acquittal on charges of piracy in London in June 1682, had it published and dedicated to King Charles II. This edition includes many historical documents and records from this freebooter's campaign.

Interesting Tracts Relating to the Island of Jamaica, Consisting of Curious State Papers, Councils of War, Letters, Petitions, Narratives, etc., Which Throw Great Light on the History of That Island from Its Conquest down to the Year 1702. St. Jago de la Vega, Jamaica: Lewis, Lunan and Jones, 1800.
    A compilation including numerous interesting references to piracy, especially the "Journal Kept by Col. William Beeston, From His First Coming to Jamaica" in April 1660 until July 1680, reprinted on pages 271–300.

Johnson, Capt. Charles. *A General History of the Robberies and Murders of the Most Notorious Pirates.* London: Rivington, 1724.
    One of most influential works for the history of piracy, cobbled together by an unknown author from a variety of contemporary newspaper accounts, admiralty court trial records, and a few interviews. Its lively and colorful accounts, while not entirely reliable, produced a best-seller that was quickly followed by an expanded edition and countless later reprints.

Labat, Jean-Baptiste. *Memoirs, 1693–1705.* London: Routledge, 1970 reedition of 1931 translation by John Eaden.
    This intellectually gifted Dominican friar served as a missionary in the French Antilles from 1694 to 1705, recording descriptions of all aspects of island life, including pirates and privateers.

Lepers, Jean-Baptiste. *La tragique histoire des Flibustiers: Histoire de Saint-Domingue et de l'Île de la Tortue, repaires des flibustiers, écrite vers 1715.* Paris: 1925 reedition by Pierre-Bernard Berthelot.
    A history of the first French buccaneers on Tortuga Island and Haiti written a few decades later by a missionary and originally published in 1730.

Lussan, Ravenau de. *Journal of a Voyage into the South Seas.* Cleveland: Arthur H. Clark, 1930 translation by Marguerite Eyer Wilbur of the 1689 original.
    Excellent eyewitness account of service among the pirates by a young indentured servant who shipped out under Laurens de Graaf in November 1684, penetrated into the Pacific, and roved its waters for three years before regaining the Caribbean in March 1688 and publishing his journal in Paris the next year.

Salley, A. S., Jr., comp. and ed. *Commissions and Instructions from the Lords Proprietors of Carolina to the Public Officials of South Carolina, 1685–1715.* Charleston, SC: Historical Commission, 1916.
    Transcribes a document from 1700, describing the landing and subsequent trial of various seamen suspected of piracy.

Saunders, William L., ed. *The Colonial Records of North Carolina.* Vols. 1–2. Raleigh:
State of North Carolina, 1886.
    Includes various early documents and correspondence referring to
measures against piracy.

Sigüenza y Góngora, Carlos de. *Infortunios que Alonso Ramírez, natural de la
ciudad de San Juan de Puerto Rico, padeció.* Reprinted in *Obras históricas.*
Mexico City: Porrúa, 1960.
    Account given by a Puerto Rican seaman who had emigrated to the
Philippines of having been captured by English pirates in the Strait of
Singapore on March 4, 1687, being held prisoner for months until he
was released in the Antilles, and shipwrecking on the Yucatán Peninsula.

Vrijman, L. C. *Dr. David van der Sterre: Zeer aenmerkelijke reysen door Jan Erasmus
Reyning.* Amsterdam: P. N. van Kampen & Zoon, 1937 reedition of 1691
original.
    Biography of the Dutch-born rover Jan Erasmus Reyning, who served
in the West Indies for more than two decades under four different flags.
The original book had been very badly written by the doctor at the
slave depot of Curaçao before being republished in a more readable
version.

Wafer, Lionel. *A New Voyage and Description of the Isthmus of America.* London:
Hakluyt Society, 1933 reedition of 1699 original.
    Lively eyewitness account written by a ship's surgeon who served
under pirate captains such as Edmond Cooke and Edward Davis and
who roamed the Spanish Pacific for the better part of the 1680s.

DOCUMENTARY SOURCES

Bartlett, John R., ed. *Records of the Colony of Rhode Island and Providence Plantations, in New England.* Vol. 3, *1678–1706.* Providence, RI: State Printers,
1858.
    Contains transcriptions of various official letters complaining of
piracy.

Baxter, James Phinney, comp. and ed. *Documentary History of the State of Maine.*
Vols. 4–5. Portland: Maine Historical Society, 1869–1897.
    Among this official correspondence appear several firsthand re-
ports that mention or describe late 17th- and early 18th-century operations undertaken against pirates off the coast of Maine.

Brodhead, John R., ed. *Documents Relative to the Colonial History of the State of
New York.* 5 vols. Albany, NY: Weed, Parsons, 1853–1857.
    Includes brief annotations alluding to the activities of early Dutch
privateers and disposals of prizes.

Calendar of State Papers, Colonial Series, America and West Indies. Vols. 1, 5–34. London: Her Majesty's Stationery Office, 1860–1936.

A major documentary collection that contains thousands of transcribed summaries of firsthand reports or accounts, many related to piratical depredations and trials.

Fernow, Berthold, ed. *The Records of New Amsterdam: From 1653 to 1674 Anno Domini.* 7 vols. New York: Knickerbocker Press, 1897; reissued in 1976 by Syracuse University Press and in 2008 by BiblioLife.

Mentions a few documents concerning early Dutch privateering activities.

"Fragmentos del testimonio de los autos hechos con motivo de la invasión de la provincia de Costa Rica por los piratas Mansfelt y Henry Morgan en 1666." *Revista de los Archivos Nacionales* (Costa Rica) 1, no. 1–2 (November–December 1936): 5–33.

Partial Spanish records made in the wake of Edward Mansfield's failed attempt to penetrate Costa Rica in April 1666.

Gehring, Charles T., and Jacob A. Schiltkamp, trans. and eds. *Curaçao Papers, 1640–1665.* Vol. 17, *New Netherland Documents.* Interlaken, NY: Heart of the Lakes Publishing, 1987.

Transcribes a few original Dutch documents referring to early piracy and privateering.

Howell, Thomas Bayly, and William Cobbett, comps. and eds. "The Trials of Major Stede Bonnet and Thirty-Three Others, at the Court of Vice-Admiralty at Charleston in South Carolina, for Piracy [October–November 1718]." In *A Complete Collection of State Trials and Proceedings for High Treason and Other Crimes and Misdemeanors, from the Earliest Period to the Year 1783,* pp. 1231–302. London: Longman, Rees, Rome, Brown & Greene, 1816.

Reproduces extensive transcripts from these hearings.

Jameson, John Franklin. *Privateering and Piracy in the Colonial Period: Illustrative Documents.* New York: Macmillan, 1923.

An excellent collection of transcribed colonial-era records, still useful today.

Janisch, Hudson Ralph, comp. and ed. *Extracts from the St. Helena Records.* St. Helena: Guardian Office, 1885.

Reproduces a few scattered references to transient pirates and privateers.

Journals of the Board of Trade and Plantations. Vols. 3 and 4: March 1715–October 1718 and November 1718–December 1722. London: His Majesty's Stationery Office, 1924–1925.

Includes various pieces of official correspondence, legal documents, and proclamations pertaining to piracy.

Marsden, Reginald G., comp. and ed. *Documents Relating to Law and Custom of the Sea*. Clark, NJ: Lawbook Exchange, 1999 reissue of Navy Records Society edition of 1915–1916, 2 vols.
>   Classic collection of records describing and reflecting on various aspects of maritime history, including piracy.

Nelson, William, ed. *Documents Relating to the Colonial History of the State of New Jersey*. Vol. 1, *1704–1739, Extracts from American Newspapers*. 1st ser., Vol. 11, Paterson: Archives of the State of New Jersey, 1894.
>   Includes numerous reports of piratical depredations.

Piracy and Privateering catalog, Vol. 4, National Maritime Museum Library. London: Her Majesty's Stationery Office, 1972.
>   Compilation of a vast collection of rare and early works on piracy, with pertinent annotations as to their contents and publishing history.

Sir Henry Morgan's Voyage to Panama, 1670. London: Thomas Malthus, 1683.
>   Published on pages 55–97 of Malthus's larger *The Present State of Jamaica*, furnishing many transcribed documents from that famous expedition.

Taylor, John. *Jamaica in 1687: The Taylor Manuscript at the National Library of Jamaica*. Kingston: University of the West Indies Press, Mill Press, and the National Library of Jamaica, 2008 edition by David Buisseret.
>   Publication of a 17th-century description of this burgeoning English colony, complete with illustrations, compiled by a young teacher of mathematics who resided on the island.

Thornton, Diana Vida. "The Probate Inventories of Port Royal, Jamaica." Master's thesis, Anthropology Department, Texas A&M University, August 1992.
>   Contains a wealth of detail on everyday life in 17th-century Jamaica, including many privateers and seamen.

Thurloe, John. *A Collection of the State Papers of John Thurloe*. 7 vols. London: privately printed, 1742.
>   Correspondence sustained by this influential Puritan secretary of state and spymaster, with many letters on the conquest and early occupation of Jamaica.

Updike, Wilkins, ed. *Memoirs of the Rhode Island Bar*. Boston: Thomas H. Webb, 1842.
>   Pages 260–94 contain a transcript of the *Trials of Thirty-Six Persons for Piracy* at Newport in July 1723 who had been captured aboard Ned Low's accompanying sloop *Fortune* by the British warship *Greyhound*.

MODERN WORKS ON PIRACY

Arana, Luis R. "Aid to St. Augustine after the Pirate Attack, 1668–1670." *El Escribano* 7 (July 1970): 11–21.

Baer, Joel H. "'Captain John Avery' and the Anatomy of a Mutiny." *Eighteenth-Century Life* 18 (February 1994): 1–23.

Barbour, Violet F. "Privateers and Pirates of the West Indies." *American Historical Review* 16, no. 3 (April 1911): 529–66.

Barnes, Clementine. "Curiosity, Wonder, and William Dampier's Painted Prince." *Journal for Early Modern Cultural Studies* 6, no. 1 (Spring/Summer 2006): 31–50.

Beattie, Tim. "Adventuring Your Estate: The Origins, Cost and Rewards of Woodes Rogers' Privateering Voyage of 1708–1711." *Mariner's Mirror* 93 (2007): 143–55.

Bensusan, Harold G. "The Spanish Struggle against Foreign Encroachment in the Caribbean, 1675–1697." Unpublished PhD thesis, University of California, Los Angeles, 1970.

Bodge, Rev. George M. "The Dutch Pirates in Boston, 1694–95." *Bostonian Society Publications* 7 (1910): 31–60.

Bonner, W. H. *Captain William Dampier, Buccaneer-Author.* Stanford, CA: Stanford University Press, 1934.

Botting, Douglas. *The Pirates.* Alexandria, VA: Time-Life Books, 1978.

Bradley, Peter T. *The Lure of Peru: Maritime Intrusion into the South Sea, 1598–1701.* New York: St Martin's Press, 1989.

Bradley, Peter T. "The Ships of the Viceroyalty of Peru in the Seventeenth Century." *The Mariner's Mirror* 79, no. 4 (November 1993): 393–402.

Bradley, Peter T. *Society, Economy and Defence in 17th Century Peru: The Administration of the Count of Alba de Liste (1655–1661).* Liverpool, UK: Institute of Latin American Studies, 1992.

Bromley, John Selwyn. *Corsairs and Navies, 1660–1760.* London: Hambledon, 1988.

Burgess, Douglas R. *The Pirates' Pact: The Secret Alliances between History's Most Notorious Buccaneers and Colonial America.* New York: McGraw-Hill, 2008.

Buisseret, David J. "Edward D'Oyley, 1617–1675." *Jamaica Journal* (1971): 6–10.

Butler, Lindley S. *Pirates, Privateers, and Rebel Raiders of the Carolina Coast.* Chapel Hill: University of North Carolina Press, 2000.

Carr, H. Gresham. "Pirate Flags." *Mariner's Mirror* 29 (1943): 131–34.

Chapin, Howard Millar. *Privateer Ships and Sailors: The First Century of American Colonial Privateering, 1625–1725.* Toulon, France: G. Mouton, 1926.

Chapin, Howard Millar. "Captain Paine of Cajacet," *Rhode Island Historical Society Collections,* Vol. XXIII, No. 1 (January 1930), 19-32.

Cordingly, David. *Under the Black Flag: The Romance and Reality of Life among the Pirates.* New York: Random House, 1995.

Cordingly, David, and John Falconer. *Pirates.* New York: Abbeville Press, 1992.

Crouse, Nellis M. *The French Struggle for the West Indies, 1665–1713.* New York: Octagon, 1966.

Cruikshank, E. A. *The Life of Sir Henry Morgan.* Toronto: Macmillan, 1935.

Crummey, Jason. *Pirates of Newfoundland.* St. John's, Newfoundland: Jeremiah, 2006.

Crump, Dr. Helen J. *Colonial Admiralty Jurisdiction in the Seventeenth Century.* London: Longmans Green, 1931.

Dow, George Francis, and John Henry Edmonds. *The Pirates of the New England Coast, 1630–1730.* Salem, MA: Marine Research Society, 1923 edition reissued in 1996 by Dover.

Driscoll, Charles B. "Finale of the Wedding March." *American Mercury* (July 1928): 355–63.

Dyer, Florence E. "Captain Christopher Myngs in the West Indies, 1657–1662." *Mariner's Mirror* 18 (April 1932): 168–87.

Dyer, Florence E. "Captain John Strong, Privateer and Treasure Hunter." *Mariner's Mirror* 13 (1927): 145–58.

Earle, Peter. *The Sack of Panama: Captain Morgan and the Battle for the Caribbean.* New York: St. Martin's Press, 2007.

Earle, Peter. *The Sack of Panamá: Sir Henry Morgan's Adventures on the Spanish Main.* New York: Viking, 1981.

Earle, Peter. *The Treasure of the* Concepción: *The Wreck of the Almiranta.* New York: Viking, 1980.

Ellms, Charles. *The Pirates Own Book: Authentic Narratives of the Most Celebrated Sea Robbers.* Salem, MA: Marine Research Society, 1837; also republished in facsimile by Courier Dover in 1993.

Floyd, Troy S. *The Anglo-Spanish Struggle for Mosquitia.* Albuquerque: University of New Mexico Press, 1967.

Fraser, C. Lovat, illus. *The Lives and Adventures of Sundry Notorious Pirates.* New York: Robert M. McBride, 1922.

Freire Costa, Leonor. "Privateering and Insurance: Transaction Costs in Seventeenth-Century European Colonial Flows." *Ricchezza del mare,* 703–26.

Fuller, Basil, and Ronald Leslie-Melville. *Pirate Harbours and Their Secrets.* London: Stanley Paul, 1935.

Galvin, Peter R. "The Pirates' Wake: A Geography of Piracy and Pirates as Geographers in Colonial Spanish America, 1536–1718." Unpublished PhD thesis, Louisiana State University, 1991.

Gerhard, Peter. *Pirates on the West Coast of New Spain, 1575–1742.* Glendale, CA: Arthur H. Clark, 1960.

Gerhard, Peter. *The Southeast Frontier of New Spain.* Princeton, NJ: Princeton University Press, 1979.

Goodman, David. *Spanish Naval Power, 1589–1665: Reconstruction and Defeat.* Cambridge: Cambridge University Press, 1998.

Goslinga, Cornelis Ch. *The Dutch in the Caribbean and in the Guianas, 1680–1791.* Dover, NH: Van Gorcum, 1985.

Goslinga, Cornelis Ch. *The Dutch in the Caribbean and on the Wild Coast, 1580–1680.* Gainesville: University Press of Florida, 1971.

Gosse, Dr. Philip Henry George. *The Pirates' Who's Who.* London: Dulau, 1924.

Gosse, Dr. Philip Henry George. *The History of Piracy.* London: Longmans Green, 1932.

Gosse, Dr. Philip Henry George. *My Pirate Library.* London: Dulau, 1926.

Gosse, Dr. Philip Henry George. "Piracy." *Mariner's Mirror* 36 (1950): 337–49.

Hamilton, Archibald, Lord. *Articles Exhibited against Lord Archibald Hamilton, Late Governour of Jamaica, With Sundry Depositions and Proofs Relating to the Same.* London: Author, 1717.

Hamshere, C. E. "Henry Morgan and the Buccaneers." *History Today* 16 (1966): 406–414.

Haring, Clarence Henry. *The Buccaneers in the West Indies in the XVII Century.* London: Methuen, 1910.

Harvey, John H. "Some Notes on the Family of Dampier." *Mariner's Mirror* 29 (1943): 54–57.

Higginbotham, Jay. *Old Mobile: Fort Louis de la Louisiane, 1702–1711.* Mobile: University of Alabama Press, 1991 reprint of 1977 original published by the Museum of the City of Mobile.

Holm, John. "The Creole English of Nicaragua's Miskito Coast: Its Sociolinguistic History and a Comparative Study of Its Lexicon and Syntax." PhD dissertation, University of London, 1978.

Huetz de Lemps, Christian. "Indentured Servants Bound for the French Antilles in the Seventeenth and Eighteenth Centuries." In *"To Make America": European Emigration in the Early Modern Period,* edited by Ida Altman and James P. P. Horn, 175–203. Berkeley: University of California Press, 1991.

Hussey, Roland D. "Spanish Reaction to Foreign Aggression in the Caribbean to about 1680." *Hispanic American Historical Review* 9, no. 3 (August 1929): 286–302.

Ingram, Kenneth E. *Manuscript Sources for the History of the West Indies, With Special Reference to Jamaica.* Kingston, Jamaica: University of the West Indies Press, 2000.

Kemp, Peter K., and Christopher Lloyd. *The Brethren of the Coast: The British and French Buccaneers in the South Seas.* London: Heinemann, 1960.

Konstam, Angus. *Blackbeard: America's Most Notorious Pirate.* New York: John Wiley, 2007.

Lane, Kris E. *Blood and Silver: A History of Piracy in the Caribbean and Central America.* Oxford, England: Signal Books, 1999.

Lane, Kris E. "Buccaneers and Coastal Defense in Late-Seventeenth-Century Quito: The Case of Barbacoas." *Colonial Latin American Historical Review* 6, no. 2 (Spring 1997): 143–73.

Leamon, James S. "Governor Fletcher's Recall." *William and Mary Quarterly,* 3rd ser., 20, no. 4 (October 1963): 527–42.

Lee, Robert E. *Blackbeard the Pirate: A Reappraisal of His Life and Times.* Winston-Salem, NC: John F. Blair, 1995.

Le Pelley, John. "Dampier's Morgan and the Privateersmen." *Mariner's Mirror* 33 (1947): 170–78.

Leslie, Edward E. *Desperate Journeys, Abandoned Souls.* New York: Houghton Mifflin, 1998.

Little, Benerson. *The Buccaneer's Realm: Pirate Life on the Spanish Main, 1674–1688.* Washington, DC: Potomac Books, 2007.

Little, Benerson. *The Sea Rover's Practice: Pirate Tactics and Techniques, 1630–1730.* Washington, DC: Potomac Books, 2005.

Livingstone, Noël B. *Sketch Pedigrees of Some of the Early Settlers in Jamaica, Compiled from the Records of the Court of Chancery of the Island, With a List of the Inhabitants in 1670 and Other Matter Relative to the Early History of the Same.* Kingston, Jamaica: Educational Supply Company, 1909.

Lloyd, Christopher. *William Dampier.* London: Faber & Faber, 1966.

McPhail, Bridget. "Through a Glass Darkly: Scots and Indians Converge at Darién." *Eighteenth-Century Life,* new ser. 18, no. 3 (November 1994): 129–47.

Malt, Ronald A. "Lionel Wafer: Surgeon to the Buccaneers." *Journal of the History of Medicine* 14, no. 10 (October 1959): 459–74.

Marcus, Linda C. "English Influence on Belize and the Petén Region of Northern Guatemala, 1630 to 1763.' Unpublished PhD thesis, Southern Methodist University, 1990.

Margolin, Samuel G. "Lawlessness on the Maritime Frontier of the Greater Chesapeake, 1650–1750 (Smuggling, Wrecking, Piracy)." Unpublished PhD thesis, College of William and Mary, 1992.

Marley, David F. "La désertion du boucanier breton Jean Villebon au Costa Rica, 1669." *Généalogie et Histoire de la Caraïbe* (France) 215 (June 2008): 5585–87.

Marley, David F. "Nau l'Olonnais à Maracaibo : un rapport espagnol, janvier 1667." *Généalogie et Histoire de la Caraïbe* (France) 217 (September 2008): 5638–40.

Marley, David F. *Pirates: Adventurers of the High Seas.* London: Arms and Armour Press, 1995.

Marley, David F. *Pirates and Engineers: Dutch and Flemish Adventurers in New Spain (1607–1697).* Windsor, Ontario: Netherlandic Press, 1992.

Marley, David F. *Sack of Veracruz: The Great Pirate Raid of 1683.* Windsor, Ontario: Netherlandic Press, 1993.

Matar, Nabil. *Britain and Barbary, 1589–1689.* Gainesville: University Press of Florida, 2005.

Mitchell, David. *Pirates.* London: Thames & Hudson, 1976.

Moore, David D. "Blackbeard's *Queen Anne's Revenge.*" *Tributaries* 11 (October 2001).

Moore, David D. "Blackbeard the Pirate Historical Background and the Beaufort Inlet Shipwrecks." *Tributaries* 7 (October 1997): 31–34.

Ollard, Richard. *Man of War: Sir Robert Holmes and the Restoration Navy.* London: Hodder & Stoughton, 1969.

Pawson, Michael, and David J. Buisseret. *Port Royal, Jamaica.* Oxford: Clarendon Press, 1975.

Pawson, Michael, and David J. Buisseret. "A Pirate at Port Royal in 1679." *Mariner's Mirror* 57 (1971): 303–5.

Pope, Dudley. *Harry Morgan's Way: The Biography of Sir Henry Morgan, 1635–1684.* London: Secker & Warburg, 1977.

Prebble, John. *The Darien Disaster.* London: Secker & Warburg, 1968.

Pringle, Patrick. *Jolly Roger: The Story of the Great Age of Piracy.* Mineola, NY: Dover, 2001.

Rankin, Hugh F. *The Pirates of Colonial North Carolina.* Raleigh, NC: State Department of Archives and History, 2001.

Rediker, Marcus. *Between the Devil and the Deep Blue Sea: Merchant Seamen, Pirates and the Anglo-American Maritime World, 1700–1750.* Cambridge: Cambridge University Press, 1987.

Ritchie, Robert C. *Captain Kidd and the War against the Pirates.* Cambridge, MA: Harvard University Press, 1986.

Shomette, Donald G. *Pirates on the Chesapeake: Being a True History of Pirates, Picaroons, and Raiders on Chesapeake Bay, 1610–1807.* Centreville, MD: Tidewater Publishers, 1985.

Shomette, Donald G., and Robert D. Haslach. *Raid on America: The Dutch Naval Campaign of 1672–1674.* Columbia: University of South Carolina Press, 1988.

Snow, Edward R. *Pirates and Buccaneers of the Atlantic Coast.* Dublin, NH: Yankee Publishing, 1944.

Spencer, J. J., ed. "Some Darién Letters, by Lieut. Robert Turnbull." *Scottish Historical Review* 11 (1914): 404–8.

Storrs, Christopher. "Disaster at Darién (1698–1700): The Persistence of Spanish Imperial Power on the Eve of the Demise of the Spanish Habsburgs." *European History Quarterly* 29 (January 1999): 5–38.

Taylor, S.A.G. *The Western Design: An Account of Cromwell's Expedition to the Caribbean.* London: Solstice Productions, 1969.

Thomson, Janice E. *Mercenaries, Pirates, and Sovereigns: State-Building and Extraterritorial Violence in Early Modern Europe.* Princeton, NJ: Princeton University Press, 1994.

Thornton, A. P. "The Modyfords and Morgan." *Jamaican Historical Review* 2 (1952): 36–60.

Thornton, A. P. "Spanish Slave-Ships in the English West Indies, 1660–85." *Hispanic American Historical Review* 35, no. 3 (August 1955): 374–85.

Thornton, A. P. *West-India Policy under the Restoration.* Oxford: Clarendon Press, 1956.

Tuttle, Charles W. *Capt. Francis Champernowne: The Dutch Conquest of Acadie, and Other Historical Papers.* Boston: Wilson & Son, 1889; republished in 2000 by Heritage Books and in 2007 by Kessinger.

Weddle, Robert S. *Wilderness Manhunt: The Spanish Search for La Salle.* Austin: University of Texas Press, 1973.

Westergaard, Waldemar. *The Danish West Indies under Company Rule (1671–1754), with a Supplementary Chapter, 1755–1917.* New York: Macmillan, 1917.

Wilkins, H. T. *Captain Kidd and His Skeleton Island.* London: Cassell's, 1935.

Williams, Gary C. "William Dampier: Pre-Linnean Explorer, Naturalist, Buccaneer." *Proceedings of the California Academy of Sciences* 55, supplement 2, no. 11 (November 2004): 146–66.

Wright, Irene Aloha. *Spanish Narratives of the English Attack on Santo Domingo, 1655.* London: Royal Historical Society, 1926.

Woodard, Colin. *The Republic of Pirates.* New York: Houghton Mifflin Harcourt, 2008.

Woodard, Colin. "Blackbeard in the Bay Islands." *Bay Islands Voice* 6, no. 8 (August 2008).

Yetter, George H. "When Blackbeard Scourged the Seas." *Colonial Williamsburg Journal* 15, no. 1 (Autumn 1992): 22–28.

Young, Everild, and Kjeld Helweg-Larsen. *The Pirates' Priest: The Life of Père Labat in the West Indies, 1693–1705.* London: Jarrolds, 1965.

Zahedieh, Nuala. "'A Frugal, Prudential and Hopeful Trade': Privateering in Jamaica, 1655–89." *Journal of Imperial and Commonwealth History* 18, no. 2 (1990): 145–68.

Zahedieh, Nuala. "The Merchants of Port Royal, Jamaica, and the Spanish Contraband Trade, 1655–1692." *William and Mary Quarterly* 43, no. 4 (October 1986): 570–93.

FOREIGN WORKS ON PIRACY

Alsedo y Herrera, Dionisio de. *Piraterías y agresiones de los ingleses y de otros pueblos de Europa en la América Española desde el siglo XVI al XVIII.* Madrid: Manuel G. Hernández, 1883 extracts compiled from Alsedo's 18th-century writings by Justo Zaragoza.

Alsedo y Herrera, Dionisio de. *Compendio histórico de la provincia, partidos, ciudades, astilleros, ríos y puerto de Guayaquil en las costas de la Mar del Sur.* Madrid: Manuel Fernández, 1741; reprinted in Guayaquil by Pedro Carbo in 1879, as well as in Quito in 1938 and 1946.

Araúz Monfante, C. A. *El contrabando holandés en el Caribe durante la primera mitad del siglo XVIII.* Caracas, Venezuela: Academia Nacional de Historia, 1984.

Auffret, Pierre Jean. "Le Père Labat: 'Critique sous toutes les formes, il n'a que peu de temps à vivre' 1663–1738." Lyon, France: *Documents pour Servir l'Histoire de Saint Domingue en France* 8 (1973): 11–24.

Baudrit, André. *Charles de Courbon, Comte de Blénac, 1622–1696.* Fort-de-France: Société d'Histoire de la Martinique, 1967.

Bernal Ruiz, María del Pilar. *La toma del puerto de Guayaquil en 1687.* Seville, Spain: Escuela de Estudios Hispano-americanos, 1979.

Binaud, Daniel. *Les corsaires de Bordeaux et de l'estuaire.* Gradignan, France: Atlantica, 1999.

Binder, Franz. "Die Zeelandische Kaperfahrt, 1654–1662." *Archief: Mededelingen van het Koninklijk Zeeuws Genootschap der Wetenschappen* (1976): 40–92; later reissued as a monograph.

Blanc, Gérard. "Dampier, ou la relation des Îles aux tortues." *Dix-huitième siècle* 22 (1990): 159–70.

Brenes Castillo, María Eugenia. "Matina, bastión de contrabando en Costa Rica." *Anuario de Estudios Centroamericanos* 4 (1979): 393–450.

Buchet, Christian. *La lutte pour l'espace caraïbe et la façade atlantique de l'Amérique centrale et du Sud (1672–1763).* Paris: Librairie de l'Inde, 1991.

Calderón Quijano, José Ignacio. *Historia de las fortificaciones en Nueva España.* Seville, Spain: Escuela de Estudios Hispano-americanos, 1953.

Camus, Michel Christian. "Une note critique à propos d'Exquemelin." *Revue française d'histoire d'outre-mer* 77, no. 286 (1990): 79–90.

Civeira Taboada, Miguel, and Luis Fernando Álvarez Aguilar, eds. *Testimonios de la Isla Triste: Isla del Carmen, Campeche, documentos históricos del siglo XVIII.* Ciudad del Carmen, Campeche: Universidad Autónoma del Carmen, 1996.

De la Matta Rodríguez, Enrique. *El asalto de Pointis a Cartagena de Indias.* Seville, Spain: Escuela de Estudios Hispano-americanos, 1979.

Ducère, Edouard. "Un corsaire basque sous Luis XIV, d'après des documents inédits." *Revue Internationale des Etudes Basques* (1908): 76–82, 222–29, and 302–12.

Ducère, Edouard. *Histoire maritime de Bayonne: Les corsaires sous l'ancien régime.* Bayonne, France: E. Hourquet, 1895.

Ducère, Edouard. *Journal de bord d'un flibustier (1686–1693).* Bayonne, France: A. Lamaignère, 1894.

Eugenio Martínez, María Ángeles. *La defensa de Tabasco, 1600–1717.* Seville, Spain: Escuela de Estudios Hispano-americanos, 1971.

García Fuentes, Lutgardo. *El comercio español con América (1650–1700).* Seville, Spain: Escuela de Estudios Hispano-americanos, 1980.

Garmendia Arruabarrena, José. "Armadores y armadas de Guipúzcoa (1689–1692)." *Boletín de Estudios Históricos de San Sebastián* (San Sebastián: Biblioteca de la Sociedad Bascongada de los Amigos del País, 1985): 259–77.

Gemelli Careri, Giovanni Francesco. *Viaje a la Nueva España.* Mexico City: Universidad Nacional Autónoma de México, 1976.

Goddet-Langlois, Jean, and Denise Goddet-Langlois. *La vie en Guadeloupe au XVIIe siècle, suivi du Dictionnaire des familles guadeloupéennes de 1635–1700.* Fort-de-France, Martinique: Editions Exbrayat, 1991.

Hasenclever, Adolf. "Die flibustier Westindiens im 17 jahrhundert." *Preussische Jahrbuch* (Germany) 203 (1926): 13–35.

Hayet, Armand. "Officiers rouges, officiers bleus." *Revue maritime* (France) (April 1960).

Incháustegui Cabral, Joaquín Marino. *La gran expedición inglesa contra las Antillas Mayores*. Mexico City: Gráfica Panamericana, 1953.

Izquierdo, Ana Luisa, ed. *El abandono de Santa María de la Victoria y la fundación de San Juan Bautista de Villahermosa*. Mexico City: Universidad Nacional Autónoma de México, 1995.

Journal du Philippe de Courcillon, Marquis de Dageneau, Vol. 6. Paris: Firmin Didot Frères, 1856.

Juárez Moreno, Juan. *Piratas y corsarios en Veracruz y Campeche*. Seville, Spain: Escuela de Estudios Hispano-americanos, 1972.

Laburu Mateo, Miguel. *Breve vocabulario que contiene términos empleados en documentos marítimos antiguos*. San Sebastián, Spain: Departamento de Cultura y Turismo, Diputación Foral de Gipuzkoa, 1990.

La Fontaine Verwey, Herman de. "De scheepschirurgijn Exquemelin en zijn boek over de flibustiers." *Jahrboek van het Genootschap Amstelodamum* (1972): 94–116, and also in *Quaerendo* 4 (1974): 109–31.

Laprise, Raynald. "Descente d'un flibustier anglais en Acadie en 1688." *Cahiers de la Société historique acadienne* (Canada) 33, no. 1–2 (March–June 2002): 33–40.

LeBland, Robert. "Un corsaire de Saint-Domingue en Acadie: Pierre Morpain, 1707–1711." *Nova Francia* (Canada) 6, no. 4 (1931): 195–203.

LeBland, Robert. "Un Officier Béarnais à Saint-Domingue: Pierre Gédéon Ier de Nolivos, Chevalier de l'Ordre Royal et Militaire de Saint-Louis, Lieutenant du Roy, puis Major du Petit-Goâve et commandant la partie Ouest de Saint-Domingue, 1706–1732." *Extrait de la Revue Historique & Archéologique du Béarn et du Pays Basque*. Pau, France: Lescher-Moutou, 1931.

López Cantos, Ángel. *Historia de Puerto Rico (1650–1700)*. Seville, Spain: Escuela de Estudios Hispano-americanos, 1975.

Lugo, Américo. *Recopilación diplomática relativa a las colonias española y francesa de la isla de Santo Domingo, 1640–1701*. Ciudad Trujillo, Dominican Republic: Editorial "La Nación," 1944.

Moya Pons, Frank. *Historia colonial de Santo Domingo*. Santiago, Dominican Republic: Universidad Católica Madre y Maestra, 1977.

Nerzic, Jean-Yves. "Le service de santé de la marine française au temps de la guerre de la Ligue d'Augsburg." *Neptunia* (France), 240 (2005): 20–27.

Peña Batlle, Manuel Arturo. *La isla de la Tortuga: plaza de armas, refugio y seminario de los enemigos de España en Indias*. Madrid: Ediciones Cultura Hispánica, 1951.

Pérez-Mallaína Bueno, Pablo Emilio, and Torres Ramírez, Bibiano. *Armada del Mar del Sur*. Seville, Spain: Escuela de Estudios Hispano-americanos, 1987.

Petitjean Roget, Jacques, and Eugène Bruneau-Latouche. *Personnes et familles à la Martinique au XVIIe siècle, d'après recensements et terriers nominatifs*. Fort-de-France: Société d'histoire de la Martinique, 1983.

Poirier, M. "Une grande figure antillaise: le R. P. Labat, aventurier, aumônier de la flibuste." *Annales de la Société des Lettres, Sciences et Arts des Alpes-Maritimes* 61 (1969–1970): 83–94.

Rodríguez Demorizi, Emilio. *La era de Francia en Santo Domingo; contribución a su estudio.* Ciudad Trujillo, Dominican Republic: Editora del Caribe, 1955.

Rodríguez Demorizi, Emilio. *Invasión inglesa de 1655; notas adicionales de Fray Cipriano de Utrera.* Ciudad Trujillo, Dominican Republic: Montalvo, 1957.

Rodríguez Demorizi, Emilio. "Invasión inglesa en 1655." *Boletín del Archivo General de la Nación* (Dominican Republic) 20, no. 92 (January–March 1957): 6–70.

Rodríguez Demorizi, Emilio. "Acerca del tratado de Ryswick." *Clio* (Dominican Republic) 22, no. 100 (July–September 1954): 127–32.

Rubio Mañé, José Ignacio. *El virreinato III.* Mexico City: Fondo de Cultura Económica y Universidad Nacional Autónoma de México, 1983.

Rubio Mañé, José Ignacio. "Las jurisdicciones de Yucatán: la creación de la plaza de teniente de Rey en Campeche, año de 1744." *Boletín del Archivo General de la Nación* (Mexico) 2nd ser., 7, no. 3 (July–September 1966): 549–631.

Rubio Mañé, José Ignacio. "Ocupación de la Isla de Términos por los ingleses, 1658–1717." *Boletín del Archivo General de la Nación* (Mexico) 1st ser., 24, no. 2 (April–June 1953): 295–330.

Saint-Yves, G. "La flibuste et les flibustiers. Documents inédits sur Saint Domingue et la Tortue." *Bulletin de la Société de géographie de Paris* (France) 38 (1923): 57–75.

Sáiz Cidoncha, Carlos. *Historia de la piratería en América Española.* Madrid: Editorial San Martín, 1985.

Saugera, Eric. *Bordeaux, Port Négrier: Chronologie, Économie, Idéologie, XVIIe–XVIIIe siècles.* Paris: Karthala, 1995.

Seitz, Don Carlos, Howard F. Gospel, and Stephen Wood. *Under the Black Flag: Exploits of the Most Notorious Pirates.* Mineola, NY: Courier Dover, 2002.

Serrano Mangas, Fernando. *Los galeones de la carrera de Indias, 1650–1700.* Seville, Spain: Escuela de Estudios Hispano-americanos, 1985.

Serrano Mangas, Fernando. "El proceso del pirata Bartholomew Sharp, 1682." *Temas americanistas* (Spain), no. 4 (1984): 14–18.

Sigüenza y Góngora, Carlos de. *Relación de lo sucedido a la Armada de Barlovento.* Reprinted in *Obras históricas.* Mexico City: Porrúa, 1960.

Sigüenza y Góngora, Carlos de. *Trofeo de la justicia española en el castigo de la alevosía francesa.* Reprinted in *Obras históricas.* Mexico City: Porrúa, 1960.

Solórzano, Juan Carlos. "El comercio de Costa Rica durante el declive del comercio español y el desarrollo del contrabando inglés: Período 1690–1750." *Anuario de Estudios Centroamericanos* 20, no. 2 (1994): 71–119.

Sucre, Luis Alberto. *Gobernadores y capitanes generales de Venezuela.* Caracas, Venezuela: Litografía Tecnocolor, 1964.

Szaszdi Nagy, Adam. "El comercio ilícito en la provincia de Honduras."
    Revista de Indias (Spain) 17 (1967): 271–83.
Taillemite, Étienne. *Dictionnaire des Marins Français.* Paris: Editions Maritimes
    et d'Outre-mer, 1982.
Tejera, Emiliano. "Gobernadores de la isla de Santo Domingo, siglos XVI-XVII."
    Boletín del Archivo General de la Nación (Dominican Republic) 18, no. 4
    (1941): 359–75.
Thilmans, Guy. "La relation de François de Paris, 1682–1683." *Bulletin de
    l'Institut fondamental de l'Afrique Noir* (Senegal) 38, no. 1 (January 1976):
    1–51.
Torres Ramírez, Bibiano. *La Armada de Barlovento.* Seville, Spain: Escuela de
    Estudios Hispano-americanos, 1981.
Tribout de Morembert, Henri. "À Saint-Domingue, le Major Bernanos, capit-
    aine de flibustiers." *Connaissance du Monde* (Paris) 78 (1965): 10–19.
Valery Salvatierra, Rafael. *La familia tachirense Moreno Pacheco: anotaciones
    sobre sus ascendientes y descendientes.* Caracas, Venezuela: privately pub-
    lished, 2000.

REGIONAL HISTORIES AND GENERAL
MARITIME BACKGROUND

Amussen, Susan Dwyer. *Caribbean Exchanges: Slavery and the Transformation of
    English Society, 1640–1700.* Chapel Hill: University of North Carolina
    Press, 2007.
Beeston, Sir William. "A Letter from Sir William Beeston, Governor of Jamaica,
    to Mr. Charles Bernard, Containing Some Observations about the Ba-
    rometer, and of a Hot Bath in That Island." *Philosophical Transactions of
    the Royal Society of London* 19 (1695–1697): 225–28. (Written from Jamaica
    on April 8, 1696, O.S.)
Bell, Winslow M., comp. "Minutes of Their Majesties' Council (1690)." *Ber-
    muda Historical Quarterly* 14, no. 3 (Autumn 1957): 72–79.
Bell, Winslow M., comp. "Minutes of Their Majesties' Council (Wm. & Mary)."
    Bermuda Historical Quarterly 14, no. 4 (Winter 1957): 102–7.
Bennett, J. Harry. "Cary Helyar, Merchant and Planter of Seventeenth-Century
    Jamaica." *William and Mary Quarterly*, 3rd ser., 21, no. 1 (January 1964),
    pp. 53–76.
Bruce, Philip A. *Institutional History of Virginia in the Seventeenth Century: An
    Inquiry into Religious, Moral and Educational, Legal, Military, and Political
    Conditions of the People, Based on Original and Contemporaneous Records.*
    New York and London: G.P. Putnam's Sons, 1910.
Calendar of State Papers, Domestic: Charles II, 1663–1664. London: Her Majesty's
    Stationery Office, 1862.
Calendar of State Papers, Domestic: Charles II, 1667 and 1672. London: Her Maj-
    esty's Stationery Office, 1866 and 1899.
Calendar of State Papers, Domestic Series, Interregnum, 1653–1660. London: Her
    Majesty's Stationery Office, 1879–1886.

Calendar of State Papers, Domestic: William III, 1698. London: His Majesty's Stationery Office, 1933.

Calendar of State Papers, Domestic: William III, 1700–1702. London: His Majesty's Stationery Office, 1937.

Calendar of State Papers, Domestic: William and Mary, 1689–1690. London: Her Majesty's Stationery Office, 1895.

Craton, Michael. *A History of the Bahamas.* London: Collins, 1968.

Davies, K.G. *The Royal African Company.* London: Longman, Grion, 1957.

De Ville, Winston. *Saint Domingue: Census Records and Military Lists (1688–1720).* Ville Platte, LA: Author, 1988.

Duncan, T. Bentley. *The Atlantic Islands: Madeira, the Azores, and Cabo Verde in the Seventeenth Century.* Chicago: University of Chicago Press, 1972.

Dunn, Richard S. "The Barbados Census of 1680: Profile of the Richest Colony in English America." *William and Mary Quarterly,* 3rd ser., 26 (1969): 3–30.

Dwyer Amussen, Susan. *Caribbean Exchanges: Slavery and the Transformation of English Society, 1640–1700.* Chapel Hill: University of North Carolina Press, 2007.

Govier, Mark. "The Royal Society, Slavery, and the Island of Jamaica: 1660–1700." *Notes and Records of the Royal Society of London* 53, no. 2 (May 1999): 203–17.

Hayton, David, et al. *The History of Parliament: the House of Commons, 1690–1715.* Cambridge: Cambridge University Press, 2002.

Insh, G.P., ed. *Papers Relating to the Ships and Voyages of the Company of Scotland Trading to Africa and the Indies, 1696–1707.* Edinburgh: Scottish History Society, 1924.

Israel, Jonathan I. *Empires and Entrepôts: The Dutch, the Spanish Monarchy, and the Jews, 1585–1713.* London: Hambledon, 1990.

Law, Robin. *The English in West Africa, 1681–1683: The Local Correspondence of the Royal African Company of England, 1681–1699.* Oxford: Oxford University Press, 1997.

McCrady, Edward. *The History of South Carolina under the Proprietary Government.* Vol. 1, *1670–1719.* Westminster, MD: Heritage Books, 2008; reedition of 1901 original published in New York by Macmillan.

McJunkin, David M. "Logwood: An Inquiry into the Historical Biogeography of *Haematoxylum campechanium L.* and Related Dyewoods of the Neotropics." Unpublished PhD thesis, University of California, Los Angeles, 1991.

Marshall, Rosalind K. *The Days of Duchess Anne: Life in the Household of the Duchess of Hamilton, 1656–1716.* New York: St. Martin's Press, 1973.

Memoirs of the Historical Society of Pennsylvania, Vol. 9. Philadelphia: Lippincott, 1870.

Mercer, Julia A. *Bermuda Settlers of the 17th Century: Genealogical Notes from Bermuda.* Baltimore: Genealogical Publishing, 1982.

Middleton, Arthur Pierce. *Tobacco Coast: A Maritime History of Chesapeake Bay in the Colonial Era.* Newport News, VA: Mariners' Museum, 1953.

Munford, Clarence J. *The Black Ordeal of Slavery and Slave Trading in the French West Indies, 1625–1715*, 3 vols. Lewiston, NY: Edwin Mellen Press, 1991.

Pritchard, James. *In Search of Empire: The French in the Americas, 1670–1730.* Cambridge: Cambridge University Press, 2004.

Radell, David R., and James J. Parsons. "Realejo: A Forgotten Colonial Port and Shipbuilding Center in Nicaragua." *Hispanic American Historical Review* 51, no. 2 (May 1971): 295–312.

Rivas, Christine. "The Spanish Colonial Military: Santo Domingo, 1701–1779." *The Americas* (American Academy of Franciscan History) 60, no. 3 (October 2003): 249–72.

Sanders, Joanne McRee, ed. *Barbados Records: Baptisms, 1637–1800.* Baltimore: Genealogical Publishing Company, 1984.

Sanders, Joanne McRee, ed. *Barbados Records: Baptisms, 1693–1800.* Houston: Sanders Historical Publications, 1982.

Sanders, Joanne McRee, ed. *Barbados Records: Marriages, 1693–1800.* Houston: Sanders Historical Publications, 1982.

Schomburgk, Robert H. *The History of Barbados: A Geographical and Statistical Description of the Island.* London: Routledge, 1971.

Seliger, William G. *Isla El Muerto and the Treasures of the "Consolación."* Ecuador, privately published, 2008.

Sheridan, Richard B., and McDonald, Roderick A., editors. *West Indies Accounts: Essays on the History of the British Caribbean and the Atlantic Economy.* Kingston, Jamaica: University of the West Indies Press, 1996.

Walduck, Thomas. "Thomas Walduck's 'Letters from Barbados, 1710–1712.'" *Journal of the Barbados Museum and Historical Society* 15, no. 1 (1947–1948): 27–51, 84–88, and 137–49.

Walsh, Micheline. *Spanish Knights of Irish Origin: Documents from Continental Archives.* Dublin: Irish Manuscripts Commission, 1960–1970.

Ward, Eliot D.C. "Imperial Panama: Commerce and Conflict in Isthmian America, 1550–1750." Unpublished PhD thesis, University of Florida, 1988.

Webster, John Clarence. *Cornelis Steenwyck: Dutch Governor of Acadie.* Ottawa: Canadian Historical Association, 1929.

Weeks, Daniel J. *Not for Filthy Lucre's Sake: Richard Saltar and the Antiproprietary Movement in East New Jersey, 1665–1707.* Bethlehem, PA: Lehigh University Press, 2001.

INDEX

About the Author

DAVID F. MARLEY is an award-winning naval historian, who lived for most of his life in Latin America and has written several of the official catalogs of the maritime collections in the Mexican National Archives, where Spanish colonial documents on piracy are housed. He is also the author of ABC-CLIO's *Pirates of the Americas* and *Wars of the Americas*.